KARLO BROUSSARD

MEETING
the
PROTESTANT
CHALLENGE

HOW TO ANSWER
50 BIBLICAL OBJECTIONS
TO CATHOLIC BELIEFS

Catholic
Answers
Press

Published by Catholic Answers, Inc.
2020 Gillespie Way
El Cajon, California 92020
1-888-291-8000 orders
619-387-0042 fax
catholic.com

Printed in the United States of America

Cover design by eBookLaunch.com
Interior design by Russell Graphic Design

978-1-68357-144-5
978-1-68357-145-2 Kindle
978-1-68357-146-9 ePub

Contents

Introduction 9

I
Church Hierarchy & Authority

1. "James Led the Council" 14
2. "No Other Foundation but Jesus" 19
3. "Paul Rebuked Peter" 23
4. "Where Two or Three Are Gathered" 26
5. "All Are One in Christ" 32
6. "The Anointing Teaches Us" 39

II
Scripture & Tradition

7. "Traditions Nullify God's Word" 44
8. "Scripture Makes the Man of God Complete" 49
9. "The Noble Bereans" 54
10. "Don't Go Beyond What Is Written" 58
11. "Don't Add to God's Word" 62

III
Salvation

12. "We Are Justified All at Once" 68
13. "Not Because of Works" 73

14. "Justified by Faith, Not Works" 78
15. "We Know That We Have Eternal Life" 83
16. "No One Can Snatch Us" 88
17. "Sanctified for All Time" 92

IV

The Sacraments

18. "Up out of the Water" 98
19. "Believer's Baptism" 103
20. "Cornelius Received the Spirit First" 110
21. "Not to Baptize but to Preach" 118
22. "God Will Cut Off the Person Who Eats Blood" . . 123
23. "Do This in Remembrance" 127
24. "Once and For All" 134
25. "The Fruit of the Vine" 140
26. "God Alone Can Forgive Sins" 145
27. "We Confess Our Sins Directly to God" 149
28. "We're All Priests" 153
29. "Except for Unchastity" 158

V

Mary

30. "All Have Sinned" 168
31. "Mary Needed a Savior" 173
32. "The Lord's Brothers" 176
33. "He Knew Her Not . . . *Until*" 182
34. "'Queen of Heaven' Condemned" 186

VI
The Saints

35. "One Mediator".......................... 192
36. "Invoking the Dead Is an Abomination"......... 196
37. "The Dead Know Nothing" 199
38. "God Alone Knows Our Hearts"............... 206
39. "*We* Are the Saints" 210

VII
The Last Things

40. "Today You Will Be with Me" 216
41. "At Home with the Lord" 221
42. "Caught Up with the Lord in the Air" 224
43. "A Thousand-Year Reign".................... 229

VIII
Catholic Life & Practice

44. "Doctrines of Demons" 236
45. "Call No Man Father"....................... 243
46. "It Is Finished"............................ 248
47. "Yoke of Slavery".......................... 255
48. "Vain Repetitions"......................... 262
49. "Wine Is a Mocker"........................ 266
50. "No Graven Images" 270

After the Challenge............................. 275

About the Author............................ 278

Endnotes 279

ACKNOWLEDGMENTS

I would like to thank Todd Aglialoro, Catholic Answers Press director and editor, for his acceptance of this book and for all his hard work in editing it. I am also grateful to Tim Staples, Trent Horn, and Doug Beaumont for their help in research for this book. I am *most* grateful to Jimmy Akin, senior apologist at Catholic Answers, for his generosity in the amount of time that he spent to review the manuscript and for his helpful suggestions.

Introduction

"You have a fine way of rejecting the commandment of God, in order to keep your tradition ... thus making void the word of God through your tradition which you hand on." —Mark 7:9,13

"Where's that in the Bible?"

Any Catholic who talks religion with Protestants has at some time been challenged with this question. It stems from the Protestant belief that we shouldn't accept any doctrine that isn't explicitly found in the Bible since it alone is our infallible rule of faith—a belief known as *sola scriptura* (Latin, "Scripture alone").

Much of Catholic apologetics, especially since its revival in the late eighties, has centered on answering that question, offering positive arguments for the biblical basis of Catholic doctrine. But, since Catholics don't operate on the principle of *sola scriptura*, we don't believe that every Christian truth has to be explicitly found in Scripture. We also appeal to truths revealed by God and preserved outside of the Bible in *Sacred Tradition*.

For example, Protestants may ask, "Where is Mary's bodily assumption in the Bible?" But a Catholic can simply reply, "I don't need to justify it with Scripture since I can accept it on the basis that it's a part of Sacred Tradition as infallibly defined by Pope Pius XII (*Munificentissimus Deus*, 1950)."

Of course, a Protestant is not going to find the above response persuasive (and it would open up other debates about Christian teaching authority). But at least he can't charge a Catholic with incoherence in his belief.

There is another kind of Protestant challenge, however. This kind *does* charge a Catholic with incoherence: "How can the Catholic Church teach X when the Bible says Y?"

For example, how can the Catholic Church teach that Mary remained a virgin after Jesus' birth when the Bible says that Jesus had brothers (Matt. 13:55)? Or how can the Catholic Church teach that works have a role to play in our salvation when the Bible says in Romans 3:28 that "a man is justified by faith apart from works of law."

This is the kind of challenge that a Catholic *must* meet because whatever the Church teaches, even if derived principally from Sacred Tradition and not the Bible, cannot *contradict* the Bible. Scripture and Tradition are two streams of revelation that flow from the same source: God.

Our task as Catholics, therefore, is to show that Catholic teaching doesn't contradict those Bible passages that some Protestants think pose a threat to it. The purpose of this book is to help you fulfill this task.

We will examine fifty challenges that Protestants commonly make from the Bible, covering a variety of topics concerning Church authority, Scripture and Tradition, salvation, the sacraments, Mary and the saints, eschatology, and Catholic life and practice. Most of the challenges come from mainstream Protestantism, but some come from smaller groups within Protestantism, such as Seventh-day Adventists.

Each chapter offers you a series of ways to meet these challenges, ultimately showing that the challenges don't succeed in proving Catholic beliefs to be contrary to the Bible. Following these is a counter-challenge you can propose to help your Protestant friend think more critically about his own assumptions.

Of course, these fifty biblical challenges don't exhaust the challenges that Protestants make against Catholic teaching. But they do offer a good sampling of what a Catholic might encounter.

I hope this book will help you be more efficient in your conversations with Protestants. Also, I hope it will strengthen your own faith, helping you to know that in embracing Catholic teaching you are *not* "making void the word of God through your tradition which you hand on" (Mark 7:13).

I

Church Hierarchy
& Authority

Many Protestants don't think Jesus established a church with *any* hierarchical structure, much less with a single figure who has the highest rank of authority, like a pope. They argue that Jesus' Church is merely an *invisible community of believers* united by grace rather than a society with visible markers.

Their motivation for this belief is commendable because they think it's what the Bible teaches. And there are certain biblical passages they commonly bring up as evidence for their belief.

As we'll see, though, it's not a matter of *either* a hierarchical and visible Church *or* an invisible community, but of both/and. As you meet these challenges, you may help Protestants come to a fuller, more biblically accurate view of the Church that Jesus established.

"James Led the Council"

Acts 15:13-29 and Peter's Primacy

How can the Catholic Church teach that Peter was the leader of the first-century Church when the Bible teaches that *James* was the leader of the Council of Jerusalem?

The *Catechism of the Catholic Church* (CCC) teaches that Christ instituted Peter as "the head" of the college of the apostles (880), and therefore that the *pope*, Peter's successor as the bishop of Rome, "is the perpetual and visible source and foundation of the unity both of the bishops and of the whole company of the faithful" (882).

But Protestants argue that the Bible teaches otherwise. Some appeal to the proceedings of the Council of Jerusalem recorded in Acts 15.[1] The council was convened due to an early Church debate over how a person is to be saved. According to Acts 15:1, some of the Jewish converts to Christianity were teaching that circumcision was necessary for salvation. Luke (the author of Acts) tells us that Paul and Barnabas "had no small dissension and debate with them" (v.2), and that in order to settle the question they were appointed to go and meet with the apostles and elders in Jerusalem.

Some Protestants, appealing to Acts 15, argue that James the Just (aka "the Lord's brother") was in charge of the council, proving that Peter could not have been head of the early Church as the first "pope." They point to James's use of the imperative mood for "listen" (Greek, *akouō*) as proof for this: "Brethren, listen [*akousate*] to me" (v.13).[2] Moreover, they assert that James decides the results of the council when he says, "Therefore my *judgment* is that we should not trouble those of the Gentiles who turn to God" (v.19).

MEETING THE CHALLENGE

1. The imperative mood for *akouō* doesn't necessarily connote authority over the group.

Imagine that everyone is throwing around ideas in a business meeting, and you say, "Listen!" and then go on to share your ideas. This doesn't necessarily mean that you are in charge of the meeting. You may be simply trying to get the others there to pay attention to what you have to say.

This is how the imperative of *akouō* is used later, in Acts 22:1, where Paul says to his Jewish brethren, "Brethren and fathers, hear [*akousate*] the defense which I now make before you." Paul wasn't exercising authority over the group; he merely was asking for their undivided attention. The following verse bears this out: "And when they heard that he addressed them in the Hebrew language, they were the *more quiet*" (v.2).

Given that the imperative mood of *akouō* doesn't necessarily connote authority, its use in Acts 15 doesn't establish that James had authority over the council proceedings. Context must be taken into consideration in order to determine the force of the imperative.[3]

So what does the context tell us? Let's move to our other ways of meeting the challenge and see.

2. **Peter is the one who speaks first and settles the substance of the debate.**

Luke sets up Peter's speech by highlighting the tension among the apostles and presbyters in verse 6: "There was much debate." And subsequent verses reveal that it is *Peter's* speech that settles the debate:

> Brethren, you know that in the early days God made choice among you, that by my mouth the Gentiles should hear the word of the gospel and believe. And God who knows the heart bore witness to them, giving them the Holy Spirit just as he did to us; and he made no distinction between us and them, but cleansed their hearts by faith . . . we believe that we shall be saved through the grace of the Lord Jesus, just as they will (Acts 15:7-11).

This all happens *before* James rises and requests the assembly to listen to his words (v.13). James does direct the council proceedings after Peter's speech, but it's Peter who speaks first and settles the debate. And in verse 14 James even recognizes as much: "Simeon has related how God first visited the Gentiles, to take out of them a people for his name." If James had just as much authority over the group as Peter (or more), he would have been the one to take the initiative and settle the substance of the debate, not Peter.[4]

3. **James's speech is a pastoral proposal, whereas Peter's speech is a doctrinal declaration.**

The content of Peter's speech was a matter of divine revelation. It was *God* who chose to reveal that the Gentiles could be saved, for he had given them the Holy Spirit just as he did the apostles, cleansing their hearts by faith and making no distinction between the circumcised and the uncircumcised (Acts 15:8-9). Based on that revelation, Peter makes a doctrinal statement that is more than mere opinion: "We *believe* that we shall be saved through the grace of the Lord Jesus, just as they [the Gentiles] will" (v.11). Peter doesn't offer this view as what he thinks *should* be believed. He offers it as what *is* believed.

James's speech stands in stark contrast with Peter's. First, it was for the most part pastoral in nature,[5] intended to address the problem of how to unify Jewish and Gentile Christians (Acts 15:1-5). It's a practical problem that only arises because of the theological issue *already settled by Peter.*

Gentile converts were coming into a community of Jewish Christians who were still holding fast to many of the Old Testament precepts (Acts 21:15-26). And in order to keep the Gentiles from offending Jewish sensibilities, James proposes that the Gentile converts adhere to certain precepts that Jewish converts would have considered it scandalous to violate: abstinence from "the pollutions of idols and from unchastity and from what is strangled and from blood" (Acts 15:20). Of these four precepts, only one is of a moral nature, namely "unchastity" (Greek, *porneia*), which may refer to invalid marital unions that the Gentiles contracted before becoming Christian.

James's speech also stands in contrast to Peter's because unlike Peter, who stated what *is* the case, James offers his ideas for consideration: "Therefore my judgment is that we should not trouble those of the Gentiles who turn to God, but should write to them" (Acts 15:19-20). In fact, the Greek word translated "judgment" in verse 19 (*krinō*) means "to hold a view or have an opinion with regard to something—'to hold a view, to have an opinion, to consider, to regard.'"[6]

COUNTER-CHALLENGE

Does your church believe that someone has authority to settle a theological controversy in a definitive way? If not, why not?

AFTERTHOUGHT

The first century Christians believed that the Holy Spirit guides the Church *through* judgments made by the body of authoritative officials, not apart from them. For example, concerning the decisions of the council, the council fathers state in Acts 15:28: "For it has seemed good to the Holy Spirit *and to us* to lay upon you no greater burden than these necessary things." This is a far cry from the belief that all we need is the Holy Spirit to guide us, which is common among those who promote the doctrine of *sola scriptura*.

"No Other Foundation but Jesus"

1 Corinthians 3:11 and Peter the Rock

How can the Catholic Church teach that Peter is the rock or the foundation of the Church when Paul teaches that there is no other foundation except Jesus?

The *Catechism* teaches, "The Lord made Simon alone, whom he named Peter, the 'rock' of his Church" (881). But as some Protestants[7] are quick to point out, Paul says in 1 Corinthians 3:11, "For no other foundation can anyone lay than that which is laid, which is Jesus Christ." On the surface, it seems that the Catholic Church is contradicting the Bible in saying that Peter is the foundation of the Church.

MEETING THE CHALLENGE

Fundamentally, this argument commits what philosophers call a *non sequitur*, which is Latin for "it does not follow." Just because Jesus is called the one foundation in one passage, it doesn't follow that Peter can't be the foundation of Jesus' Church in other passages. Here are three ways to show this:

1. In the Bible, metaphors and symbols are often used in more than one way.

In Matthew 16:18, Jesus says he is the builder, yet elsewhere Paul tells us that ministers are builders as well: "Like a skilled master builder I laid a foundation, and another man is building upon it. Let each man take care how he builds upon it" (1 Cor. 3:10).[8] Is Paul wrong for saying that ministers build up the Church when Jesus says that *he's* the one who will build his Church?

Other examples abound. Jesus is the "living stone, rejected by men" (1 Pet. 2:4), but the next verse says that *Christians* are "living stones . . . built into a spiritual house" (1 Pet. 2:5). Jesus says that he is the "Good Shepherd" (John 10:11), yet he makes Peter the shepherd of his flock on earth, telling him to tend his sheep (John 21:15-17). Jesus calls himself the "light of the world" (John 9:5), but this doesn't stop him from teaching that *we* are "the light of the world" as well (Matthew 5:14).

If we were to apply the logic of this challenge elsewhere, we would have to say that Peter is wrong for teaching that Christians are "stones" and that Jesus is confused about who is supposed to be shepherding and shining light in the world. But no Christian draws those conclusions. We recognize that metaphors are used in different ways according to their context.

2. The Bible depicts the foundation of the Church in a variety of ways.

In 1 Corinthians 3:11, Paul says that Christ is the one foundation, but in Ephesians 2:19-20 he also identifies *apostles and prophets* as the foundation of the Church: "You are fellow citizens with the saints and members of the household of God, built upon the foundation of the apostles and prophets, Christ Jesus himself being the cornerstone."

Paul's reference to the prophets likely refers to those of the New Testament age. This is made clear by Paul's other two references to such prophets in Ephesians 3:5 and 4:11.[9] Paul sees no contradiction between Jesus being the foundation in one sense and the apostles and prophets being the foundation in another.

John also doesn't see a contradiction in Revelation 21:14 when he describes the foundation of the heavenly city of Jerusalem as having twelve stones with the apostles' names inscribed upon each of them.

And as we saw above, Peter doesn't see a contradiction in Christ being the "living stone" and Christians being "living stones."

If neither Paul, Peter, nor John saw a contradiction between Jesus being the foundation of the Church and at the same time others being the foundation of the Church, why should we say that there is a contradiction in Matthew 16:18–19? That the metaphor of being the foundation of the Church can be used in various ways should impress upon us the importance of considering carefully what Jesus says to Peter about being the "rock" of the Church.

3. Peter's role as the foundation of the Church is not apart from Jesus but only *in* and *through* Jesus.

In all the examples above, the roles that Christians share with Jesus ("living stones," "builders," "shepherding," "the light of world") do not take away from Jesus. We only have such roles inasmuch as we are in Christ. We participate in these roles that Christ possesses in full.

Perhaps one more example will help. We're told in 1 Timothy 2:5 that Jesus is our "one mediator." Yet in 1 Timothy 2:1, Paul exhorts Christians to intercede (or mediate) for one another, and in Philippians 1:4 he practices intercessory prayer. Such Christian mediation doesn't take away from the unique role of Christ as mediator. The prayers of Christians are efficacious only inasmuch as they are *in* Christ, as members of his mystical body (1 Cor. 12:12-13). The same principle can be applied to Peter's role of being the "rock" of the Church. Peter's *rockness* doesn't rob Jesus of his glory as the power on which the whole Church is built and depends. Peter is rock only as Christ grafts Peter into himself, delegating a role to Peter in his own image and likeness.

COUNTER-CHALLENGE

Must biblical metaphors be restricted to a single use? Can't they be used in a variety of ways?

AFTERTHOUGHT

The name *Peter* (Greek, *petros*) means "rock." St. John confirms this in John 1:42 when he explains that the Aramaic equivalent of the Greek word *petros* is *kephas*, which means "rock." John quotes Jesus saying to Simon, "You shall be called Cephas [Aramaic for rock]," and then John interjects, "which means Peter [*petros*]."

"Paul Rebuked Peter"

Galatians 2:11 and Papal Infallibility

How can the Catholic Church teach that Peter is infallible when Paul rebukes Peter for not eating with the Gentiles? Doesn't this further show that Peter had no more authority than Paul?

The *Catechism* teaches that the "Roman pontiff, head of the college of bishops, enjoys . . . infallibility in virtue of his office" (891). The office that the *Catechism* speaks of is the See of Peter, the bishopric of Rome. The Church teaches that the pope's authority is derived from the authority that Jesus gave to Peter.

But some Protestants[10] argue that Paul's rebuke of Peter in Galatians 2:11 not only disproves the Catholic doctrine of papal infallibility—it shows that Peter didn't have any more authority than St. Paul!

Paul describes how Peter withdrew from table fellowship with the Gentiles in Antioch out of fear of giving offense to the new Jewish converts arriving from Jerusalem (v. 12). Because of the scandal that Peter's actions created—causing other Jewish Christians to avoid table fellowship with Gentile converts and giving the wrong signal that Gentile converts had to live like Jews (vv.13-14)—Paul says that he rebuked Peter: "But when Cephas came to Antioch I opposed him to his face, because he stood condemned" (v.11).

How could Peter have been infallible when he led believers astray? How could Peter have had more authority than Paul when Paul was the one doing the correcting?

MEETING THE CHALLENGE

1. The rebuke was for inappropriate behavior and not for teaching erroneous doctrine.

This Protestant challenge reveals a lack of understanding of the Catholic doctrine of papal infallibility. The *Catechism* lays out the conditions that must be met for the pope to exercise the gift of infallibility: "When, as supreme pastor and teacher of all the faithful—who confirms his brethren in the faith—he [the pope] proclaims by a definitive act a doctrine pertaining to faith or morals" (891).

Peter's actions in Galatians 2 doesn't meet this condition for infallibility. Peter wasn't even proclaiming a doctrine. He simply stopped eating a meal with Gentile converts in order to save face with Jewish converts.

Paul even highlights that the mistake was behavioral. In verse 13, he says that the rest of the Jews, along with Barnabas, "acted insincerely" with Peter. Paul uses the Greek word *sunupokrinomai*, which literally means "to act hypocritically along with others—'to pretend together, to join in hypocrisy.'"[11] It also has the connotation to act with cowardice.[12]

Again, in verse 14, Paul emphasizes that the failure was in moral *action*: "But when I saw that they were not straightforward about the truth of the gospel." The phrase "were not straightforward" translates the Greek phrase *ouk orthopodousin. Ouk* means "not" and *orthopodousin* is a form of the verb *orthopodeō*, meaning "to live a life of moral correctness."[13]

This challenge thus attacks a straw man. It targets Peter's action as if papal infallibility should apply to it, extending the conditions of papal infallibility way beyond what the Church actually says. Peter may have made a mistake, but the Church has never said that popes are unable to make mistakes. The Church simply says that a pope can't err when he definitively proclaims a doctrine of faith and morals. Choosing lunch companions is hardly a dogmatic declaration.

2. The rebuke actually implies Peter's special authority.

Far from proving that Paul didn't consider Peter to have any higher-ranking authority than him, Paul's rebuke suggests the opposite. If Peter didn't have a special authority, there would be no need for Paul to record the rebuke. It would be no big thing, not worth the ink and the space on the scroll.

Protestant scholars Albright and Mann, in their commentary on Matthew in the *Anchor Bible Commentary*, concur:

> To deny the pre-eminent position of Peter among the disciples or in the early Christian community is a denial of the evidence . . . The interest in Peter's failures and vacillations does not detract from the pre-eminence; rather, it emphasizes it. Had Peter been a lesser figure his behavior would have been of far less consequence.[14]

COUNTER-CHALLENGE

Can a rebuke of Peter's behavior refute papal infallibility if infallibility has nothing to do with papal behavior?

AFTERTHOUGHT

If a Protestant wants to blame Peter for unnecessary compliance to Jewish law for the sake of facilitating relations in the Church, he will have to blame Paul as well. For example, Paul had Timothy circumcised for the sake of peace (Acts 16:3), yet he had been preaching that circumcision doesn't matter (1 Cor. 7:18-19; Gal. 6:12-15).

"Where Two or Three Are Gathered"

Matthew 18:20 and the Visible Church

How can Catholics believe that the Church is a visible hierarchical institution when Jesus says that the Church is an invisible union of believers?

Citing the Second Vatican Council's Dogmatic Constitution on the Church, *Lumen Gentium*, the *Catechism* teaches that Christ's Church is a "visible organization through which he communicates truth and grace to all men" and is at the same time "a society structured with *hierarchical* organs and the Mystical Body of Christ, the *visible* society *and* the spiritual community" (771; emphasis added).

But some Protestants[15] use Matthew 18:20 to challenge this belief. Matthew records Jesus' teaching, "For where two or three are gathered in my name, there am I in the midst of them." Since the Church is where Christ is, and Christ says he is present where Christian believers are present, the Church must be merely an invisible community of believers who are united by grace.

But these words from Jesus come by way of a conclusion to his preceding instructions about how to deal with a sinner among the brethren (Matt. 18:15-18). And these instructions reveal the *visible* nature of the Church.

MEETING THE CHALLENGE

1. **That a Christian can be separated from the Christian community for refusal to accept the Church's judgment reveals the visible nature of the Church.**

In Matthew 18:15, Jesus instructs his disciples to approach the sinner personally and try to win him over. If the sinner refuses, then the disciples must take one or two others with him to try and convince the brother (v.16). And if the two or three are unable to win over their brother, Jesus says, "Tell it to the church; and if he refuses to listen even to the church, let him be to you as a Gentile and a tax collector" (v.17).

The first thing to note is the gravity of this consequence. Gentiles were non-Jews and consequently were not beneficiaries of the blessings of God's family. Jewish tax collectors were considered traitors because they were assisting the very enemy that Jews were praying to be delivered from, namely the Romans.

So Jesus is saying that he who disobeys the Church is considered an outcast, a non-beneficiary of the new covenantal blessings of God's family, and a traitor. That's a pretty serious consequence, which suggests that the Church's decision is to be taken very seriously.

Moreover, it argues against the idea that the Church is merely invisible. How can Jesus' Church not have visible boundaries of membership if Jesus is saying that disobedient members can be cast out? You can't be cast out of something that doesn't have demarcated boundaries of membership.

2. **That the Church has the authority to "bind and loose" shows that it has judicial authority, which suggests a visible nature.**

Jesus tells the disciples gathered, "Whatever you bind on earth shall be bound in heaven, and whatever you loose on earth shall be loosed in heaven" (Matt. 18:18). In Jewish tradition, this language denotes judicial authority—deciding what was forbidden or allowed according to the law.[16] But rabbis were also said to bind and loose when they would "pronounce and revoke an anathema upon a person," thus excluding or restoring a person from or to membership in the faith community.[17]

How could the Church be merely invisible when Jesus clearly invests it with judicial authority? Also, how could the Church exercise that judicial authority to excommunicate someone if there were no visible boundaries of membership in it?

3. **The parallels that exist between Jesus' instructions for the Church's governing activity in Matthew 18:15-17 and Moses' instructions for Israel's governing activity in Deuteronomy 17:6-12 reveal the visible nature of the Church.**

Deuteronomy 17:6-12 spells out the decision-making process for Israel:

> On the evidence of two witnesses or of three witnesses he that is to die shall be put to death; a person shall not be put to death on the evidence of one witness. The hand of the witnesses shall be first against him to put him to death, and afterward the hand of all the people. So you shall purge the evil from the midst of you.
>
> If any case arises requiring decision between one kind of homicide and another, one kind of legal right and another, or one kind of assault and another, any case within your towns which is too difficult for you, then you shall arise and go up to the place which the LORD your God will choose, and coming to the Levitical priests, and to the judge who is in office in those days, you shall consult them, and they shall

declare to you the decision. Then you shall do according to what they declare to you from that place which the LORD will choose; and you shall be careful to do according to all that they direct you; according to the instructions which they give you, and according to the decision which they pronounce to you, you shall do; you shall not turn aside from the verdict which they declare to you, either to the right hand or to the left. The man who acts presumptuously, by not obeying the priest who stands to minister there before the LORD your God, or the judge, that man shall die; so you shall purge the evil from Israel.

Notice the parallels with Christ's instructions in Matthew 18:15-17:

1. There is a governing body that has authority to make judgments on certain matters.
2. There is a need to employ the testimony of two or three witnesses.
3. Obedience to the authoritative judgment is necessary.
4. There are severe consequences for not obeying the proper authoritative judgment.

These parallels strongly suggest that the New Israel, the Church, is just as much a visible society as the Old Israel was. Just as the Old Israel was not merely an "invisible body of persons faithful to Yahweh," neither is the New Israel merely an invisible body of persons faithful to Christ.

4. When read within its immediate context, the "two or three gathered" in Jesus' name in verse 20 can be applied to the governing body who gather in the name of Jesus—with Jesus' authority—to bind and loose.

The "two or three gathered" that Jesus speaks of in verse 20 seems to be identified with the "two of you" spoken of in verse 19: "If *two of you* agree on earth about anything they ask, it will be done for them by my Father in heaven." It's likely that "two of you" in verse 19 refers to those who "bind and loose" in verse 18 since Jesus says in verse 19 that the Father in heaven will do for them that which they agree upon on earth. This is similar language to what Jesus says in verse 18 concerning the church: "whatever you bind on earth shall be bound *in heaven*," and "whatever you lose on earth shall be loosed *in heaven*." Therefore, it seems the "two or three gathered" that Jesus speaks of in verse 20 refers to those who "bind" and "loose" in verse 18.

Given this connection, it's plausible to read Jesus' statement in verse 20 to mean that when the Church convenes to tackle difficult matters and pronounce judgments in his *name*—that is, with his authority—he will be with them, ensuring that whatever they (the "two or three gathered in his name") bind and loose on earth is bound and loosed in heaven.

Bible scholar J. MacEvilly explains the argument this way:

[Some] connect this [v.19] with verse 18, as if it meant to prove, that whatever they shall bind on earth, shall be bound in heaven, &c., because, he is in the midst of them, binding and loosing, as if he said: since the aid of heavenly light is necessary for the right government of the Church; therefore, if two of those, charged with the government of the Church, agree upon anything appertaining to the exercise of the keys, they shall obtain it of his Father. "For, where there are two or three gathered together in my name," &c., representing his name and power for governing the Church, "there he is in the midst of them," hearing their prayers, judging, decreeing with them, governing the Church with them.[18]

Therefore, rather than disproving the visible nature of the Church, when read in context this verse actually supports it.[19]

COUNTER-CHALLENGE

Does instruction to oversee the behavior of members of a community suggest a hierarchical structure? What about instruction to discipline a member who refuses to obey judgments?

AFTERTHOUGHT

The Council of Jerusalem in Acts 15 is an example of how the early Church followed Jesus' prescription when it came to doctrinal matters. Luke tells us in Acts 15:1-2 that Paul and Barnabas "had no small dissension and debate" with those Jewish converts who were teaching that circumcision was necessary for salvation. And in order to settle the debate, Paul and Barnabas were appointed to go and meet with the apostles and elders in Jerusalem. In other words, they took it to the Church, just as Jesus told them to do.

"All Are One in Christ"

Galatians 3:28 and Church Hierarchy

How can the Catholic Church teach that some Christians have more authority than others when Scripture says that we're all one in Christ?

The *Catechism* teaches that in the Church there are "hierarchy and laity" (873) and that the Lord wills such differences between the members of his body. Paragraphs 874 and 877 speak of the Church as having a "variety of offices" and being constituted with a "sacred hierarchy."

But for some Protestants,[20] this teaching on hierarchy contradicts what Paul writes in Galatians 3:28: "There is neither Jew nor Greek, there is neither slave nor free, there is neither male nor female; for you are all one in Christ Jesus." To Paul, we're all equal, which disproves the Catholic belief that the Church is constituted with a hierarchy.

MEETING THE CHALLENGE

1. Paul can't be denying the hierarchical nature of the Church because there is evidence that both Jesus and Paul understood the Church to be hierarchical.

We can start with Jesus. That Jesus selects twelve men to be his "apostles" apart from all other believers reveals his intention to establish his Church with a hierarchy (Matt. 10:1-4). In Luke 22:29-30, we discover that he makes these apostles rulers in his kingdom. Jesus promises to assign his kingdom to the apostles (as the Father assigned it to him) and give them the authority to "sit on thrones judging the twelve tribes of Israel" (v.30).

A possible background for the imagery of *sitting on thrones to judge* is Psalm 122:5, which speaks of the "thrones for judgment . . . of the house of David." Such thrones were seats for the royal ministers of the Davidic kingdom that governed Israel. With this background in mind, it's possible that when Jesus speaks of his apostles sitting on thrones to judge in his kingdom he intends his apostles to be for the *new* Davidic kingdom, the Church, what the royal ministers were for the old Davidic kingdom: rulers who govern. And if they are rulers who govern, they constitute a hierarchy in Jesus' Church.

Jesus' intention for his Church to be hierarchical is further supported by his appointment of Peter as head of the Twelve. Consider what Jesus tells Peter in Matthew 16:18-19:

> And I tell you, you are Peter, and on this rock I will build my church, and the powers of death shall not pre-vail against it. I will give you the keys of the kingdom of heaven, and whatever you bind on earth shall be bound in heaven, and whatever you loose on earth shall be loosed in heaven.

There are three clues that suggest Peter's superior rank of authority. First, Peter is the foundational "rock" of the Church. As we noted previously, the name *Peter* (Greek, *petros*) means "rock," as John the evangelist confirms in John 1:42. If Peter is the visible foundation of Jesus' Church on earth, that makes him the visible source of unity. Wherever the foundation is, there is the true Church of Jesus.

Second, Peter is given the "keys of the kingdom." In the Jewish tradition, this imagery signifies an institutional office in the Davidic kingdom known as the *royal steward* or *master of the palace.* This official had royal authority second to no one except the king himself (Isa. 22:15-22). Therefore, Jesus' handing over the keys to Peter signifies Peter as the royal steward, second in authority only to king Jesus.

The third clue is Jesus' exclusive instruction for Peter to "bind and loose." We know from Matthew 18:18 that the Church as a whole has authority to bind and loose as well. But notice here that Jesus *singles out Peter.* This suggests that Peter has a unique authority to bind and loose, an authority that he can exercise on his own, which ranks him above the collegial authority of the Church.

This higher rank that Peter has among the Twelve explains why Matthew lists Peter as "first" in Matthew 10:2. The Greek word used here, *protos,* can be used either to connote a chronological order or to suggest a primacy of place, like "first and foremost," or "most prominent."[21]

It doesn't seem that Matthew is using *protos* in a chronological sense. He can't be using it to refer to the chronological order of the apostles' *calling* because Andrew was called first, not Peter (John 1:42). Nor can he be using it to refer to an order in a *list,* since he doesn't speak of a "second," "third," etc. Therefore, Matthew must intend *protos* to refer to Peter having a primacy of place among the Twelve, the "first and foremost," or "most prominent" apostle. That's hierarchy!

We can turn to Paul himself for evidence of the hierarchical nature of the Church. In Acts 14:23 we read that Paul appointed "elders" (Greek, *presbuteroi*; "presbyters" or "priests") in every church throughout their apostolic journeys. In Acts 20, he convenes the presbyters of the church in Ephesus and confirms them in their leadership role: "Take heed to yourselves and to all the flock, in which the Holy Spirit has made you guardians, to feed the church of the Lord" (v.28).

The office of the bishop is another hierarchical office that Paul gives instructions about—for example, in 1 Timothy 3:1-3, calling the office of the bishop a "noble task." The Greek word that Paul uses for "office of bishop" is *episkopē,* which is the same word used to describe the apostolic office in Acts 1:20. This suggests that the bishops (*episkopoi;* "overseers") of the early Church, like the apostles, were to exercise oversight in the Church, which proves its hierarchical nature.

The other role that constituted part of the hierarchy in the early Church was that of the deacon. In 1 Timothy 3:8-13, Paul gives Timothy instructions about this office as well, immediately after he gives instructions concerning the office of the bishop.

For Paul, the ministers that occupy these various offices were to be given special honor. He writes to Timothy concerning the presbyters: "Let the elders who rule well be considered worthy of double honor, especially those who labor in preaching and teaching" (1 Tim. 5:17). Paul gives the same instruction to the Christians in Thessalonica, telling them to "esteem them [those who labor over us in the Lord] very highly in love" (1 Thess. 5:13).

We can also include the book of Hebrews, although we don't know if Paul wrote it. For example, it says in 13:17, "Obey your leaders and submit to them; for they are keeping watch over your souls." Just a few verses earlier, in verse 7, the author writes, "Remember your *leaders,* those who spoke to you the word of God; consider the outcome of their life, and imitate their faith."

That bishops, presbyters, and deacons exercised oversight and governing authority in the early Church and that such ministers were to be given honor and obedience, allows us to conclude that not every member of the Christian community had equal roles, but rather that there was a hierarchy of authority.

2. **Membership in the hierarchy for the early Church was objectively verifiable through the rite of ordination by the laying on of hands and their commission to appoint others to the hierarchy and teach with authority.[22]**

Just as Moses laid hands on Joshua as a visible sign of the conferring of authority (Num. 27:22-23; cf. Deut. 34:9), so too, the apostles laid hands on men as a sign of conferring apostolic authority.

For example, Paul speaks of how he laid hands on Timothy: "Hence I remind you to rekindle the gift of God that is within you through the laying on of my hands" (2 Timothy 1:6). This suggests an ordination to a specific ministerial office in the hierarchy.

Timothy's position in the hierarchy is further supported by the fact that Paul tasks him with appointing other men to hierarchical roles in the Church: "Do not be hasty in the laying on of hands" (1 Tim. 5:22).

This follows upon Paul's instructions to Timothy about how we should consider "elders" as "worthy of double honor" (1 Tim. 5:17) and how Timothy is to discern which men are worthy to be "bishops" (1 Tim. 3:1-7) and "deacons" (1 Tim. 8-13). That Timothy is to oversee these ministries suggests that he belongs to the hierarchy of the early Church.

Timothy is also given the authoritative task to "command and teach" (1 Tim. 4:11), along with *rebuking* those who come along and teach things contrary to sound teaching (2 Tim. 4:1-5).

Titus is given similar instructions to Timothy's. For example, in Titus 1:5, Paul instructs him to "appoint elders in every town." A few verses later, Paul gives Titus authority to "rebuke sharply" (v.13) and "silence" (v.11) those "insubordinate men, empty talkers and deceivers" of the "circumcision party" (v.10). That Titus has authority to appoint elders and authoritatively rebuke those who teach contrary to sound doctrine reveals that he too belongs to the hierarchy in the early Church.

3. **Equality in dignity and diversity in roles among members of the Body of Christ are not mutually exclusive.**

Paul, indeed, teaches that we are all one in Christ, yet this doesn't mean that everyone has the same role to play. There is a difference between equality in dignity and equality in roles. The Bible affirms the former but denies the latter.

The above passages prove as much. But there are more. Consider, for example, Paul's list of ministries in the Church:

> And God has appointed in the Church first apostles, second prophets, third teachers, then workers of miracles, then healers, helpers, administrators, speakers in various kinds of tongues. Are all apostles? Are all prophets? Are all teachers? Do all work miracles? Do all possess gifts of healing? Do all speak with tongues? Do all interpret? But earnestly desire the higher gifts (1 Cor. 12:28-31).

Notice that Paul lists the ministries in a ranking order, thus revealing that he believes the Church is hierarchical.

Similarly, Paul writes in Ephesians 4:11, "And his gifts were that some should be apostles, some prophets, some evangelists, some pastors and teachers." For Paul, the purpose of these distinct ministries is to equip the saints for the work of ministry, for building up the body of Christ until we all attain to the unity of the faith and of the knowledge of the Son of God, to mature manhood, to the measure of the stature of the fullness of Christ (Eph. 4:12-13).

These passages show that not everybody in the Church has the same function and that the different functions in the Church are ranked according to their importance. Thus, Scripture teaches that the early Church was hierarchical.

COUNTER-CHALLENGE

Why must unity and diversity of roles in the Church be mutually exclusive? Can't they exist together?

AFTERTHOUGHT

The threefold hierarchical nature of the Church—bishops, priests, and deacons—is confirmed in early post-apostolic writings as early as A.D. 107 or 110. The early Church Father Ignatius of Antioch writes, "In like manner, let all reverence the deacons as an appointment of Jesus Christ, and the bishop as Jesus Christ, who is the Son of the Father, and the presbyters as the Sanhedrin of God, and assembly of the apostles. Apart from these, there is no Church."[23]

"The Anointing Teaches Us"

1 John 2:27 and the Magisterium

How can the Catholic Church teach that we need a Magisterium (a living teaching authority) when John says that we have no need for a man to teach us since the Holy Spirit will teach us?

The *Catechism* teaches that the "task of giving authentic interpretation of the word of God, whether in its written form or in the form of Tradition, has been entrusted to the living, teaching office of the Church alone" (85). It identifies this living, teaching office as residing in the pope and the bishops in communion with him (100).

But some Protestants will argue that such a teaching office is a Catholic invention that contradicts what the Bible teaches. For evidence, they turn to 1 John 2:27,[24] where John teaches,

> But the anointing [the Holy Spirit—see 1 John 2:20] which you received from him abides in you, and you have no need that any one should teach you; as his anointing teaches you about everything, and is true, and is no lie, just as it has taught you, abide in him.

If John says that Christians have *no* need that any man should teach them (since they have the "anointing," or the Holy Spirit), then how can the Catholic Church say that they do have such a need? Doesn't this Catholic belief contradict the Bible?

MEETING THE CHALLENGE

1. This interpretation can't be right because it doesn't cohere with the beliefs and practices of the author himself.

Do we want to say that John is contradicting the command that Jesus gives the apostles in Matthew 28:19-20? "Go therefore and make disciples of all nations . . . *teaching* them to observe all that I have commanded you." Do we think John doesn't want his audience to accept Peter's teaching in Acts 15 that Gentiles don't have to be circumcised in order to be saved because that was a teaching given by a man? Surely not.

Also, considering that he's writing the epistle, John is *teaching* the Christian community. Even the instruction, "You have no need that anyone should teach you" (1 John 2:27), is in and of itself a teaching that the author is giving!

Moreover, just three verses earlier in 1 John 2:24, he instructs his readers to "let what you heard from the beginning abide in you" and "if what you heard from the beginning abides in you, then you will abide in the Son and in the Father." If John meant for Christians to follow only the testimony of the Spirit—which is what he refers to when he speaks of "the anointing" in verse 27—he would be contradicting himself here in verse 24. The instruction to let what they have heard abide in them implies they received instruction from *men*.

1 John 4:6 is another example: "We are of God. Whoever knows God listens to us, and he who is not of God does not listen to us. By this we know the spirit of truth and the spirit of error." That John speaks of some listening and some not listening implies that there is some sort of teaching activity

going on in the Christian community by which one is able to know the spirit of truth and the spirit of error.

Unless we're willing to say that John is contradicting his own beliefs and practices, we must reject the interpretation that the challenge offers for 1 John 2:27.

2. **There are additional acknowledgments of a divinely appointed teaching ministry in the New Testament.**

For example, in 1 Corinthians 12:28 Paul writes, "And God has appointed in the Church first apostles, second prophets, third teachers."

Similarly, he writes to the Ephesians, "And his gifts were that some should be apostles, some prophets, some evangelists, some pastors and teachers" (4:11). The purpose for such ministries is to "attain to the unity of the faith and of the knowledge of the Son of God" (v.13) and "that we may no longer be children, tossed to and fro and carried about with every wind of doctrine, by the cunning of men, by their craftiness in deceitful wiles" (v.14).

Hebrews 13:7 reads, "Remember your leaders, those *who spoke to you the word of God*; consider the outcome of their life, and imitate their faith."

Given that it's unlikely John, the author, would contradict the above passages, we can conclude that the interpretation of 1 John 2:27 that the challenge purports misses the mark.

3. **What John intends to say in 1 John 2:27 is that his readers must be on guard against false teachers, and he uses hyperbole to do it.**

Since we know that John thinks teachers have an essential role in the Church, he must be using hyperbole (purposeful exaggeration) here. But what message is he conveying with such exaggeration?

The context bears out that John is concerned with those who "went out from us, but they *were not of us*" (1 John 2:19). In other words, he's warning his audience against false teachers, those who are deceiving Christians (v.26) by denying "that Jesus is the Christ" (v.22).

It's in response to such deception that he says, "You have no need that anyone should teach you; as his anointing teaches you about everything" (v. 27). What John means is that his Christian audience should know that what these "antichrists" (v.18) are teaching is false because as Christians they have the Spirit of God, or "the anointing," within them. He's not saying that the Spirit is all we need to discern the truth about God's revelation.

COUNTER-CHALLENGE

How can you tell if the Holy Spirit is leading you to truth without some standard outside yourself to judge whether you have the truth or not?

AFTERTHOUGHT

The idea that the secret testimony of the Spirit is all we need to interpret God's word runs contrary to Peter's teaching in 2 Peter 1:20: "You must understand this, that no prophecy of Scripture is a matter of one's own interpretation." His reason for such a command is that "no prophecy ever came by the impulse of man, but men moved by the Holy Spirit spoke from God" (v.21). Notice that, for Peter, the Holy Spirit doesn't lead us only in a private manner but also does so *through* God's ordained ministers.

II

Scripture & Tradition

Catholics believe that Scripture, Sacred Tradition, and the Magisterium together make up the infallible rule of faith and morals for Christians. But Protestants believe that Scripture *alone* (Latin, *sola scriptura*) is our infallible religious authority and, consequently, view the Catholic position as unbiblical.

The passages that Protestants appeal to in order to prove this alleged contradiction vary in form. Some attempt to show that belief in Sacred Tradition directly contradicts the Bible; others are indirect, taking a positive approach to establish a biblical basis for *sola scriptura* and thereby refute the idea that Tradition also serves as a rule of faith.

But, as in our previous section, meeting these challenges will reveal that Scripture and Tradition don't have to be pitted against each other but together make up the fullness of God's public, authoritative revelation.

"Traditions Nullify God's Word"

Mark 7:8 and Sacred Tradition

How can the Catholic Church teach that Christians are bound to accept Sacred Tradition when Jesus teaches that traditions must be measured by the word of God, thus making the *Bible* the only binding authority for Christians?

The Catholic Church teaches that a Christian must accept and honor "both Scripture and Tradition" (CCC 82). Yet, as some Protestants will challenge,[25] Jesus' condemnation of the pharisaical traditions in Mark 7:8-13 shows otherwise. Jesus condemns the Pharisees' traditions because they "reject the commandment of God" (v.9) and "make void the word of God" (v.13).

Since Jesus judges the Pharisees' traditions based on what Scripture says, it follows that Scripture is our sole infallible rule of faith. Therefore, no tradition can be binding on a Christian.

MEETING THE CHALLENGE

1. Just because Jesus measures a tradition of *men* by Sacred Scripture, it doesn't follow that there is no Tradition from *God* that Christians are bound to accept.

When you read this text carefully, you discover that the type of tradition that Jesus refers to is a "tradition of men" (Mark 7:8). This leaves open the possibility that there may be some Tradition that is of *divine* origin and thus would be binding for Christians.

Moreover, Jesus' condemnation doesn't concern just *any* tradition of men but a tradition that makes "void the word of God" (v.13). In particular, it's a tradition that "rejects the *commandment* of God" (v.9).

Which commandment? Jesus makes it explicit which commandment he has in mind in verses 9-10:

You have a fine way of rejecting the commandment of God, in order to keep your tradition! For Moses said, *"Honor your father and your mother"* and, "He who speaks evil of father or mother, let him surely die."

As to the nature of the tradition itself, Jesus identifies it as *Corban*:

For Moses said, "Honor your father and your mother" and, "He who speaks evil of father or mother, let him surely die"; but you say, "If a man tells his father or his mother, What you would have gained from me is *Corban*" (that is, given to God)—then you no longer permit him to do anything for his father or mother (Mark 7:10-12).

Kittel's Theological Dictionary of the New Testament explains that *Corban* is a Hebrew word that in the Old Testament meant "what is offered."[26] Such an offering could take various forms, including food or possessions. *Corban* would later come to denote offerings made as donations to the temple, which was appropriate since *korbanas* is the word that described the temple's treasury (Matt. 27:6).[27] This kind of offering is what Jesus is referring to in Mark 7:11.

What sends Jesus in an uproar is the first century religious leaders' allowance of men to designate their assets to the temple as *Corban* to free them from supporting their aging parents, a precept that falls under the fourth commandment. It's this nullification of God's word that Jesus condemns. And rightfully so!

Knowing that Jesus' condemnation specifically involved a tradition that some were using to disobey God's word, we can see how this Protestant challenge lacks persuasive force. This passage from Mark 7 only proves that *traditions can't contradict Scripture*, something the Catholic Church agrees with wholeheartedly. It doesn't prove that there can be *no* traditions that Christians are bound to accept.

2. **Paul teaches that there are apostolic traditions that Christians are required to follow.**

One example is 2 Thessalonians 2:15. Right after he speaks of the Thessalonians being saved through "belief in the truth" (v.13) to which they were called through the "gospel" (v.14), Paul writes, "Stand firm and hold to the traditions [Greek, *paradoseis*] which you were taught by us, either by word of mouth or by letter" (2 Thess. 2:15). For Paul, the truth of Jesus' gospel is to be found in Sacred Tradition equally along with Sacred Scripture.

The narrative flow of the chapter shows that the reason Paul instructs the Thessalonians to "hold fast to the traditions" is so that they may be protected from the deception of the "man of lawlessness" and "obtain the glory of our Lord Jesus Christ" (v.14) at the "coming of our Lord Jesus Christ" (v.1). Since Paul nowhere says that this command is *only* for the Thessalonians, we can apply the principle to *all* Christians and say that holding fast to the apostolic traditions is essential to a Christian's salvation and thus is binding for a Christian.

In the next chapter of the same epistle, Paul instructs the Thessalonians again about the binding power of apostolic Tradition: "Now we command you, brethren, in the name of our Lord Jesus Christ, that you keep away from any brother who is living in idleness and not in accord with the Tradition [Greek, *paradosin*] that you received from us" (2 Thess. 3:6). That Paul commands the Thessalonians "in the name of our Lord Jesus Christ" signals that this is not a mere pastoral suggestion.

With such a formula, Paul is exercising his authority as an apostle. This authoritative instruction to reject a brother who fails to live in accord with the received Tradition implies the positive instruction that Christians are *bound* to live in accord with it. For Paul, therefore, the Sacred Tradition is binding and authoritative just as the scriptures are binding and authoritative.

Yet another Pauline text that reveals the existence of apostolic Tradition is 1 Corinthians 11:2. Paul writes, "I commend you because you remember me in everything and maintain the traditions [Greek, *paradoseis*] even as I have delivered them to you." Paul was *delivering* such traditions, suggesting that there existed an *apostolic* Tradition apart from what was written in Scripture. And Paul's praise for the Corinthians for holding fast to those traditions implies that Christians were expected to keep them. Therefore, the Catholic teaching that all Christians must accept and honor "both Scripture and Tradition" (CCC 82) is right in line with Paul's teachings.

COUNTER-CHALLENGE

Does biblical condemnation of one kind of tradition require us to condemn all kinds of traditions?

AFTERTHOUGHT

Jesus' condemnation of a *bad* tradition doesn't preclude the possibility of *good* apostolic traditions "any more than the existence of forged apostolic writings (2 Thess. 2:2) invalidate genuine apostolic writings."[28]

"Scripture Makes the Man of God Complete"

2 Timothy 3:16-17 and the Rejection of Sola Scriptura

How can the Catholic Church teach that we need Tradition as well as Scripture when the Bible says that Scripture is sufficient as a rule of faith and for making a man "complete"?

The *Catechism* teaches that the Church "does not derive her certainty about all revealed truths from the holy scriptures alone" (82). The Church looks to both Scripture *and* Sacred Tradition.

But many Protestants argue that this teaching contradicts what Paul tells Timothy in 2 Timothy 3:16-17:

All Scripture is inspired by God and profitable for teaching, for reproof, for correction, and for training in righteousness, that the man of God may be complete, equipped for every good work.

Many argue that because Scripture is inspired (Greek, *theopneustos*),[29] along with being profitable for teaching and making a man of God complete, it is sufficient as a rule for faith and morals. As Protestant apologist James White puts it, this "passage literally [*sic*] screams sufficiency."[30] On this account there is no need for Sacred Tradition or the Magisterium to know the truth of God's revelation, whether that revelation concerns what we must believe (faith) or do (morals). All we need is the Bible.

MEETING THE CHALLENGE

1. That the scriptures are profitable doesn't mean they are sufficient.

The point of Paul's instruction is to help Timothy be "complete" (Greek, *artios*; to be well-fitted for some function[31]) and "equipped" (Greek, *exērtismenos*; to make ready for service[32]) for his work as an ordained minister to teach, reprove, correct, and train in righteousness. These are the "good works" that Paul is referring to.

That the instruction is for Timothy as an ordained minister is suggested by Paul's use of the phrase "man of God." The only other time this phrase appears in the New Testament is in 1 Timothy 6:11, where Paul refers to Timothy as "man of God" within the context of giving Timothy a series of instructions for his ministry.

For example, after explaining how a slave is to behave toward his believing master, Paul tells Timothy, "Teach and urge these duties" (v.2). Paul then gives a litany of vices that false teachers embody (vv.3-10), instructs Timothy, "But as for you, man of God, shun all this" (v.11), and then gives a list of virtues that Timothy should aim to develop as a teacher of the Faith (vv.11-14). Paul completes his counsel by instructing Timothy to charge the rich to focus on God (vv.17-19), to guard what has been entrusted to him (v.20), and to avoid godless chatter (v.21).

Paul says that Scripture is "profitable" in accomplishing the good works that Timothy is called to perform in his ministry. But *profitable* (Greek, *ophelimos*; pertaining to a benefit to be derived from some object, event, or state—advantage, benefit, beneficial[33]) doesn't equal *sufficient*. Studying a handbook on how to be a police officer is *profitable* to becoming a complete, thoroughly equipped police officer. But there's a whole lot of other stuff we'd also need to undergo: physical training, firearm instruction, real-world experience, etc.

Similarly, just because Paul says that Scripture is profitable for Timothy to fulfill his tasks as an ordained minister, it doesn't follow that it's sufficient all by itself. Even if we grant that what Paul writes can apply to *any* "man of God" and that Scripture is profitable for any Christian to be "complete" and "equipped" for any good work, it still wouldn't follow that Scripture alone is sufficient to achieve these goals.

Sometimes, Protestants will point to the word *complete* and say that this somehow implies the sufficiency of Scripture, but this doesn't follow. A collector may say he needs a certain stamp to make his collection "complete," yet no one takes that to mean that one stamp by itself results in a complete collection. We understand that other stamps are also needed to make the collection complete.

Similarly, the inspired scriptures may lead to the end of Christian perfection. But that doesn't mean that the Bible by itself is sufficient to achieve the end of Christian perfection because we know that other things are needed as well, like obeying decisions made by the authoritative Church (see Matt. 18:15-17; cf. Acts 15) and living in accord with the standard of Tradition (see 2 Thess. 3:6).

2. To read this passage as teaching *sola scriptura* would imply that the *Old Testament* by itself is sufficient.

Recall that Paul is giving Timothy counsel that Scripture is "profitable for teaching, for reproof, for correction, and for training in righteousness." But note that the New Testament did not yet exist. Some of its letters and books hadn't even been written yet, and we were still centuries away from a complete canon of Scripture.

And in case that's not enough, the immediate context (vv.14–15) reveals that Paul is talking *explicitly* about the Old Testament. He tells Timothy to "continue in what you have learned" (v.14) and "know from whom you learned it . . . how from childhood you have been acquainted with the sacred writings" (2 Tim. 3:15). So, at least in Paul's mind, the "profitable" scriptures to which he is referring don't include the non-existent New Testament; they can't even be said to refer in a vague way to all possible scriptures, past and future (Paul could have said that if he meant that). The "sacred writings" that Timothy was "acquainted with" in childhood can only refer to the Old Testament.

If we granted the interpretation that Paul is teaching *sola scriptura* in this passage, then we'd have to conclude that the *Old Testament* alone is a sufficient rule of faith. But no Protestant would say this.

Since we know Paul cannot be encouraging Timothy to embrace the doctrine of *sola Old Testament*, we know that he's not teaching the doctrine of *sola scriptura* either.

3. **To read this passage as teaching *sola scriptura* makes each individual book of Scripture a sufficient rule of faith.**

The Greek *pasa graphē*, which the RSV translates as "all scripture" in 2 Timothy 3:16, is more commonly translated as "every Scripture." Whenever *pasa* is used with a singular noun without the article, like *graphē*, it usually means "every."[34] Given that "every scripture" is likely the more appropriate translation, it's reasonable to conclude that Paul may very well be referring to how each individual book of Scripture is inspired.

Of course, Christians do believe that every book of Scripture is inspired by God. But this causes a problem for a Protestant who uses this passage to support *sola scriptura* since he would have to say likewise that each individual book is also *sufficient* as a rule of faith. In the words of Jimmy Akin, he would have to "do theology by 'Genesis alone,' 'Isaiah alone,' and so forth."[35]

COUNTER-CHALLENGE

If something is profitable for attaining a goal, does that mean that nothing else can be profitable—or even necessary—to attain it?

AFTERTHOUGHT

Notice that the challenge from 2 Timothy 3:16-17 assumes that we know what inspired Scripture is in the first place. But the only way to know what counts as Scripture is to appeal to some source outside Scripture. In making this appeal, though, we make something outside Scripture a rule of faith, thus invalidating *sola scriptura*.

"The Noble Bereans"

Acts 17:11 and the Rejection of Sola Scriptura

How can the Catholic Church teach that Scripture is not our sole infallible source for doctrine when the book of Acts praises the Bereans for using Scripture alone to determine the truth?

In Acts 17, Luke records Paul and Silas's trips to various places, two of which were Thessalonica and Berea. We're told that Paul argued with the Jews in the synagogues of each city, explaining to them where in the scriptures it spoke of the Christ having to die and rise.

Although Paul and Silas converted some "devout Greeks" and "not a few of the leading women" in Thessalonica (v.4), the Jews there were jealous and led a huge riot, forcing the Christian "brethren" to send Paul and Silas away in the middle of the night lest they be handed over to the city authorities.

Things were different in Berea. Luke tells us that the Bereans were "more noble than those in Thessalonica" because "they received the word with all eagerness, examining the scriptures daily" to see if what Paul taught was true (v.11).

Many Protestants[36] argue that the Berean response to Paul implies that Scripture is the final authority since for them it was the measure for determining the truth of Paul's teaching. And since the Bereans didn't appeal to anything *except* Scripture, it was sufficient for them to verify or disprove Paul's teaching. Therefore, it's sufficient for us, too—contrary to what the Catholic Church teaches.

MEETING THE CHALLENGE

1. The conclusion that Scripture is sufficient as an infallible rule for faith and morals doesn't follow from the Bereans' behavior recorded in Acts 17:11.

First, the Bereans are appealing to the Old Testament. Even if we granted for argument's sake that ancient Jews looked to Scripture as their only infallible rule for faith and morals (which they didn't), it wouldn't necessarily follow that *Christians* would be bound by that same principle.

Like other things that are new in Christian revelation (e.g., baptism, the Lord's Supper, love of enemies), Christians could have been given a new source of truth that along with Scripture constituted *their* infallible rule for faith and morals. It's futile to appeal to a Jewish practice alone in order to establish a formal Christian principle.

Furthermore, even if we took Luke's statement about the Berean nobility to be a reference to their appeal to Scripture (in a moment we'll see that there's reason to doubt this), the fact that examining the scriptures is a noble act doesn't lead us to conclude that Scripture is the only infallible rule of faith. Of course, examining Scripture to see if a teaching harmonizes with it is noble (and wise!). But there may be other authoritative sources of religious truth that it's also noble to examine.

Ultimately, the Bereans' behavior proves nothing more than that Christian doctrine shouldn't contradict definitive truth articulated in the Old Testament. The Catholic

Church has no beef with this since it professes the Old Testament books to be inspired and accepts as divinely revealed its teachings on faith and morals. So it makes perfect sense for those teachings to be in harmony with the new revelation of Jesus Christ.

2. **The nobility of the Bereans wasn't due to their appeal to Scripture but to their lack of hostility, unlike the Jews in Thessalonica.**

Luke's statement about the Bereans' nobility comes after his description of the hostile behavior of the Jews in Thessalonica. We're told in Acts 17:4 that some Jews were persuaded by Paul's teaching. But then, in verse 5, Luke highlights how these conversions led to much Jewish conflict: "And taking some wicked fellows of the rabble, they gathered a crowd, set the city in an uproar, and attacked the house of Jason, seeking to bring them out to the people" (Acts 17:5).

The "wicked fellows" then dragged Jason and some of the new Christians before the city authorities and charged them with acting against the decrees of Caesar by claiming Jesus to be king (Acts 17:6-7). The situation caused such panic on the part of the Christians that they sent Paul and Silas away to Berea during the night (the most dangerous time to travel). The Jews in Thessalonica, however, didn't give up. Enraged with Paul's actions in Thessalonica, they sent men to pursue Paul to Berea and provoked the crowd against him.

This is the background against which Luke says the Bereans were "more noble than those in Thessalonica, for they received the word with all eagerness" (Acts 17:11). The nobility doesn't have to do with examining the scriptures. It has to do with the Bereans' lack of hostility and their open-mindedness to the gospel message.

This is further supported by the Greek word translated as "noble": a form of *eugenēs*. The word originally referred to noble birth[37] but came to be used more generally to refer to open-minded behavior and a willingness to learn, which at the time were qualities associated with the upper class.[38]

3. The "word" that the Bereans received was the apostolic preaching, which is called the "word of God."

Luke tells us that the Bereans received "the word with all eagerness" (Acts 17:11), and he identifies that *word* as the "word of God" (v.13). But the "word of God" here can't mean the Old Testament since the Bereans had already accepted that word. It can't be referring to the New Testament, because it wasn't written yet. The only reference possible is the content of Paul's *preaching*, namely the apostolic Tradition.

Paul didn't merely parrot what was found in the Old Testament. He preached new revelation, namely that Jesus was the Messiah. *That* is the word that the Bereans received with eagerness, the word that Luke labels the "word of God" (v.13). The Bereans simply did what the believing Thessalonians did: they accepted Paul's preaching not as the word of men but as the "word of God" (1 Thess. 2:13).

COUNTER-CHALLENGE

What if the Bereans had concluded that Paul was wrong? Should they have stuck with their interpretation of the Old Testament? Or should they have gone with Paul's interpretation?

AFTERTHOUGHT

Consider what it would mean for us if we followed the Bereans' example. If someone came and proposed an extrabiblical Tradition for Christian belief, we would need to examine it to see if it coheres with Scripture.

"Don't Go Beyond What Is Written"

1 Corinthians 4:6 and the Rejection of Sola Scriptura

How can the Catholic Church reject the Protestant doctrine of *sola scriptura* when Paul instructs us "not to go beyond what is written"?

As we've seen, the Church doesn't teach *sola scriptura*. Catholics also look to Sacred Tradition as part of the one divine source of God's revelation.

But for some Protestants,[39] this contradicts Paul's teaching "not to go beyond what is written" (1 Cor. 4:6). They think it couldn't be any clearer: Paul makes *written Scripture* the parameter beyond which we are not free to go in order to derive knowledge about God's revelation.[40] Appealing to Sacred Tradition to gain such knowledge violates this clear command.

MEETING THE CHALLENGE

1. The *sola scriptura* interpretation of 1 Corinthians 4:6 doesn't fit with Paul's positive attitude to traditions that *do* go beyond what is written.

The instruction not to go beyond what is written comes at the end of a long discourse starting in chapter three of the same letter in which Paul chastises the Corinthians for creating factions in their church. Some were saying, "I belong to Paul," and others, "I belong to Apollos" (1 Cor. 3:4). Paul sees such factionist activity as destructive.

This seems to be what motivates Paul to give his instruction not to go beyond what is written because he tells the Corinthians right afterward, "I have applied all this to myself and Apollos for your benefit . . . *that none of you may be puffed up in favor of one against another*" (4:6). It seems reasonable, therefore, to conclude that Paul appeals to "what is written" as his justification for telling the Corinthians to cease their factionist activity.

But what does Paul mean by "what is written"? Let's say for argument's sake that Paul meant the scriptures as a whole, both Old and New Testaments. If the *sola scriptura* interpretation of this passage were correct, though, it would conflict with the positive attitude to and teaching about Christian Tradition that Paul exhibits elsewhere.

Luke tells us that Paul visited the Christians in Corinth a few years before he wrote his first letter to them, staying there for a year and six months, "teaching the word of God among them" (Acts 18:11). Surely, not *everything* he taught the Corinthians during his visit ended up in his epistles written to them. And it's unlikely that the entirety of what he taught outside his written epistles ended up in other apostolic epistles.

According to the logic of this challenge, though, we'd have to conclude that Paul wanted Christians to reject the majority of what he taught for a year and a half prior to his letters and hold only to the parts that made it into writing!

Not only does this seem unlikely, we know that it wasn't Paul's intention. In 1 Corinthians 11:2, he writes,

"I commend you because you remember me in everything and maintain the *traditions* even as I have delivered them to you." Paul wouldn't be saying in 1 Corinthians 4:6 not to go beyond what is written and then a few chapters later praise the Corinthians for doing that very thing. This shows that Paul was not operating on the principle of *sola scriptura* and that he didn't want the Corinthians operating on it either.

2 Thessalonians 2:15 is further evidence that Paul didn't intend the churches to follow *sola scriptura*. He instructs the Thessalonians, "So then, brethren, stand firm and *hold to the traditions* which you were taught by us, *either by word of mouth or by letter.*"

Any tradition that is not taught by "letter" (for example, knowledge of which books are inspired by God) would constitute something that goes beyond "what is written." The logic embedded in the challenge using 1 Corinthians 4:6, therefore, creates a dilemma: either give up the *sola scriptura* interpretation of 1 Corinthians 4:6 and keep Paul's instruction in 2 Thessalonians 2:15 or give up Paul's instruction in 2 Thessalonians 2:15 and keep the *sola scriptura* spin on 1 Corinthians 4:6. I think Paul would want us to go with keeping his instruction in 2 Thessalonians 2:15!

2. **The meaning of "not to go beyond what is written" in 1 Corinthians 4:6 is too ambiguous to be used as a prooftext for *sola scriptura*.**

Respected Protestant scholar Fee Gordon writes that "this clause is particularly difficult to pin down" and that some see it "as so obscure that they despair of finding its meaning."[41]

Here are some of the options that people have proposed for what "beyond what is written" might refer to:[42]

- the scriptures in general concerning conduct for preachers

- the Old Testament passages Paul already quoted in 1 Corinthians 1:19, 31; 2:16; 3:19-20
- the metaphors of planting and building used in 1 Corinthians 3:15-17, the implication being that we should avoid false teachers who add to the gospel
- more generally, to everything Paul himself wrote in the preceding chapters of the same epistle concerning Christian conduct
- a Christian slogan or proverb used to address those causing discord in the community, a slogan that meant something akin to, "Keep within the rules"
- a public document for the Corinthian church that Paul modeled on cultic bylaws in order to lay out guidelines and principles necessary to preserve peace and prosperity

Given the ambiguity of what is meant by "what is written," as evident in the diversity of theories even among Protestant scholars, 1 Corinthians 4:6 can't be used to challenge Catholic belief in Sacred Tradition and support the doctrine of *sola scriptura*.

COUNTER-CHALLENGE

If Paul instructed Christians to look to traditions beyond the written scriptures, shouldn't we?

AFTERTHOUGHT

You can point out to those who make this challenge that not even John Calvin, a staunch defender of the doctrine of *sola scriptura*, thought 1 Corinthians 4:6 supported it. He thought Paul's use of the phrase "what is written" probably referred either to "proofs from Scripture" which he brought forward or his "own writings."[43]

"Don't Add to God's Word"

Revelation 22:18-19 and the Deuterocanonical Books

How can the Catholic Church add books to the biblical canon when the book of Revelation expressly forbids adding to God's word?

Catholic Bibles are bigger than Protestant ones. The *Catechism* teaches that the canon of Scripture includes "forty-six books for the Old Testament (forty-five if we count Jeremiah and Lamentations as one) and twenty-seven for the New" (120). Although Protestants agree with Catholics on the books that make up the New Testament, there are seven books in the Catholic Old Testament canon that they reject: Tobit, Judith, Wisdom, Sirach, Baruch, and 1 and 2 Maccabees. They also reject portions of the books of Daniel and Esther.[44] Catholics refer to these seven books as the *deuterocanonical* (second-canon) books and Protestants call them the *Apocrypha*.

You may run across a Protestant[45] who rejects the deuterocanonical books because he thinks the Catholic Church added these books in violation of John's prohibition to add to the Bible:

I warn everyone who hears the words of the prophecy of this book: if anyone adds to them, God will add to him the plagues described in this book, and if anyone takes away from the words of the book of this prophecy, God will take away his share in the tree of life and in the holy city, which are described in this book (Rev. 22:18-19).

John says not to add to Scripture, yet the Catholic Church literally added seven whole books and more!

MEETING THE CHALLENGE

1. **If we granted for argument's sake that John here is referring to the entire canon of Scripture, then Protestants would be guilty for removing the deuterocanonicals.**

If we suppose that John is talking about the biblical canon (the list of all the books that make up the Bible) in Revelation 22:18-19, then the challenge becomes a two-edged sword. A Protestant may argue that the Catholic Church added books to the Bible, but a Catholic can just as easily argue that the Protestant community took some books away.

The seven books found in the Catholic Old Testament that are not found in the Protestant Old Testament were widely held as Scripture all throughout Christian history, and it was not until the Protestant Reformation that their canonicity was called into question and rejected on a major scale.

Prior to the Reformation, some individuals did question the canonicity of these books, but for the most part Christians as a whole accepted them. Numerous fourth and fifth-century Church councils authoritatively declared them to be inspired: the Synod of Rome (A.D. 382), Council of Hippo (393), Third Council of Carthage (397), and Sixth Council of Carthage (419). Protestant scholar J.N.D. Kelly affirms the major consensus on these books in the early Church: "For the great majority, however, the deuterocanonical writings ranked as Scripture in the fullest sense."[46]

Such historical evidence makes this challenge difficult for a Protestant. If Revelation 22:18-19 refers to the canon, then the prohibition of "taking away" from it is just as strong as the prohibition of adding to it. So how can Protestants reject seven books from the Bible when Revelation 22:18-19 forbids it?

2. This passage is not even discussing the canon of Scripture but merely the book of Revelation.

These verses, however, don't even refer to the entire Bible. The Greek word used here for *book, bibliou,* can mean "small book" or "scroll."[47] In the ancient world, it was impossible to fit the entire Bible on a single scroll. The books of the Bible were originally individual compositions, such as an individual scroll, and the biblical canon as we know it was a collection of individual scrolls, a library of books. That's why they are called the "books" (plural) of the Bible. These books would not be put into a single volume until centuries later.

Therefore, it makes most sense to read the phrase "book of this prophecy" as referring to the scroll *in which John is recording his prophecy,* namely the book of Revelation. As such, John's instruction not to add or remove anything refers to the book he was writing—Revelation—and not the future canon of Scripture (which wouldn't be authoritatively settled for centuries after).

A similar instruction is given in Deuteronomy 4:2, where Moses says, "You shall not add to the word which I command you, nor take from it; that you may keep the commandments of the LORD your God which I command you." Moses wasn't referring to the whole Old Testament canon; otherwise we would have to side with the Saddu-cees and reject every Old Testament book outside the Pen-tateuch. He was merely prohibiting adding or taking away from the "statutes and the ordinances" that constitute the Mosaic Law.

Since we now know that John was not giving instruc-tions concerning the biblical canon but instructions govern-ing the book of Revelation (don't add to the prophetic text of Revelation and don't take away from it), it becomes clear that Revelation 22:18-19 doesn't undermine the Catholic canon, regardless of whether the Catholic Church added books to the biblical canon or Protestants subtracted from it. Of course, we must not add to or subtract from the canon of Scripture. But that is not what John is talking about in this passage.

COUNTER-CHALLENGE

How could John be referring to the entire biblical canon in Revelation 22:18-19 when the canon wouldn't be settled for another several hundred years?

AFTERTHOUGHT

Your Protestant friend might argue that because the New Testament doesn't quote any of the deuterocanonical books[48] we have good reason to exclude them from the canon of Scripture. This is common among some Protestants.[49] But this logic would demand that we also exclude from the canon Song of Songs, Ecclesiastes, Esther, Obadiah, Zephaniah, Judges, 1 Chronicles, Ezra, Nehemiah, Lamentations, Nahum, Joshua, Obadiah, and Zephaniah since the New Testament doesn't quote any of these. I don't think your Protestant friend wants to make his biblical canon any smaller!

III

Salvation

The biblical challenges we encountered in the previous section have their roots in the Protestant Reformation, of which *sola scriptura* was one of two "pillars." The other pillar was the doctrine of salvation by faith alone, known as *sola fide*. A great many Protestants to this day adhere to the belief that a person is saved, justified, made righteous by faith alone, and that no actions he performs can have any impact on his salvation.

Related to this doctrine is the idea that justification is a one-time event that secures us in a saving relationship with Jesus, a relationship that no sinful deeds can break.

There is no lack of Bible passages that Protestants cite in support of these beliefs. Some passages seem to show that works, indeed, play no part in our salvation. Others seem to suggest that our salvation is a one-time event and can never be lost. Protestants also hold fast to these beliefs because they think that to deny them somehow undermines the sufficiency of Jesus' work on the cross.

But, as we'll see, the Scripture passages that Protestants raise in order to challenge Catholic teaching on salvation do not pose a real threat to it. (Properly understood, they harmonize with it.) And we'll see that Catholic teaching on salvation in no way detracts from Jesus' saving death on the cross but manifests and honors it.

"We Are Justified All at Once"

Romans 5:1 and the Process of Justification

How can the Catholic Church teach that our justification is a process when the Bible says that our justification is a one-time event?

The Catholic Church distinguishes between different stages of justification. In chapter ten of its decree, "The Increase of the Justification Received," the Council of Trent speaks of those who have "been thus justified and made the friends and domestics of God," thereby recognizing an initial stage of justification in which a person first comes into relationship with Christ.

The council then says that such justified Christians "increase in that justice received through the grace of Christ and are further justified" through the "observance of the commandments of God and of the Church" and by "faith cooperating with good works." This "increase in justice" that makes a Christian "further justified" signifies an *ongoing* stage of justification.

For some Protestants,[50] this idea of increasing in justice and furthering our justification contradicts the teaching of the Bible since Paul tells us that justification is a one-time event that occurs when we first express faith: "Therefore, since we are justified by faith, we have peace with God through our Lord Jesus Christ" (Rom. 5:1).

Some argue that we know Paul is referring to an action in the past because the Greek word for "we are justified" (*dikaiōthentes*) can literally be translated as "we *have been declared* righteous."[51] *Dikaiōthentes* is a passive participle in a simple past tense, which usually refers to an antecedent time with respect to the main verb,[52] which in this case is *dikaioō*, "justify; declare righteous."[53]

Moreover, Paul says this in the context of quoting Genesis 15:6, which speaks of Abraham's justification: "Abraham believed God, and it was reckoned to him as righteousness"[54] (Rom. 4:3). If Abraham was justified once and for all at the moment of faith, and Paul is drawing a parallel between his justification and our justification, it follows that we are justified once and for all at the moment when we profess faith in Christ, contrary to what the Catholic Church teaches about an ongoing process of justification.

MEETING THE CHALLENGE

1. Paul can't mean that justification is a one-time completed action of the past because elsewhere he teaches that there are multiple stages of justification.

Consider what Paul says in Romans 2:13: "For it is not the hearers of the law who are righteous before God, but the doers of the law who will be justified." The future tense, "*will be* justified," suggests that justification doesn't merely occur in the past.

Another example of this future dimension of justification is Romans 6:16. Here Paul juxtaposes sin and obedience and teaches that obedience "*leads to* righteousness [*eis dikaiosunēn*]." And he's not just talking about obedience prior to faith—he's talking about obedience leading to righteousness *after* we already have believed.

In Galatians 5:5, Paul writes, "For through the Spirit, by faith, we wait for the hope of righteousness (*dikaiosunēs*)." Paul's use of *hope* indicates that there is some aspect to our justification that is not yet complete since you can only hope for that which you don't yet possess (cf. Rom. 8:24). Moreover, Paul speaks of those who have such hope as having faith and *already* being in the Spirit. How could Paul speak of justified Christians having a hope of righteousness if there were not some future aspect to our justification?

2. **The parallel to Abraham's justification supports the multiple-stages view of justification.**

The challenge says that justification is a one-time event of the past because Paul parallels our justification with Abraham's justification by faith. But rather than this parallel undermining Catholic belief, it weighs in favor of it.

In Romans 4:3, when Paul speaks of Abraham believing God and its being reckoned to him as righteousness, Paul is quoting Genesis 15:6. The context of that verse shows that Abraham was justified because he believed God's promise concerning his offspring. But what many fail to recall is that Abraham had *already been* justified many years before when he followed God's call to leave his home in Haran and journey to a then-unknown land promised to him by God (Gen. 12:1-3).

The author of Hebrews is our guiding light here. In Hebrews 11:8, we discover that Abraham obeyed God's call "by faith," and the type of faith that he had was a faith "without [which] it is impossible to please God" (v.6) and a faith by which "men of old received divine approval" (v.2). This means that Abraham responded to God's call with a faith that justifies—a *saving* faith.

So, the righteousness that was reckoned to Abraham later, when he believed God's promise in Genesis 15:6, was not his initial stage of justification. It was a *new* act of belief that God reckoned as a *new* act of righteousness.[55] The New American Bible translation brings this point out better, saying that the Lord "attributed it to him [Abraham] as an *act* of righteousness."

Abraham's justification didn't stop there. James tells us that Abraham was justified yet again in Genesis 22 when he obeyed God's command to offer his son Isaac in sacrifice—years after the events recorded in Genesis 15. James writes,

> Was not Abraham our father justified by works, when he offered his son Isaac upon the altar? You see that faith was active along with his works, and faith was completed by works, and the Scripture was fulfilled which says, "Abraham believed God, and it was reckoned to him as righteousness"; and he was called the friend of God (2:21-23).

This text shows that a believer can increase in righteousness even *after* he is initially justified.

With this added piece to the puzzle, we have a total of three moments in Abraham's life when he was justified through his faith: when he obeyed God's call in Genesis 12, when he believed God's promise concerning his offspring in Genesis 15:6, and when he began to offer Isaac in sacrifice in Genesis 22. If Abraham's justification is the paradigm for our justification, as our Protestant friends like to say, then our justification is not a one-time event of the past. Rather, as it was for Abraham, it's an ongoing process for a person who *lives* by faith continuously throughout his life.

COUNTER-CHALLENGE

Does affirming one stage of justification mean we have to deny others?

AFTERTHOUGHT

Protestants should be glad to know that the Catholic Church agrees that when we are justified in the initial stage of justification we are *fully* justified. The Council of Trent taught that believers "are made innocent, immaculate, pure, guiltless and beloved of God, heirs indeed of God, joint heirs with Christ; so that there is nothing whatever to hinder their entrance into heaven."[56] That justification, or righteousness, then grows by the performance of good works throughout a Christian's life.[57]

"Not Because of Works"

Ephesians 2:8-9 and the Role of Works for Our Salvation

Why do Catholics believe that works contribute to our salvation, when Scripture teaches that we are not saved by works lest anyone should boast?

In chapter twenty-six of its *Decree on Justification,* the Council of Trent taught that eternal life will be given at our judgment as a reward for our good works. It states, "Unto them who work well *unto the end,* and hoping in God, life eternal is to be proposed, both as a grace mercifully promised to the sons of God through Jesus Christ, and as a recompense which is to be faithfully rendered to their good works" (emphasis added).

But for some Protestants,[58] this contradicts Scripture because Paul makes it clear that we are saved by grace and *not* by works: "For by grace you have been saved through faith; and this is not your own doing, it is the gift of God—not because of works, lest any man should boast" (Eph. 2:8-9).

Paul says plainly that works have nothing to do with our salvation, so the Catholic Church's teaching that good works contribute to our final salvation is unbiblical.

MEETING THE CHALLENGE

1. Paul can't be saying that works have nothing to do with our salvation *in any sense* because he elsewhere teaches that works do contribute to our salvation.

Take the next verse of the passage in question: "For we are his workmanship, created in Christ Jesus *for good works*, which God prepared beforehand, that we should walk in them" (Eph. 2:10). We also know that Paul can't be denying works in an absolute sense because elsewhere in his writings he affirms that works do have some role to play in our salvation. The following passages are illustrative:

-   Philippians 2:12: "Work out your own salvation with fear and trembling."

-   Galatians 5:6: "For in Christ Jesus neither circumcision nor uncircumcision is of any avail, but faith working through love."

-   2 Corinthians 6:1: "Working together with him, then, we entreat you not to accept the grace of God in vain."

-   Romans 2:6-7: "For he will render to every man according to his works: to those who by patience in well-doing seek for glory and honor and immortality, he will give eternal life."

Either Paul is contradicting himself, or the claim that Ephesians 2:8-9 says works are not necessary for salvation *in any sense* must be wrong.

So why would Paul say that works have nothing to do with our salvation and then in the same breath say that they do? Our next response to this challenge will show how Paul's statements can be reconciled.

2. Paul is referring to the initial stage of salvation, which according to Catholic teaching cannot be merited by works of any kind.

The key to understanding Paul's apparent contradiction lies in Paul's references to different *stages* of salvation. Verses 8-9 of the passage in question, where Paul says we're not saved by works, refer to that initial stage of salvation—the salvation we receive when we initially enter into relationship with Christ. The Catholic Church teaches that good works *cannot* obtain the grace for this stage of salvation (CCC 1996, 2010, 2022).

The preceding context (vv. 1-6) supports this view. Paul describes himself and the Ephesians as "dead in their offenses, and sins" (v.1) while they were "children of unbelief" (v.2) and "children of wrath" (v.3). Then in verses 5-6, Paul describes their passage from unbelief to belief:

> Even when we were dead through our trespasses, [God] made us alive together with Christ (by grace you have been saved), and raised us up with him, and made us sit with him in the heavenly places in Christ Jesus.

For Paul, therefore, the grace by which they were saved apart from works is the grace of initial conversion. It is only after they are "made alive in Christ" (v.5) that they can walk in the works that God prepared for them and "reap eternal life" (Gal. 6:8).

3. The "works" that Paul says we're saved apart from may be a different kind of works from the "good works" that God has prepared for us to walk in.

The above interpretation solves the apparent contradiction. But there is an additional and complementary way to explain it.

Upon first reading, we might think that what Paul has in mind for "works" is the same before and after initial salvation. But it's possible that "works" (v.9) and "good works" (v.10) are different things: "works" referring to the precepts of the Mosaic Law and "good works" referring to acts of charity.

This interpretation is, in fact, probable, given that in verses 11-22 of the same chapter Paul addresses Gentiles (v.11), telling them that they are united to God through the "blood of Christ" (v.13) and that the "dividing wall" (v.14), the "law of commandments and ordinances" (v.15), has been broken down. On this interpretation, Paul is telling the Jews that they can't boast because they are saved by the free gift of grace through faith and not by their performance of the works of the Mosaic Law.[59]

Apologist Jimmy Akin makes the argument that this interpretation appears even more probable when you consider that Paul commonly uses the Greek word for *boast* (*kauchaomai*) in reference to Jews boasting of their special relationship with God through the law (see Rom. 2:17, 23) and Christians boasting of their special relationship with God through Christ (Rom. 5:2; 5:11). Therefore, he concludes, Paul's saying that salvation is "not because of works, lest any man should boast" "means neither Jew nor Gentile can boast of having a special, saving relationship with God in preference to the other: both are saved through faith in Christ."[60]

COUNTER-CHALLENGE

If Ephesians 2:8-9 only proves that works have nothing to do with receiving salvation initially, isn't it possible that works could play a role in other stages of our salvation, such as when we're judged to receive eternal life at the end of our lives?

AFTERTHOUGHT

The Catholic Church only sees works as contributing to our salvation *after* we are initially saved. In fact, the Council of Trent teaches that James 2:24, which states that "by works a man is justified, and not by faith only," applies only to those who have already been initially justified and seek to increase in that justice.[61]

"Justified by Faith, Not Works"

Romans 3:28 and the Relation Between Works and Justification

How can the Catholic Church teach that good works play a role in our justification when Paul insists that we're not justified by works?

As we saw, the Council of Trent taught that eternal life is given to those "who work well *unto the end*." Protestants like to challenge this belief with Ephesians 2:8-9, which on the surface seems to teach that works have nothing to do with our salvation.

There is another Bible passage that some Protestants think poses a serious challenge to the Catholic belief concerning works: Romans 3:28.[62] Here, Paul writes, "For we hold that a man is justified by faith apart from works of law." Paul can't be any clearer: works have nothing to do with our justification or salvation. We are justified by faith alone.

MEETING THE CHALLENGE

1. If Paul were teaching that works have no relation to our justification in any sense, then he would be contradicting James 2:24.

James makes it clear that works *do* have some relation to man's justification: "You see that a man is justified by works and not by faith alone" (James 2:24). He even goes so far as to say that if a person's faith lacks works it can't save him: "What does it profit, my brethren, if a man says he has faith but has not works? Can his faith save him?" (v.14).

Of course, the answer is no, for "faith by itself, if it has no works, is dead" (v.17). The relationship between faith and works is so profound for James that he compares it to the union of a body and soul in a human being: "For as the body apart from the spirit is dead, so faith apart from works is dead" (v.26).

James's connection of works to our justification means that Paul can't be denying works as necessary for our justification in any sense because biblical teaching can't contradict itself.

But how are we to reconcile the two passages? One way is to say that Paul and James are referring to two different stages of justification. The Council of Trent teaches that James 2:24 applies to those who have *already been initially justified* and seek to increase in that justice (*Decree on Justification* 10). In other words, the Church teaches that James 2:24 refers to works that apply to the *ongoing* dimension of justification.

Paul, on the other hand, could be referring only to the *initial* stage of justification in which good works do not apply but only God's gratuitous gift. As the *Catechism* teaches, "Since the initiative belongs to God in the order of grace, *no one can merit the initial grace* of forgiveness and justification" (2010; emphasis in original).

Another way to solve the apparent contradiction is that Paul and James may be referring to two different kinds of works.

We know that James is referring to works that belong to the *moral* sphere—that's to say, works of charity. The two that he lists are feeding the hungry and clothing the naked: "If a brother or sister is ill-clad and in lack of daily food, and one of you says to them, 'Go in peace, be warmed and filled,' without giving them the things needed for the body, what does it profit?" (James 2:15).

Obedience is another kind of work that James has in mind, for he names Abraham's offering of Isaac as the example *par excellence* of a work that justifies:

> Was not Abraham our father justified by works, when he offered his son Isaac upon the altar? You see that faith was active along with his works, and faith was completed by works, and the Scripture was fulfilled which says, "Abraham believed God, and it was reckoned to him as righteousness"; and he was called the friend of God (vv.21-23).

If James is referring to works that belong to the *moral* sphere, and Paul can't be contradicting James, then in Romans 3:28 Paul must be referring to a different kind of works. What kind of works? We'll see in the next response.

2. **In Romans 3:28, Paul refers to works that belonged to the Law of Moses: circumcision, kosher laws, ritual washings, precepts governing the offering of sacrifices, and other rules that Jews had to observe.**

There are two clues that suggest this interpretation. First, in Romans 2:28-29 Paul disabuses members of his audience of the idea that someone has to be a Jew outwardly, via circumcision, in order to be saved. He writes,

> For he is not a real Jew who is one outwardly, nor is true circumcision something external and physical. He is a Jew who is one inwardly, and real circumcision is a matter of the heart, spiritual and not literal. His praise is not from men but from God.

Paul's instruction here was meant to counter the claim of some first-century Christians that being a Jew and all of the Mosaic precepts that come with such a status (e.g., circumcision) are necessary for salvation (see Acts 15:1-2). Paul's point is that salvation is not restricted to the visible boundaries of the Jewish people. It is a gift offered to all, the non-circumcised (Gentiles) included.

This is the general context in which Paul says that "a man is justified by faith *apart from the works of law.*" Justification (right relationship with God) is not determined by some standard that belongs only to Jews, like the precepts codified in the Mosaic Law (or the Torah). Since membership in God's family is being offered to all men, the standard by which one is measured to be a member of God's family (justified) must be something that can apply to all peoples. That universal standard is faith.

The two verses immediately following Romans 3:28 bear this out. Right after juxtaposing the standards of faith and "works of law," Paul writes in verse 29, "Is God the God of Jews only? Is he not the God of Gentiles also? Yes, of Gentiles also, since God is one." This is the premise that leads Paul to the conclusion that God will "justify the circumcised on the ground of their faith and the uncircumcised through their faith" (v.30). If Paul is juxtaposing faith and circumcision here in verse 30, we can conclude that circumcision is the kind of thing he has in mind when he juxtaposes faith with "works of law" in verse 28.

We see the coherence of this interpretation in the next chapter (Romans 4) where Paul talks about Abraham's justification. Paul begins by saying how Abraham has no reason to boast because he was justified apart from works (v.2), and God reckoned him as righteous because of his faith (v.3). He then quotes David's blessing from Psalm 32:1-2 as evidence for the type of blessing that God pronounces on those whom God reckons as righteous apart from works (v.6-8).

But then Paul asks, "Is this blessing pronounced upon the circumcised, or also upon the uncircumcised?" (v.9). This continues the theme of Romans 2:28-29 and Romans 3:28.

Paul then goes on to establish that Abraham's faith was reckoned to him as righteousness *before* he was circumcised (v.10). The point that Paul is making is that circumcision and adherence to the Mosaic Law are not necessary for being reckoned as righteous, and his primary argument for this is the justification of Abraham. It's faith that justifies, not the law.

COUNTER-CHALLENGE

If Romans 3:28 is saying that only a particular type of "work"—obedience to the Mosaic Law—has no relation whatsoever to our justification, then isn't it possible that works of love could have a role to play?

AFTERTHOUGHT

Another text that reveals the problems that Paul was facing with those who thought circumcision was necessary for salvation is Galatians 5:4-6: "You are severed from Christ, you who would be justified by the law; you have fallen away from grace. For through the Spirit, by faith, we wait for the hope of righteousness. For in Christ Jesus neither circumcision nor uncircumcision is of any avail, but faith working through love."

"We Know That We Have Eternal Life"

1 John 5:13 and the Hope of Salvation

How can the Catholic Church teach that we can't have absolute assurance that we're going to heaven when the Bible says that we can *know* we have eternal life?

The *Catechism* defines the theological virtue of *hope* as "the confident expectation of divine blessing and the beatific vision of God" (CCC 2090). It also identifies hope in the fear one has of "offending God's love" and "incurring punishment." To have a *confident* expectation of heaven and *fear* of incurring the punishment of hell implies that a person can't have absolute assurance of his salvation.

But some Protestants[63] argue that this teaching contradicts the Bible. They quote 1 John 5:13 as a prooftext: "I write this . . . that you may *know* that you have eternal life." *Knowledge* that we have eternal life is mutually exclusive from the Catholic teaching that we can only have a "confident expectation" that we're going to heaven.

MEETING THE CHALLENGE

1. Just because John says that we can "know" we have eternal life, it doesn't follow that we can know with absolute certitude.

The term "knowledge" can be used for different kinds of intellectual certainty. Sometimes, it is used to convey absolute certitude. For example, I "know" that 1+1 = 2.

But "knowledge" can also be used in a way that doesn't imply having absolute certitude. For example, I may say that I "know" I'm going to make an A on my philosophy exam because I've studied hard and I'm familiar with the material. But that doesn't mean that I have infallible knowledge without the possibility of error since I could very well goof up and get a B. Rather, I have a *confident expectation.*

Since the term *knowledge* can take the form of either absolute certitude or confident expectation, it's wrong to conclude that we can have absolute assurance that we're going to heaven just because John says that his readers can "know" they have eternal life.

2. The context of 1 John 5:13 reveals that *confident assurance* is what John has in mind when he speaks of our knowledge that we have eternal life.

Consider the immediate context. In verse 11, John reminds his readers of the good news that God has given us eternal life in his Son, Jesus: "And this is the testimony, that God gave us eternal life, and this life is in his Son." He then says in verse 12, "He who has the Son has life; he who has not the Son of God has not life." So, for John, the condition for having eternal life is to have the Son, Jesus, dwelling within us.

John sets forth other conditions for salvation within the wider context of the epistle. For example, in 1 John 2:3, John says that we may be sure that we know him "if we keep his commandments." Then, in verse five, John writes that we can have assurance that we're in God and that his love dwells in us if we keep his word: "Whoever keeps his word, in him truly love for God is perfected. By this we may be sure that we are in him."

John further stipulates in 1 John 3:23 that we must believe in Jesus and love each another: "And this is his commandment, that we should believe in the name of his Son Jesus Christ and love one another, just as he has commanded us."

John's statement about knowing we have eternal life in 1 John 5:13 is based on the supposition that all the above conditions are met. But how can we be absolutely certain that we currently meet these conditions? How can we be absolutely certain that we will *continuously* meet these conditions until the moment of death?

There is no passage in the Bible that says, "Karlo, you have the Son of God dwelling in you because you have perfectly kept my word, believed in my name, and loved others as I have commanded you, and you will continue to do so every single hour until your death." Nor have I received any private visits from Jesus telling me as much.

Without God telling us through some special revelation, we can't be *absolutely* certain that we currently meet the above conditions necessary for salvation or that we will *continue* to do so until death. We can only have a *confident* assurance. And if we can only have a confident assurance concerning the conditions for salvation, then we can only have a confident assurance that we have eternal life.

3. If absolute assurance were what John had in mind, then he would be contradicting Paul's teaching about our knowledge of salvation.

It's clear from Paul's writings that he didn't have absolute assurance that he was going to receive his eternal reward. Consider, for example, 1 Corinthians 4:4: "I am not aware of anything against myself, but I am not thereby acquitted." Paul refrains from making a definitive judgment that he's in a state of grace, thereby indicating that he doesn't have absolute certitude that he's saved.

Another example is 1 Corinthians 9:27. Paul writes, "I pommel my body and subdue it, lest after preaching to others I myself should be disqualified." Within context, Paul compares his work as an evangelist to that of an athlete who competes in a race to receive a prize. He speaks of how he became "all things to all men" that he might "by all means save some" (v.22), doing it "all for the sake of the gospel" in order that he might "share in its blessings" (v.23).

Paul then writes, "Do you not know that in a race all the runners compete, but only one receives the prize?" (v.24). He contrasts the "perishable wreath" that the runner seeks with the "imperishable" one that he seeks (and all Christians seek) in his apostolic endeavors (v.25). That the wreath for which Paul runs is *imperishable* tells us that Paul has eternal life in mind.

If the prize is eternal life, and Paul fears being disqualified from the race to obtain such a prize, then Paul fears losing the gift of eternal life. And since Paul fears losing the gift of eternal life, we can conclude that Paul himself doesn't have absolute assurance that he will be finally saved.

If Paul doesn't think he can make a definitive judgment on the state of his own soul, then why should we think we could do so for ours?

COUNTER-CHALLENGE

If Paul didn't have absolute certitude of his salvation, how can we?

AFTERTHOUGHT

After listing the sins that the Israelites fell into while in the wilderness, Paul warns the Corinthians, "Let anyone who thinks that he stands take heed lest he fall" (1 Cor. 10:12). If the Corinthians had absolute certitude that they would be finally saved, there would be no need for such a warning. Similarly, Paul warns the Philippians to "work out your salvation with fear and trembling" (Phil. 2:12).

"No One Can Snatch Us"

John 10:27-29 and the Fear of Losing Salvation

How can the Catholic Church teach that it's possible for us to lose our salvation when Jesus says that his sheep always hear his voice and that no one can snatch us out of his hand?

Recall that the *Catechism* warns of "offending God's love" and "incurring punishment" (2090). To fear incurring the punishment of hell implies that a person can't have absolute assurance of his salvation.

We saw how to respond to a Protestant's use of 1 John 5:13 to challenge this belief. But there is another Bible passage that some Protestants[64] use to mount the challenge: John 10:27-29:

> My sheep hear my voice, and I know them, and they follow me; and I give them eternal life, and they shall never perish, and no one shall snatch them out of my hand. My Father, who has given them to me, is greater than all, and no one is able to snatch them out of the Father's hand.

If Jesus says that no one shall snatch Christians out of his and the Father's hand, doesn't it follow that we are eternally secure?

MEETING THE CHALLENGE

1. Jesus' promise to protect his sheep is on the condition that his sheep remain in the flock. It doesn't exclude the possibility that a sheep could wonder off and thus lose the reward of eternal life.

The condition for being among Jesus' sheep and being rewarded with eternal life is that we *continue* hearing Jesus' voice and following him. Jesus teaches this motif of continued faithfulness a few chapters later with his vine and branch metaphor in John 15:4-6:

> Abide in me, and I in you. As the branch cannot bear fruit by itself, unless it abides in the vine, neither can you, unless you abide in me. I am the vine, you are the branches. He who abides in me, and I in him, he it is that bears much fruit, for apart from me you can do nothing. If a man does not abide in me, he is cast forth as a branch and withers; and the branches are gathered, thrown into the fire and burned.

Just as we the branches must *remain* in Christ the vine lest we perish, so, too, we the sheep must *continue* to listen to the voice of Jesus the shepherd lest we perish.

Even the verbs suggest continuous, ongoing action by the sheep and the shepherd, not a one-time event in the past.[65] Jesus doesn't say, "My sheep *heard* my voice, and I *knew* them." Instead, he says, "My sheep hear my voice, and I know them" (v.27). His sheep are those who hear his voice in the present.

2. Jesus only says that no *external power* can snatch a sheep out of his hands. He doesn't say that a sheep couldn't exclude itself from his hands.

The passage says that no one shall snatch—take away by force—Christians out of the hands of Jesus and the Father. This doesn't preclude the possibility that we can take *ourselves* out of Jesus' protecting hands by our sin. A similar passage is Romans 8:35-39 where Paul lists a series of external things that can't take us out of Christ's loving embrace. But he never says that our own *sin* can't separate us from Christ's love.

Like Paul in Romans 8:35-39, Jesus is telling us in John 10:27-29 that no external power can snatch us out of his hands. But that doesn't mean we can't voluntarily leave his hands by committing a sin "unto death" (1 John 5:16-17). And if we were to die in that state of spiritual death without repentance, we would forfeit the gift that was promised to us: eternal life.

3. There is abundant evidence from Scripture that Christians do, in fact, fall from a saving relationship with Christ due to sin.

The Bible teaches that sheep *do* go astray. Consider, for example, Jesus' parable about the lost sheep whom the shepherd goes to find (Matt. 18:12-14; Luke 15:3-7). Sure, the shepherd finds the sheep (Jesus never stops trying to get us back in his flock). But the point is that the sheep can wander away.

The same motif is found in Jesus' parable about the wicked servant who thinks his master is delayed and beats the other servants and gets drunk (Matt. 24:45-51). Notice that the servant is a member of the master's household. But because of his failure to be vigilant in preparing for his master's return, he was found wanting and was kicked out with the hypocrites where "men will weep and gnash their teeth" (v.51). Similarly, Christians can be members of Christ's flock and members of his household, but if we don't persevere in fidelity to him we will lose our number among the elect.

That Christians can fall out of Christ's hands due to sin is evident in Paul's harsh criticism of the Galatians:

> Now I, Paul, say to you that if you receive circumcision, Christ will be of no advantage to you . . . You are severed from Christ, you who would be justified by the law; you have fallen away from grace (Gal. 5:2,4).

If some of the Galatians were "severed from Christ" and "fallen from grace," then they were first *in Christ* and *in grace*. They were counted among the flock, but they later went astray. Not because they were snatched but by their own volition.

COUNTER-CHALLENGE

Didn't Jesus give a parable about a sheep *wondering away from the flock? (Matt. 18:10-14).*

AFTERTHOUGHT

Peter teaches that those who "have escaped the defilements of the world through the knowledge of our Lord and Savior Jesus Christ"— that's to say born-again Christians—can return back to their evil ways: "They are again entangled in them and overpowered" (2 Pet. 2:20). Peter identifies their return to defilement as being worse than their former state, saying, "The last state has become worse for them than the first. For it would have been better for them never to have known the way of righteousness than after knowing it to turn back from the holy commandment delivered to them" (vv.20-21). He adds salt to the wound by comparing their return to defilement to a dog returning to its vomit (v.22). Clearly, Peter didn't believe in the doctrine of eternal security.

"Sanctified for All Time"

Hebrews 10:10,14 and the Possibility of Losing Salvation

How can the Catholic Church teach that we need to worry about losing our salvation through mortal sin when the Bible teaches that we have been sanctified once and for all?

The *Catechism* teaches that mortal sin "destroys charity in the heart of man" (1855) and that "to die in mortal sin without repenting and accepting God's merciful love means remaining separated from him forever by our own free choice" in a state of existence that we call "hell" (1033). This means that even a Christian who commits a mortal sin can lose his salvation.

But some Protestants[66] think that Hebrews 10:10,14 contradicts this belief, which is held not only by Catholics but by many Protestants.[67] The author of Hebrews says that we "have been sanctified through the offering of the body of Jesus Christ *once for all*" (v.10). The author then says similarly in verse 14, "For by a single offering he has perfected *for all time* those who are sanctified."

If Christ's offering has sanctified us "once for all" and "for all time," then we don't need to worry about mortal sins causing us to lose our salvation since when God justifies us he forgives all our sins—past, present, and *future*.

MEETING THE CHALLENGE

1. This passage can't mean that all future sins are automatically forgiven because the Bible elsewhere teaches that there are conditions for having our future sins forgiven.

Consider, for example, Jesus' teaching in the Our Father: "Forgive us our debts, as we also have forgiven our debtors" (Matt. 6:12). Jesus then gives us commentary, saying,

> For if you forgive men their trespasses, your heavenly Father also will forgive you; but if you do not forgive men their trespasses, neither will your Father forgive your trespasses" (vv.14-15).

According to Jesus, a condition for having our sins forgiven is that we forgive others. But by making reception of the forgiveness of sins conditional, it can't possibly be true that all our future sins are forgiven. What if we don't forgive others in the future? Jesus seems to imply that it's possible for a Christian to choose not to forgive his debtors and thus not be forgiven himself. If our future sins were already forgiven, then such hypotheticals would be unintelligible.

Other elements in the Our Father give support for the ongoing need for forgiveness. Consider that Jesus also instructs us to pray for our "daily bread," that God's "will be done on earth as it is in heaven," that God "lead us not into temptation," and "deliver us from evil." Are these requests that we make only once in our Christian life?

If Jesus intends us to make these petitions in the Our Father on an ongoing basis, then it stands to reason that he wants us to pray for forgiveness on an ongoing basis, too. But Jesus wouldn't intend for us to continuously pray that

God forgive our sins if all our future sins are forgiven from the moment we're "saved."

What Jesus teaches about forgiveness in the Our Father is concretized in his parable about the unforgiving servant in Matthew 18. Jesus tells the story of the servant whose debt of 10,000 talents (worth 164,000 years of daily wages![68]) was forgiven by the king and how the servant didn't extend the same mercy to those who owed him much smaller debts. Upon discovering the wicked servant's actions, the king threw the servant into prison.

Given that it would have been impossible for the servant to pay back 10,000 talents, which according to late Anglican New Testament scholar R.T. France is like saying he owed "zillions,"[69] the "prison" most likely represents hell. Similar to his teaching in the Our Father, Jesus then tells his audience, "So also my heavenly Father will do to every one of you, if you do not forgive your brother from your heart."

This parable not only teaches us that there are conditions for receiving God's mercy but also that it's possible for future sins not to be forgiven if the condition of forgiving others is not met. Jesus' audience consists of those who already had their sins forgiven, his *disciples*: "At that time the disciples came to Jesus, saying, 'Who is the greatest in the kingdom of heaven?'" (Matt. 18:1). If Jesus threatens his *disciples* with hell for not forgiving their brethren, then he doesn't intend for their future sins to have already been forgiven.

Notice that the king forgave the servant's debts, which according to the parable means he was saved—the eternal debt of sin was wiped away. If it were true that all future sins of saved Christians are forgiven, it wouldn't have been possible for the servant to be thrown in jail for not forgiving his debtors. How could hell be the destiny of a disciple whose sins had already been forgiven?

We can also look at another passage from the book of Hebrews itself. Verse 4:16 reads, "Let us then with confidence draw near to the throne of grace, that we may receive mercy and find grace to help in time of need." If our future sins were already forgiven, this instruction would be unintelligible since there would be no need to approach God's throne in order to receive his mercy.

2. **The true meaning of the passage is that the grace Christ won on the cross for the forgiveness of sins can be applied to sinners at all times, on the condition that they repent.**

The meaning of "once for all" in verse 10 becomes clear in verses 11–12 where the author contrasts the repeated sacrifices that can't take away sins with Christ's *single* sacrifice for sins. The author of Hebrews writes,

> And every priest stands daily at his service, offering repeatedly the same sacrifices, which can never take away sins. But when Christ had offered for all time a single sacrifice for sins, he sat down at the right hand of God.

The point the author is making is that Christ's *one* sacrifice is sufficient to take away our sins (whenever we repent). He doesn't have to offer himself again to merit the grace that forgives us of any new sins we commit. His single death on the cross 2,000 years ago was sufficient.

Concerning verse 14 where the author says that Christ has "perfected [Greek, *teteleiōken*] for all time those who are sanctified," in light of the above passages we know that the author can't mean that our future sins are forgiven. Therefore, he must mean something else.

A plausible reading is that Christ's sacrifice makes *complete provision* for Christians of all times to achieve their goal of perfection. Not only does the Greek word *teteleiōken* ("he has perfected") allow for such a reading,[70] it would also fit the context that speaks of Christ's death precluding any further sacrifices for sins.

Furthermore, the phrase "those who are sanctified" can be translated "those who are *being* sanctified" (as it is in the ESV translation). The present participle suggests that there is an *ongoing application* of the merits of Christ's single offering, unlike the Old Testament sacrifices, which needed to be constantly repeated. This militates against the way the challenge interprets the text since if our future sins were already forgiven there would be no need for a continuous application of Christ's merits.[71]

COUNTER-CHALLENGE

Is repentance a condition for forgiveness or not?

AFTERTHOUGHT

The author of Hebrews actually teaches that a person can lose his salvation after being a true believer. In Hebrews 10:26-27, he writes, "For if we sin deliberately after receiving the knowledge of the truth, there no longer remains a sacrifice for sins, but a fearful prospect of judgment, and a fury of fire which will consume the adversaries." Given that the author is warning his audience against going back to the Old Covenant sacrifices (vv.19-22), what the author means by "there no longer remains a sacrifice for sins" is that by going back to the Old Covenant sacrifices we can't have our sins forgiven since the Old Covenant sacrifices lack that power.

IV

The Sacraments

Of all the biblical challenges that we've considered so far in this book, only two have come from things Jesus said or did. As we start to take up the biblical challenges that Protestants pose to Catholic beliefs concerning the sacraments, this is going to change.

For example, Protestants challenge the Catholic belief that baptism is necessary for salvation by pointing out that Jesus didn't send Paul to baptize. They challenge infant baptism by insisting that Jesus says faith (which infants can't express) is necessary for baptism. They cite several things Jesus said and did against Catholic teaching about the Mass, the Eucharist, and even the indissolubility of marriage.

From the Protestant perspective, the Catholic Church's claim that Jesus instituted all seven sacraments is laughable because from their reading of Scripture he directly refutes various aspects of Catholic sacramental doctrine. These challenges are serious but, as we're going to see, answerable.

CHALLENGE 18

"Up out of the Water"

Acts 8:36-39, Mark 1:10, and Non-Immersion Baptisms

How can the Church teach that non-immersion baptisms are valid when the Bible speaks only of baptisms that were done by immersion?

The *Catechism* teaches that baptism is validly conferred "by pouring the water three times over the candidate's head" (1239). But some Protestants[72] argue that this contradicts what the Bible teaches about how a person is to be baptized.

For example, Mark tells us that when Jesus was baptized he "came up out of the water" (Mark 1:10). Luke records that the Ethiopian eunuch "went down into the water" when he was baptized by Philip (Acts 8:38). Furthermore, the Greek word for baptize, *baptizō,* which is found in Acts 8:38, means "to immerse." If immersion is the biblical mode of baptism, then any non-immersion form of baptism is un-biblical and invalid.

MEETING THE CHALLENGE

1. The narratives concerning Jesus' baptism and the baptism of the Ethiopian eunuch don't specify that immersion was the mode of baptism used.

Let's take Jesus' baptism first. All Mark tells us is that Jesus "came up out of the water." Of course, it *could* mean that he was immersed. But it could also mean that he simply came out of the water in the sense that he came up onto the shore of the Jordan River. The text itself is silent as to the mode of baptism.

With regard to the eunuch in Acts 8:38, we have a bit more detail that sheds light on what Luke meant. Notice that Luke says that "*they both* went down into the water." Then, afterward, "*they* came up out of the water." This suggests that Luke is not using that expression to convey baptism by immersion. He is simply telling us that the eunuch and Philip went down into the water together and they both came out together—not that they were both immersed. Philip would not have immersed himself as he baptized the eunuch!

2. The word *baptizō* in Scripture is associated with *pouring out* regarding the Jewish ritual washings and thus gives grounds for denying the claim that *baptizō* only means immersion baptism.

Consider, for example, a passage from Mark's Gospel that refers to Jewish ceremonial washings. In the seventh chapter, Mark records that the Pharisees and scribes were appalled at how Jesus' disciples "ate with their hands defiled, that is, unwashed" (v.2). Mark then gives a commentary on the "baptismal" washings that Jesus' apostles failed to uphold:

> For the Pharisees, and all the Jews, do not eat unless they wash their hands, observing the tradition of the elders; and when they come from the market place, they do not eat unless they purify [Greek, *baptisōntai*] themselves; and there are many other traditions which they observe, the washing [*baptismous*] of cups and pots and vessels of bronze (vv.3-4).

According to the *Jewish Encyclopedia*, the baptismal washing of hands may be performed either by pouring or immersion:

> The pouring on of water was a sign of discipleship. Thus, Scripture says of Elisha that he poured water (2 Kings 3:11) upon the hands of Elijah, meaning that he was his disciple. The hands may also be purified by immersion; but in that case the same rules must be observed as in the case of immersion of the entire body in a regular ritual bath, or *mikweh*.[73]

Since Mark describes the Jewish ritual washing of hands with the word *baptizō*, and such Jewish ritual washings could be performed either by pouring or immersion, we have biblical grounds for associating *baptizō* with the pouring. From this it follows that it's unbiblical to restrict the word *baptizō* to immersion baptisms.

3. Ezekiel 36:24-25 gives a biblical precedent for non-immersion baptisms.

In reference to the time of the Messiah, God says through the prophet Ezekiel,

> For I will take you from the nations, and gather you from all the countries, and bring you into your own land. I will *sprinkle clean water upon you*, and you shall be clean from all your uncleannesses, and from all your idols I will cleanse you. A new heart I will give you, and a new spirit I will put within you; and I will take out of your flesh the heart of stone and give you a heart of flesh. And I will put my spirit within you, and cause you to walk in my statutes and be careful to observe my ordinances.

This passage refers to baptism in the messianic age. The *Jewish Encyclopedia* says of this time:

> To receive the Spirit of God, or to be permitted to stand in the presence of God (his *Shekinah*), man must undergo baptism . . . in the messianic time God will himself pour water of purification upon Israel in accordance with Ezekiel 36:25.[74]

Since Ezekiel's prophecy refers to baptism in the messianic age, and it describes this messianic baptism as God "sprinkling" water upon his people, then we have good biblical grounds to think that baptism can be validly administered in ways other than full immersion.

4. There is a historical precedent in the early Church for the pouring method of baptism.

The earliest record is the *Didache*, which is an early Christian handbook dating to around A.D. 50 to 70. It gives the following instructions on how to baptize:

> [Y]ou baptize this way: Having first said all these things, baptize in the name of the Father, and of the Son, and of the Holy Spirit, in living water. But if you don't have living water, baptize in other water; and if you cannot baptize in cold, then baptize in warm. But if you have not either, *pour water three times on the head* in the name of Father and Son and Holy Spirit (7, emphasis added).[75]

The first few modes of baptism mentioned here *could* refer to immersion (though they don't have to). But the explicit mention of pouring that follows makes it clear that even in the mid-first century, pouring was considered a valid form.

St. Cyprian provides another historical example of the validity of the pouring method of baptism. In his *Letter to a Certain Magnus*, which dates to around A.D. 255, Cyprian addresses the specific question of whether pouring is a valid form of baptism:

> You have asked also, dearest son, what I thought about those who obtain the grace of God while they are weakened by illness—whether or not they are to be reckoned as legitimate Christians who have not been bathed with the saving water, but have had it poured over them . . . In the saving sacraments, when necessity compels and when God bestows His pardon, divine benefits are bestowed fully upon believers; nor ought anyone be disturbed because the sick are poured upon or sprinkled when they receive the Lord's grace.

So, whether you've been dunked or had water poured on your head, no need to fret, you've been validly baptized.

COUNTER-CHALLENGE

How can baptism only mean immersion when both the Bible and early Christian practice associate the word with the act of pouring?

AFTERTHOUGHT

Point out that practical difficulties make it nearly or entirely impossible for some people to undergo immersion baptism: people with medical conditions—the bedridden, quadriplegics, those who have recently undergone surgical procedure, etc. Certain environments would also make immersion baptism difficult for some people, such as nomads in the desert or inhabitants of frigid climates. If immersion were the only valid form of baptism, at certain places and times it would be a practical impossibility.

"Believer's Baptism"

Mark 16:16 and Infant Baptism

How can the Catholic Church baptize infants when Jesus makes it clear that one must believe first and then be baptized?

The *Catechism* teaches that infant baptism is an "immemorial Tradition of the Church" (1252) and that the Church baptizes "for the remission of sins even tiny infants who have not committed personal sin" (403).

But some Protestants[76] object that this belief contradicts the Bible. They appeal to Jesus' teaching in Mark 16:16 where he says, "He who *believes* and is baptized will be saved." These Protestants see this as clear evidence that baptism is to be given *only* to those who have professed faith in Christ. This is why it's sometimes called a *"believer's* baptism."

If belief must *precede* baptism, and infants can't profess belief since they can't reason yet, it follows that infants can't be baptized. To do so would be to go against the instruction of Jesus.

MEETING THE CHALLENGE

1. Jesus doesn't say that belief *precedes* baptism. He simply makes belief a condition for salvation *along with* baptism.

Nowhere in Scripture does Jesus say, "He who believes *first* and *then* is baptized will be saved." He simply made belief *and* baptism two conditions for salvation, without stipulating the order.

For an adult, of course, faith will come first because faith is what leads him to the waters of baptism (CCC 1262). But for an infant who is baptized, the faith of the parents and of the Church suffices. As St. Thomas Aquinas teaches in his *Summa Theologiae,*[77] the faith of the parents and, indeed, the whole Church "profits the child through the operation of the Holy Ghost" because the child before the use of reason "believes not by himself but by others." This being the case, the child receives salvation "not by [his] own act, but by the act of the Church."

This doesn't mean that the infant won't have to personally make an act of faith in Christ as he or she comes to the age of reason. Such a profession will be necessary on the condition that the child comes to know the truth of God's revelation. But as an infant, the faith of the parents and the Church suffices, thus meeting both of Jesus' conditions for salvation: belief and baptism.

2. The idea that the faith of the parents and the Church suffices to meet the faith condition is consistent with Jesus' practice of administering blessings on behalf of the faith of others.

Consider, first of all, how Jesus instructs his disciples: "Let the children come to me, and do not hinder them; for to such belongs the kingdom of heaven" (Matt. 19:14). Jesus is not opposed to children being members of his kingdom.

And Mark's version indicates that these probably were *little* children unable to make an act of faith since Mark says that Jesus "*took them in his arms* and blessed them, laying his hands upon them" (Mark 10:16). The act of giving our children over to Christ in baptism, even though they can't make an act of faith, is consistent with Jesus' desire for children to be brought to him.

Furthermore, there are examples in the Bible where Jesus administers blessings specifically on behalf of the faith of the parents. Take Jesus' decision to raise Jairus's daughter from the dead (Mark 5:22-23, 35-43). The young girl made no profession of faith in Christ, yet Jesus still performed the miracle. And we can infer that it was on behalf of Jairus's faith because Jesus tells Jairus, "Do not fear, only believe" (v.36). That Jesus then performed the miracle tells us that Jairus *did* believe, and Jesus performed the miracle as a result.

Similarly, in Mark 9:14-27 Jesus exorcizes a demon-possessed boy in response to his father's request, even though the boy had no faith. Mark makes explicit that Jesus performed the exorcism in response to the *father's* faith: "Jesus said to him . . . 'All things are possible to him who believes.' Immediately the father of the child cried out and said, 'I believe; help my unbelief!'" (vv.23-24). If a parent's faith sufficed for Jesus to physically raise a girl from the dead and free a boy from demonic possession, then it's reasonable to conclude that a parent's faith can suffice for a child under the age of reason to receive the blessings of baptism.

We can also take into account the household baptisms mentioned in Scripture. For example, when the Philippian jailer asks Paul what he must do to be saved (Acts 16:30), Paul responds, "Believe in the Lord Jesus, and you will be saved, you *and your household*" (v.31). We're then told that Paul spoke the "word of the Lord" to the jailer and his household that evening, after which they were all baptized (vv.32-33). Notice that the jailer's faith was sufficient to bring the blessing of baptism upon his entire family, members of which may have been children under the age of reason.

The idea of salvation being brought to the Philippian jailer *and his household* is reminiscent of Peter's words on Pentecost: "Repent, and be baptized every one of you in the name of Jesus Christ for the forgiveness of your sins; and you shall receive the gift of the Holy Spirit. For the promise is to you *and to your children* (Acts 2:38-39)." Children, no matter how old, can be recipients of the gift of the Spirit in baptism on behalf of the faith of the parents.

Other examples of household baptisms administered on behalf of the faith of the parent are Lydia's household (Acts 16:15) and the household of Stephanas (1 Cor. 1:16). It's true that we don't know for sure that these households had children under the age of reason. Nevertheless, blessings still come upon these households on behalf of the faith of the parents.

3. If baptism is the new circumcision, then children can be baptized.

Paul teaches in Colossians 2:11-12 that baptism is the New Testament fulfillment of circumcision. He writes,

> You were circumcised with a circumcision made without hands, by putting off the body of flesh in the circumcision of Christ; and you were buried with him in baptism, in which you were also raised with him through faith in the working of God, who raised him from the dead.

It's important to note here that the Greek word for *and* (*kai*) is not present in the original text. It literally reads, "You were circumcised with . . . the circumcision of Christ, *having been* buried with him in baptism."[78] Meaning, baptism *is* the "circumcision of Christ." Martin Luther acknowledged as much: "We now have baptism instead of circumcision."[79]

According to Genesis 17:10-12, every male child was to be circumcised at eight days old. Children were made members of God's covenant not by the use of their reason but based on the faith of their parents.

Given that baptism is the new circumcision—the gateway into the New Covenant—to say that children under the age of reason can't be baptized is to say that children under the age of reason could be incorporated into the Old Covenant but not the New Covenant. That would make the New Covenant less inclusive than the Old, which doesn't fit with the general theme of inclusivity that marks the New Covenant (see Matt. 28:19-20; Gal. 3:8). The New Covenant is open to every nation and people on earth—but not to little children?

We not only have Paul's teaching on baptism as the new circumcision, we also have positive evidence from Peter that children are able to be members of the New Covenant. In his sermon on the day of Pentecost, he instructs the crowd present,

Repent, and be baptized every one of you in the name of Jesus Christ for the forgiveness of your sins; and you shall receive the gift of the Holy Spirit. For the promise is to you *and to your children*" (Acts 2:38-39).

The promise of receiving the Holy Spirit is not just for those repenting and believing there at Pentecost. It extends to their children as well, which would include children under the age of reason.

4. There is historical evidence that the early Christians in the second and third centuries practiced infant baptism.

One example is that of St. Irenaeus of Lyons. In his work *Against Heresies,* which dates to about A.D. 189, he affirms that infants can be born again:

For he came to save all through himself—all, I say, who through him are born again to God—infants, and children, and boys, and youths, and old men.[80]

We know that Irenaeus has baptism in mind here because elsewhere in his writings he identifies this second birth with baptism:

And [Naaman] dipped himself . . . seven times in the Jordan [2 Kgs 5:14]. It was not for nothing that Naaman, when suffering from leprosy, was purified upon being baptized, but as an indication to us. For as we are lepers in sin, we are made clean of our old transgressions by means of the sacred water and the invocation of the Lord; we are spiritually regenerated as newborn babes, even as the Lord has declared: "Except a man be born again through water and the Spirit, he shall not enter into the kingdom of heaven" [John 3:5].[81]

Another witness to infant baptism in the early Church is St. Cyprian of Carthage. During his time, the early mid-200's, Cyprian was dealing with a controversy over whether Christians should model the Jewish practice of circumcision and hold off baptism until the eighth day after birth. Here is how Cyprian responded:

But in respect of the case of the infants, which you [Fidus] say ought not to be baptized within the second or third day after their birth, and that the law of ancient circumcision should be followed, so that one who is just born should not be baptized and sanctified within the eighth day, we all thought very differently in our council. For no one agreed with the course you thought should be taken;

rather we all judge that the mercy and grace of God is not to be refused to anyone born of man.[82]

The above passages from Irenaeus and Cyprian confirm that infant baptism is an "immemorial Tradition of the Church" (CCC 1252) to which we should hold fast.

COUNTER-CHALLENGE

How is it that children were able to be incorporated into God's family in the Old Covenant through the faith of their parents but aren't in the New?

AFTERTHOUGHT

Point out to your Protestant friend that baptism is not merely a visible sign but brings about real effects: 1) it regenerates us (John 3:3-5), 2) it buries us with Christ and raises us to a new life with him (Rom. 6:3-4), 3), it incorporates us into Christ's mystical body (1 Cor. 12:13), and 4) it saves us (1 Pet. 3:21). Who wouldn't want to give such blessings to their children?

"Cornelius Received the Spirit First"

Acts 10:45-48 and the Necessity of Baptism

How can the Catholic Church teach that baptism is necessary for salvation when the Bible relates that people can receive the Holy Spirit before baptism?

The *Catechism* teaches that baptism is "necessary for salvation" because "God has bound salvation to the sacrament" and that the Church "does not know of any means other than baptism that assures entry into eternal beatitude" (1257).

But some Protestants[83] think this teaching on the necessity of baptism contradicts Scripture. They appeal to Acts 10:45-48 where Cornelius and Gentiles receive an outpouring of the Holy Spirit *without* baptism. Luke tells us that it was only *after* they received the Spirit that Peter baptized Cornelius and the others with him.

For these Protestants, if it's not necessary to be baptized in order to receive the Spirit, this is clear evidence that baptism is not necessary for salvation.

MEETING THE CHALLENGE

1. Reception of the Holy Spirit doesn't always indicate that salvation has been accomplished.

The challenge assumes that because Cornelius and his companions received the Holy Spirit they were saved. But receiving an outpouring of the Holy Spirit doesn't necessarily mean someone is saved.

Consider, first of all, that the Spirit can be given for other things besides salvation.[84] One such thing is artistic skill. For example, God fills Bezalel, son of Uri, with "the Spirit of God" (Exod. 31:3) "to devise artistic designs, to work in gold, silver, and bronze, in cutting stones for setting, and in carving wood, for work in every craft" (vv.4–5).

To others, God gave his Spirit to empower them with special strength as exemplified in the life of Samson (Judg. 14:6, 19; 15:14) and to empower for leadership (see Num. 27:18; Deut. 34:9; Judg. 3:10; 6:34; 11:29; 1 Sam. 11:6-7; 16:13-14).

Just as in the Old Testament God gave his Spirit for purposes besides salvation, it's possible that in the New Testament God gave his Spirit to Cornelius and his companions for some purpose besides salvation.

The context of the passage in question seems to suggest this. We're told that when the Holy Spirit fell upon Cornelius and the other Gentiles present the "believers from among the circumcised who came with Peter were amazed because the gift of the Holy Spirit had been poured out even on the Gentiles" (v.45). They knew this had happened because "they heard them speaking in tongues and extolling God" (v.46).

It seems that God gave his Spirit in order to convince the circumcised what Peter had said at the outset of his speech in verse 34 that "God shows no partiality" and that "in every nation anyone who fears him and does what is right is acceptable to him."

Matthew 7:22-23 provides another example of how having the outpouring of the Spirit doesn't guarantee that someone is saved:[85]

On that day many will say to me, "Lord, Lord, did we not prophesy in your name, and cast out demons in your name, and do many mighty works in your name?" And then will I declare to them, "I never knew you; depart from me, you evildoers."

To prophesy and cast out demons requires the power of the Holy Spirit. Yet according to Jesus, having such power doesn't guarantee salvation.

Just because the power of the Holy Spirit falls upon Cornelius and his Gentile companions prior to baptism and empowers them to speak in tongues, it doesn't follow that they were saved at that moment. Therefore, this passage doesn't prove that baptism is not necessary for salvation.

2. The Catholic Church doesn't teach that baptism is necessary in an *absolute sense* since it believes that God can work beyond his sacraments.

Even if we said for argument's sake that Cornelius and his companions were saved prior to baptism when they received the outpouring of the Holy Spirit, the challenge only has force if the Church believed that the Holy Spirit and the gift of salvation *cannot* be given apart from the sacrament. But this is not true.

The *Catechism* teaches that although God "has bound salvation to the sacrament of baptism . . . he himself is not bound by his sacraments" (1257) and "in ways known to himself . . . can lead those who, through no fault of their own, are ignorant of the gospel, to that faith without which it is impossible to please him" (848). Only for those "to whom the gospel has been proclaimed and who have had the possibility of asking for [baptism]" is it necessary (1257). You might say that baptism is the *ordinary* means of salvation, which allows for God to save people in ways known only to him.

In the case of Cornelius and his Gentile friends, God could have willed to work beyond the ordinary means of salvation and gave his saving Spirit to those who through no fault of their own didn't know about baptism. In no way would this undermine the Catholic belief about the necessity of baptism for salvation.

In other words, the challenge involves a straw man of the Catholic position.

3. The exception to the norm was fitting given the circumstances.

This exception to the norm of receiving the Holy Spirit first through baptism was fitting in this case, given the need for a public demonstration of God's approval of the admission of Gentiles into the Church without the conditions of submitting to the Jewish ceremonial laws. Peter (Acts 10:9-16) and Cornelius (Acts 10:3-7) had both received private visions, but this provided public evidence.

With the public evidence of God's approval, the Jewish Christians in Jerusalem who were hesitant to admit Gentiles into the Church (see Acts 11:2,3) could no longer be reasonably opposed to their admission. Many ceased their opposition (see Acts 11:4-18), but some remained (Acts 15:1-2), which gave rise to the Council of Jerusalem where Peter settled the debate (Acts 15:6-29).

4. We can't deny that baptism is necessary for salvation *ordinarily speaking* because the Bible teaches as much.

Let's consider, for example, John 3:5 where Jesus says, "Unless one is born of water and the Spirit, he cannot enter the kingdom of God." This comes within the context of a conversation that Jesus has with Nicodemus, "a teacher of Israel" (v.10).

Jesus had told Nicodemus that in order to enter the kingdom of God, one must be "born anew" (v.3), which prompted a question: "How can a man be born when he is old? Can he enter a second time into his mother's womb and be born?" (v.4). It's in response to this question by Nicodemus that Jesus says, "Unless one is born of water and the Spirit, he cannot enter the kingdom of God" (v.5).

Jesus then tells Nicodemus, "Do not marvel that I said to you, 'You must be born anew'" (v.7), which leads Nicodemus to ask again, "How can this be?" (v.9). Jesus answers, "Are you a teacher of Israel, and yet you do not understand this?" (v.10).

The implication here is that Jesus' teaching about water, spirit, and new birth is rooted in Jewish tradition. And since Nicodemus is a teacher of that tradition, he should know about it.

But where is this found in Jewish tradition? The answer is Ezekiel 36:25-27:

> I will sprinkle clean water upon you, and you shall be clean from all your uncleannesses, and from all your idols I will cleanse you. A new heart I will give you, and a new spirit I will put within you; and I will take out of your flesh the heart of stone and give you a heart of flesh. And I will put my spirit within you, and cause you to walk in my statutes and be careful to observe my ordinances.

Notice how this passage contains the same themes that are present in Jesus' conversation with Nicodemus: water, God's spirit, and renewal. Given the combination of these themes, this is likely what Jesus expects Nicodemus to think of when he speaks of a *new* birth by *water* and *Spirit*. Jesus is teaching Nicodemus that the rebirth by water and Spirit *is* the event of cleansing and renewal that Ezekiel prophesied.

But what is this rebirth by water and Spirit, precisely? The answer is baptism. First century Jews associated the hope of the age when God would cleanse and renew his people by water and Spirit found in Ezekiel's prophecy with a baptismal ministry. The late New Testament scholar George Beasley-Murray explains,

> The conjunction of water and Spirit in eschatological hope is deeply rooted in the Jewish consciousness, as is attested by Ezekiel 36:25-27 and various apocalyptic writings (e.g., *Jud.* 1:23; *Pss. Sol.* 18:6; Test *Jud* 24:3), but above all the literature and practices of the Qumran sectaries, who sought to unite cleansing and the hope of the Spirit *with actual immersions* and repentance in a community beginning to "see" the kingdom of God (cf. 1QS 3:6-9; 1QH 11:12-14).[86]

If the Jews saw the event of Ezekiel's prophecy as a baptism for the age of cleansing and renewal, and Jesus intends Nicodemus to understand rebirth by water and Spirit in terms of that event, then it follows that Jesus intends baptism to be the new birth by water and Spirit.

This interpretation is further confirmed by the preceding and subsequent context of the passage in question. The images of Spirit and water *together* constitute the one event of Jesus' baptism, which John hints at in John 1:29-34. In John 3:23, he records how John the Baptist was baptizing at Aenon near Salim. We're also told in John 4:1-2 that the apostles went about baptizing.

If the instruction to be born again of water and spirit is surrounded both before and after by the theme of baptism, then it's reasonable to conclude that baptism is what Jesus has in mind when he speaks of the necessity to be born of water and spirit for entrance into heaven.[87]

The necessity of baptism can also be inferred from the apostolic teaching concerning the salvific effect of baptism. For example, St. Paul teaches in Romans 6:3–4 that through baptism we are buried with Christ into death and that we rise with him to new life. He writes,

> Do you not know that all of us who have been baptized into Christ Jesus were baptized into his death? We were buried therefore with him by baptism into death, so that as Christ was raised from the dead by the glory of the Father, we too might walk in newness of life.

Paul then tells us that through such a death we are "dead to sin and alive to God in Christ Jesus" (v.11). To be dead to sin and alive with Christ is the essence of being saved.

St. Peter concurs in 1 Peter 3:21: "Baptism . . . now saves you, not as a removal of dirt from the body but as an appeal to God for a clear conscience, through the resurrection of Jesus Christ." Like Paul, Peter understands baptism to be the means by which we are united to Christ in his resurrection, and as a result we receive a clear conscience. This parallels Paul's statement that we are "freed from sin" (Rom. 6:7) through the death we experience in baptism.

COUNTER-CHALLENGE

Should we base our beliefs about baptism on what God does in an extraordinary circumstance? Or should we base our belief on what the Bible says about baptism in general?

AFTERTHOUGHT

Some Protestants object that the *water* doesn't refer to the waters of baptism but to the amniotic fluid of our mother's womb, through which we passed during our biological birth. The second birth, so it's argued, is being born only of the Spirit—when you confess Jesus as Lord. But water and spirit *together* make up Jesus' answer to how a man is *born again*. Furthermore, as argued in the fourth response of this chapter, the new birth refers to the eschatological event prophesied by Ezekiel, which includes *both* water and the Spirit. Both water and the Spirit, therefore, make up the second birth.

"Not to Baptize but to Preach"

1 Corinthians 1:17 and the Necessity of Baptism

How can the Catholic Church teach that baptism is necessary for salvation when Paul tells us that Christ did not send him to baptize but to preach?

The Church teaches that baptism is "necessary for salvation" (CCC 1257). We saw that some Protestants like to use Acts 10:45–48 to claim that this teaching contradicts the Bible.

There is another passage that some Protestants[88] use to the same end: 1 Corinthians 1:17. Paul writes, "For Christ did not send me to baptize but to preach the gospel, and not with eloquent wisdom, lest the cross of Christ be emptied of its power." Those who appeal to this verse argue that Paul dissociates baptism from the gospel. And if baptism is not part of the gospel, it can't be necessary for salvation.

MEETING THE CHALLENGE

1. The challenge confuses the duty to administer the rite of baptism with baptism being essential to the gospel.

Paul doesn't say that baptism is not essential to the gospel. What does and doesn't constitute the gospel is not Paul's concern here. Rather, he is concerned with the *administration* of baptism.

Paul is addressing a problem that arose in the Corinthian church where some were identifying themselves with particular ministers and causing division within the community. Paul writes,

> For it has been reported to me by Chloe's people that there is quarreling among you, my brethren. What I mean is that each one of you says, "I belong to Paul," or "I belong to Apollos," or "I belong to Cephas," or "I belong to Christ" (1 Cor. 1:11-12).

In subsequent verses, Paul gives a hint as to why the Corinthians were identifying themselves with different ministers:

> [W]ere you baptized in the name of Paul? I am thankful that I baptized none of you except Crispus and Gaius; lest anyone should say that you were baptized in my name (vv.13-14).

Apparently, the Corinthians were adopting religious affiliations based on the minister who *baptized* them. Consequently, Paul was grateful that he hadn't baptized more people than he did among the Corinthians lest they affiliate themselves with him.

It is within this context that Paul says, "For Christ did not send me to baptize but to preach the gospel" (1 Cor. 1:17). His intent is not to separate the sacrament of baptism from the gospel but rather to clarify his own part in the *administration* of the actual rite of baptism among the Corinthians.

Even if we conceded, for argument's sake, that Paul wasn't sent to baptize in a strict, general sense, it doesn't follow that baptism is not essential to the gospel. His preaching of the gospel could have included the necessity of baptism for salvation—with the administration of the actual rite of baptism left to other ministers. Someone other than Paul performing baptism wouldn't preclude baptism from being essential to the gospel message that Paul preached.

But as we'll see below, we have good reason to not take Paul's statement in a strict sense.

2. Paul is using hyperbole to emphasize two things: 1) it doesn't matter by whom you're baptized, and (2) his apostolic role is not restricted to administering baptism but also involves preaching the gospel.

We know that Paul's statement, "For Christ did not send me to baptize," is hyperbolic because Jesus commanded *all* the apostles to make disciples of all nations by baptizing them (Matt.28:19-20). And since Paul is an apostle, it therefore belongs to his ministry to baptize.

Moreover, if Paul wasn't sent to baptize in a strict sense, then he would have acted in disobedience when he baptized Crispus, Gaius, and the household of Stephanas, which he tells us about in verse 14. Do we want to say that the great apostle Paul was disobedient to Jesus' instruction?

With this hyperbolic speech, Paul is stressing that it doesn't matter by whom you're baptized. Whether it's Apollos, Cephas, or Paul who baptizes, we're all incorporated into the same "fellowship of [God's] Son, Jesus Christ our Lord" (1 Cor. 1:9).

The use of hyperbole is similar to Jesus' teaching in John 12:44: "He who believes in me, believes not in me but in him who sent me." Of course, Jesus doesn't mean that we shouldn't believe in *him*. With the "not . . . but" formula, he is merely emphasizing the importance of the Father's authority with which he is sent and consequently that we shouldn't believe in Jesus *alone* but also in the Father.

This is the same kind of language that Paul uses in 1 Corinthians 1:17. Other examples include John 6:27; 12:44; 1 Corinthians 15:10; 1 Peter 3:3,4; Mark 9:37; Matt. 10:20; Acts 5:4; 1 Thess. 4:8; Genesis 45:8; and Titus 3:5.

3. The assertion that baptism is not essential to the gospel is inconsistent with Paul's teaching on baptism in Romans 6.

Paul introduces baptism in this chapter as the experience of death and resurrection in Christ:

> Do you not know that all of us who have been baptized into Christ Jesus were baptized into his death? We were buried therefore with him by baptism into death, so that as Christ was raised from the dead by the glory of the Father, we too might walk in newness of life (Rom. 6:3-4).

Paul goes on to articulate the effects of this baptismal death and resurrection:

> We know that our old self was crucified with him so that the sinful body might be destroyed, and we might *no longer be enslaved to sin*. For he who has died is *freed from sin* (vv.6-7).

What's interesting about this passage is that the Greek doesn't say "*freed* from sin." The Greek word translated "freed" is *dedikaiōtai*, which means "justified."[89] So the text can literally be translated, "justified from sin."

Modern translations render it as "freed from sin" because the context is clearly about sanctification. For example, in the verse before Paul speaks of baptismal death, he speaks of those in Christ as having "died to sin" (v.2). As quoted above, Paul speaks of those who have died the death of baptism as "no longer enslaved to sin" (v.6).

In verses 17-18, Paul actually uses a form of the Greek word for "free" (*eleutheroō*) in relation to the freedom from sin that we receive in Christ:

> But thanks be to God, that you who were once slaves of sin have become obedient from the heart to the standard of teaching to which you were committed, and, having been set free [*eleutherothentes*] from sin, have become slaves of righteousness.

This tells us that, for Paul, justification can include sanctification, which is the interior renewal of the soul whereby the objective guilt of sin is removed.

If justification and sanctification are essential to the gospel, and for Paul baptism justifies and sanctifies, it follows that for Paul baptism *is* essential to the gospel. The challenge that Paul's statement in 1 Corinthians 1:17 dissociates baptism from the gospel is not consistent with Paul's baptismal theology in Romans 6.

COUNTER-CHALLENGE

Do you believe that being set free from sin is essential to the gospel? If so, then wouldn't baptism be essential to the gospel if it frees a person from sin?

AFTERTHOUGHT

Paul's teaching in Romans 6:3-4 about baptism freeing us from sin follows from his experience of being forgiven of his sins through baptism in Acts 22:16: "And now why do you wait? Rise and be baptized, and wash away your sins, calling on his name."

CHALLENGE 22

"God Will Cut Off the Person Who Eats Blood"

Leviticus 17:10 and the Real Presence of Jesus' Blood

How can the Catholic Church teach that we actually eat and drink the body and blood of Jesus when Scripture forbids partaking of blood?

The Catholic Church teaches that when we partake of the Eucharist in Holy Communion we are literally consuming the blood of Jesus Christ. Paragraph 1244 of the *Catechism* says that we "receive the food of the new life, the body and *blood* of Christ" (emphasis added). In 1275, it states that the Eucharist nourishes us with "Christ's body and blood" in order for us to be transformed in Christ. According to paragraph 1335, the faithful "drink the new wine that has become the *blood* of Christ" (emphasis added).

For some Protestants,[90] this idea of drinking Christ's blood violates the Bible's prohibition of drinking blood:

> If any man of the house of Israel or of the strangers that sojourn among them eats any blood, I will set my face against that person who eats blood, and will cut him off from among his people (Lev. 17:10).

In light of this prohibition, in John 6 and at the Last Supper Jesus couldn't have possibly meant for us to *really* drink his blood, meaning that Catholic teaching on the Eucharist is unbiblical.

MEETING THE CHALLENGE

1. The dietary laws of the old law, to which the prohibition of drinking blood belonged, passed away with the advent of Christ.

The prohibition of consuming blood was not a precept rooted in the *natural* law, which is forever binding (Rom. 2:14-15). Rather, it was one of many dietary regulations that involved the *ritual* purity of Jews—disciplinary in nature, not moral, and thus subject to change.

That it did change is proven by the New Testament's affirmation that the dietary laws of the old law are no longer binding for Christians. Consider, for example, what Jesus says in Mark 7:15: "[T]here is nothing outside a man which by going into him can defile him; but the things which come out of a man are what defile him." Mark tells us that by saying this Jesus "declared all foods clean" (v.19).

This is made even clearer in God's revelation to Peter in Acts 10:9-16. We're told that Peter "fell into a trance" and saw a "great sheet" in which were "all kinds of animals and reptiles and birds of the air." Peter heard a voice command him to "kill and eat." But Peter refused, saying, "No, Lord; for I have never eaten anything that is common or unclean." The voice responded, "What God has cleansed, you must not call common." Luke tells us that this happened three times.

We find this new revelation in Paul's writings as well. For example, he instructs the Colossians,

Having canceled the bond which stood against us with its legal demands; this [Jesus] set aside, nailing it to the cross . . . Therefore let no one pass judgment on you in questions of food and drink or with regard to a festival or a new moon or a Sabbath. These are only a shadow of what is to come; but the substance belongs to Christ (Col. 2:16–17).

Similarly, Paul writes to the Corinthians: "Food will not commend us to God. We are no worse off if we do not eat, and no better off if we do" (1 Cor. 8:8).

If the dietary laws of the Old Law are no longer binding for Christians, and the prohibition of consuming blood was a part of those dietary laws, it follows that the prohibition of consuming blood is no longer binding for Christians. This challenge from Leviticus 17:10, therefore, doesn't undermine the Catholic belief that we literally partake of Jesus' blood in the Eucharist.

2. Jesus gives a positive command to drink his blood, which by nature supersedes the Old Testament precept.

Jesus says, "He who drinks my blood has eternal life" (John 6:54). At the Last Supper he instructs the apostles, "Drink it," in reference to the cup that he says contained his blood. Such a positive command tells us that the Old Testament's prohibition of partaking of blood was disciplinary in nature, for Christ could never command us to violate a precept of the natural law. And when Christ gives us a new command, it supersedes the old.

3. Given the Jewish understanding that blood contains the life of the animal, it makes sense why Jesus would command us to drink his blood in order to have his eternal life.

The reason for the ritual prohibition of drinking blood was that the life of the animal was believed to be in the blood:

For the life of the flesh is in the blood; and I have given it for you upon the altar to make atonement for your souls; for it is the blood that makes atonement, by reason of the life (Lev. 17:11).

If Jews believed that the life of an animal is in its blood, it makes sense for Jesus to say, "He who drinks my blood has *eternal* life" (John 6:54). Because Jesus is God, his blood contains the divine life. As Paul writes, "For in him the whole fullness of deity dwells bodily" (Col. 2:9).

Christ wants his disciples to have his *eternal* life. And since his divine life dwells within his blood, he commands his disciples to drink his blood. Bible scholar Brant Pitre puts it nicely: "The very reason God forbids drinking blood in the Old Covenant is the same reason Jesus commands his disciples to drink his blood."[91] Therefore, if we want Christ's life to dwell within us, we need to drink his blood in the Holy Eucharist.

COUNTER-CHALLENGE

Why should we abide by this Old Testament precept when Jesus clearly gives us a command that supersedes it? If Jesus commands us to do something new, shouldn't we follow it?

AFTERTHOUGHT

This challenge also poses a problem for Protestants who believe that the elements of the Eucharist are merely symbolic. Why would Jesus command the apostles (and all Christians) to *symbolically* do something immoral and forbidden by God? If the prohibition against "eating blood" applies to the Catholic idea of the Real Presence, it applies to the Protestant idea of a symbolic Eucharist, too.

"Do This in Remembrance"

Luke 22:19 and the Eucharistic Offering of Jesus' Body and Blood

How can the Catholic Church teach that the eucharistic celebration is the offering of Christ's actual body and blood when Jesus only intended for the apostles to perform the Last Supper as a "remembrance"?

The Church teaches that the Eucharist is "the making present and the sacramental offering of [Christ's] unique sacrifice" (CCC 1362). But many Protestants[92] argue that Jesus' instruction to "do this in remembrance of me" (Luke 22:19) contradicts this belief.

They say that Jesus didn't intend for his apostles to offer his *actual* body and blood as a sacrifice like the Catholic Church believes. Rather, Jesus simply meant for the apostles to *remember* (bring to mind) the offering of his body and blood on the cross by reenacting the Last Supper.

MEETING THE CHALLENGE

1. The Greek for "do this" suggests that Jesus intends the apostles to offer the Eucharist as a sacrifice.

The Greek for "do this" is *touto poieite*. The verb *poieō* means "do" or "make." But there is good reason to think that in this context it is charged with sacrificial overtones.

In the Septuagint (the Greek translation of the Old Testament), the word *poieō* is used in reference to offering sacrifices. For this reason, the Revised Standard Version (and others) translates the verb as "offer":

- "Now this is what you shall offer [*poieseis*] upon the altar: two lambs a year old day by day continually" (Exod. 29:38).

- "Draw near to the altar and offer [*poieson*] your sin offering and your burnt offering and make atonement for yourself and for the people" (Lev. 9:7).

- "I will offer [*poiesō*] to thee burnt offerings of fatlings, with the smoke of the sacrifice of rams" (Psalm 66:15).

Protestant scholar J.N.D. Kelly affirms the sacrificial undertones of *poieō:*

It was natural for early Christians to think of the Eucharist as a sacrifice. The fulfillment of prophecy demanded a solemn Christian offering, and the rite itself was wrapped in the sacrificial atmosphere with which our Lord invested the Last Supper. The words of institution, "Do this" (*touto poieite*), must have been charged with sacrificial overtones for second-century ears; Justin at any rate understood them to mean, "Offer this."[93]

If Jesus is commanding the apostles to *poiete* the Eucharist, and that verb elsewhere in Scripture refers to offering sacrifices, it's reasonable to conclude that Jesus intended his apostles to "offer" the Eucharist as a sacrifice.

This at least shows that the Last Supper had a sacrificial character to it, thus proving wrong the idea that the reenactment of the Last Supper was meant to be *merely* a remembrance and not a sacrifice.

2. **The act of remembrance that Jesus commands may not apply to the apostles but may refer to what the Father does when the Last Supper is offered as a memorial offering.**

The challenge's interpretation of Luke 22:19 assumes that Jesus is instructing the apostles (and by extension the believer) to be the ones doing the "remembering." But it's possible that Jesus intends to ascribe the act of remembrance to God the Father instead.

The Greek word for "remembrance," *anamnesis*, is used in the Bible to describe sacrifices that prompt *God* to engage in an act of remembrance. For example, in Numbers 10:10 of the Septuagint, the sacrifices of peace offerings are said to "serve you for remembrance [*anamnesis*] before your God." The NIV translation makes it a little clearer: the peace offerings "will be a memorial for you before your God." Notice that God is the one who remembers in response to the offering that the Israelites make.

Similarly, we read in Acts 10:4 that Cornelius's prayers and alms ascend "as a memorial before God." The act of remembrance occasioned by such an offering is not ascribed to Cornelius but to God.

Given this use of *anamnēsis* in the Bible, and given that Jesus commands the apostles to "offer" the Last Supper as a sacrifice, it's reasonable to conclude that Jesus meant for the apostles to offer the Last Supper to prompt *the Father* to remember Jesus' death on the cross and the salvation that he won for us. This would be in keeping with the biblical practice of memorial offerings.

Of course, the language of prompting the Father to remember Jesus' death on the cross is *anthropomorphic* (a

MEETING THE PROTESTANT CHALLENGE

description of God with human-like qualities). God the Father is unable to change and thus can't move from a state of not remembering to a state of remembering. But the biblical language of God "remembering" is meant to convey that God wills to continually bestow the graces of the cross in response to the eucharistic offering.

The late Lutheran Bible scholar Joachim Jeremias recognized as much:

> [T]he command for repetition [of the Lord's Supper] may be translated: "This do, that God may remember me." How is this to be understood? Here an old Passover prayer is illuminating. On Passover evening a prayer is inserted into the third benediction of the grace after the meal, a prayer which asks God *to remember the Messiah*. . . . In this very common prayer, which is also used on other festival days, God is petitioned at every Passover concerning "the remembrance of the Messiah," i.e., concerning the appearance of the Messiah, which means the bringing about of the *parousia*.[94]

Since the act of remembrance that Jesus commands doesn't necessarily have to be directed to the apostles but may instead describe a memorial placed at the Father's attention, this challenge does not disprove Catholic belief in the Real Presence.

3. Supposing that Jesus intends the *apostles* to be the ones doing the remembering, the type of remembering that Jesus commands is a liturgical remembrance that actually makes present the event remembered.

Above we quoted the *Catechism* to say that the Eucharist is the "making present and the sacramental offering of his unique sacrifice." The reason it gives is that "In all the eucharistic prayers we find after the words of institution a prayer called the *anamnēsis* or memorial" (1362; emphasis in original).

It goes on to explain why the *anamnēsis* proves what the Church claims about the Eucharist making present Christ's sacrifice:

> In the sense of Sacred Scripture the *memorial* is not merely the recollection of past events but the proclamation of the mighty works wrought by God for men. In the liturgical celebration of these events, they become in a certain way present and real. This is how Israel understands its liberation from Egypt: every time Passover is celebrated, the Exodus events are made present to the memory of believers so that they may conform their lives to them (1363).

Is there any reason to think that what the *Catechism* claims is true? For starters, let's consider the ritual words for Passover itself, which God commands in Exodus 13:8,14:

> And you shall tell your son on that day, "It is because of what the LORD did for me when I came out of Egypt . . ." And when in time to come your son asks you, "What does this mean?" you shall say to him, "By strength of hand the LORD brought us out of Egypt, from the house of bondage."

Notice that the father must say, "when *I* came out of Egypt . . . the Lord has brought *us* out of Egypt." The father is instructed to insert himself and his family into the events that the liturgical celebration commemorates, no matter how much time has passed since the days of Moses.

MEETING THE PROTESTANT CHALLENGE

The *Mishna Pesahim,* a treatise that deals with laws for the Jewish Passover and the Passover lamb offering, says, "In every generation, a Jew is obligated to regard himself as if he personally had gone out of Egypt" (10.5). The *Pesahim* goes on to instruct,

> Therefore we are bound to give thanks . . . and to bless him who wrought all these wonders for our fathers and for us. He brought us out from bondage to freedom, from sorrow to gladness, and from mourning to a festival-day, and from darkness to great light, and from servitude to redemption; so let us say before him the hallelujah (10.5).

For the ancient Jews, the Passover meal wasn't merely a theoretical or abstract remembrance of God's past saving deeds. They viewed themselves as *participants* in the events the meal recalled because they viewed those events being mysteriously made present in their liturgical commemoration. Bible scholar Max Thurian explains the Jewish belief this way:

> As they ate . . . the Jews could re-live mystically, sacramentally, the events of the deliverance and Exodus from Egypt. They became contemporaries of their forefathers and were saved with them. There was in the mystery of the paschal meal a kind of telescoping of two periods of history, the present and the Exodus. The past event became present or rather each person became a contemporary of the past event.[95]

Jesus' instruction to view the Eucharist as a memorial, therefore, doesn't have to refer merely to a mental recollection of his sacrifice on the cross. It could be that Jesus intended the "remembrance" (*anamnēsis*) of his saving act on the cross to be of the same kind as the Jewish liturgical remembrance. The difference is that the *anamnēsis* for the new Passover meal, the Last Supper, would take on a new meaning. Rather than commemorating and making present the Jewish Passover, it would commemorate *Christ's* Passover (see CCC 1364) and make it present.

We have good reason to think that Jesus intended this connection because he instituted the Eucharist within the context of the Passover meal (Matt. 26:17-19), making the Eucharist the Christian equivalent of the Passover. Paul affirms this view in 1 Corinthians 5:7-8 when he writes, "For Christ, our paschal lamb, has been sacrificed. Let us, therefore, celebrate the festival."

When we take all of this into consideration, we can conclude that the *anamnēsis* instruction in Luke 22:19 doesn't pose a threat to the Catholic belief that the Eucharist offers the actual body and blood of Jesus.

COUNTER-CHALLENGE

Shouldn't we interpret the meaning of a biblical word in light of how the Bible and Jewish tradition use it rather than how it's used in modern English?

AFTERTHOUGHT

Prominent Protestant scholar J.N.D. Kelly recognizes that the act of remembrance is not merely a mental recollection, and thus not contradictory with the Catholic view. Kelly writes, "The bread and wine, moreover, are offered 'for a memorial (*eis anamnasin*) of the Passion,' a phrase which in view of his identification of them with the Lord's body and blood implies much more than an act of purely spiritual recollection."[96]

"Once and For All"

Hebrews 7:27 and the Eucharistic Sacrifice

How can the Catholic Church teach that the Mass is Christ's sacrifice when the Bible teaches that Christ offered himself once and for all?

The *Catechism* says that in the "divine sacrifice which is celebrated in the Mass," Christ is "contained and offered" (1367). But for many Protestants,[97] this contradicts the Bible's teaching on the "once for all" nature of Christ's death on the cross. Hebrews 7:27 is one of the passages they often appeal to:

> He [Jesus] has no need, like those high priests, to offer sacrifices daily, first for his own sins and then for those of the people; he did this once for all when he offered up himself.

If Christ offered himself "once for all," but the Catholic Church says that Christ continues to offer himself in the Eucharist, it would seem that the Catholic Church is teaching something contrary to the Bible.

MEETING THE CHALLENGE

1. The Catholic doctrine of the eucharistic sacrifice doesn't entail a re-crucifixion of Jesus but a re-*presentation* of Christ's one sacrifice in an unbloody manner.

The "once for all" statement in this verse comes within the context of contrasting Jesus' sacrifice for sins with the sacrifices that the Jewish priests had to offer on a daily basis. The author of Hebrews is making the point that Jesus doesn't have to offer regular animal sacrifices because his one sacrifice was sufficient to forgive the sins of all people throughout all time: "He [Jesus] has no need, like those high priests, to offer sacrifices daily . . . he did this once *for all* when he offered up himself."

The Catholic doctrine of the eucharistic sacrifice *would* contradict this biblical teaching if it entailed a re-crucifixion of Jesus. But that is not the case. The eucharistic sacrifice is not *another* sacrifice of Christ, as if Christ were repeatedly shedding his blood and dying. His *bloody* offering on the cross was a one-time event in the past and is never to be repeated. The offering in the eucharistic celebration *re-presents*—without blood, without making Jesus suffer and die anew—that one historical sacrifice. The *Catechism* explains:

> The sacrifice of Christ and the sacrifice of the Eucharist are one single sacrifice: "The victim is one and the same: the same now offers through the ministry of priests, who then offered himself on the cross; only the manner of offering is different" (1367, citing the Council of Trent).

Inasmuch as the Church's doctrine of the eucharistic sacrifice affirms that Christ died once on the cross and that he does not and cannot die again, it in no way violates the "once for all" teaching of Hebrews 7:27.

2. **The Bible itself reveals that Christ continues to offer himself in sacrifice to the Father in an unbloody manner.**

This challenge assumes that after Christ's bloody offering on the cross, nothing remains of his sacrificial ministry. But the Bible disproves that assumption.

The letter to the Hebrews tells us that Christ "holds his priesthood permanently" (7:24) and is our high priest "in the sanctuary and the true tent, which is set up not by man but by the Lord" (8:2). And since he "always lives to make intercession" (7:25) for us as our high priest, he is "able for all time to save those who draw near to God through him."

For the author of Hebrews, Christ's sacrifice is the basis for our salvation. So the ongoing intercession that Christ makes in the heavenly sanctuary must be on account of his death on the cross.

But Christ can't be repeatedly dying in the heavenly sanctuary, for that is the thing that the author of Hebrews is denying when he speaks of Christ offering himself "once for all" (see also Heb. 9:24-25). Christ's heavenly intercession, therefore, must consist of re-presenting to the Father his single sacrifice on the cross as a memorial offering and asking the Father to save those who draw near to him on account of that sacrifice. This makes sense out of what the author of Hebrews says in 8:3: "For every high priest is appointed to offer gifts and sacrifices; hence it is necessary for this priest also to have something to offer."

If Jesus can re-present his one sacrifice to the Father in an unbloody manner for an eternity in heaven and not take away from his once-for-all bloody offering on the cross, then the eucharistic sacrifice can do the same on earth. It is the temporal and visible outworking of Christ's mystical re-presentation of his one sacrifice in the heavenly sanctuary. It's a moment when heaven and earth are united, the earthly liturgy making present in time and space the heavenly liturgy.

Another passage that suggests an ongoing aspect of Christ's sacrificial ministry in the heavenly sanctuary is

Hebrews 9:23, which reads, "Thus it was necessary for the copies of the heavenly things to be purified with these rites, but the heavenly things themselves with better sacrifices than these."

The author implies that there are sacrifices taking place in the heavenly sanctuary—and that Christ is offering them, for in the next verse he speaks of Christ's heavenly intercession: "For Christ has entered, not into a sanctuary made with hands, a copy of the true one, but into heaven itself, *now to appear in the presence of God on our behalf*" (v.24).

This at least suggests that there is an *ongoing* aspect to Christ's sacrificial ministry. But what does he mean by "sacrifices" plural?

We know for sure that he doesn't mean that Christ repeatedly offers himself like he did on the cross. For he writes, "Nor was it to offer himself repeatedly, as the high priest enters the Holy Place yearly with blood not his own; for then he would have had to suffer repeatedly since the foundation of the world." (v.25-26). In saying that Jesus does not have to "suffer repeatedly," he has Christ's earthly, bloody sacrifice in mind.

How could Christ offer multiple sacrifices in heaven without suffering and without undermining the sufficiency of his death on the cross? By re-presenting his single sacrifice to the Father in an unbloody manner. It's the same sacrifice in that it's the same priest and the same victim but a different sacrifice in that it's offered in a different manner with different acts of intercession. This would explain how there are "sacrifices" (plural) offered in the heavenly temple.

This ongoing dimension of Christ's sacrifice in heaven, taught by Scripture, shows that the "once for all" challenge doesn't prove the Catholic belief wrong.

3. Death is not essential to a sacrifice.

One of the reasons many Protestants think the "once for all" passage undermines the eucharistic sacrifice is that they think sacrifice must involve death. Therefore, they immediately think that the eucharistic sacrifice is a re-crucifixion of Jesus.

For these people, to speak of sacrifice is to speak of death. And since Jesus only died once, the Eucharist can't be his sacrifice.

But this is not the only way that the Bible views sacrifice. The Old Testament is full of drink offerings and grain offerings, for instance, neither of which involves death.

There was also the "wave" offering in which the gift was waved before God to present it to him. This type of sacrifice didn't involve the destruction of the gift.

For example, Numbers 8:11-21 records God's instructions for Aaron to "offer the Levites before the Lord as a wave offering from the people of Israel" (vv.11, 13). This act constituted the Levites as ministers of the tabernacle, bestowing upon them the duty to "do service for the people of Israel at the tent of meeting" (v.19).

Similarly, Paul tells the Christians in Rome to "present your bodies as a living sacrifice, holy and acceptable to God, which is your spiritual worship" (Rom. 12:1). We don't allow ourselves to be killed as a sacrifice; rather, we are to present ourselves as wave offerings to the Lord.[98]

It's this type offering that Jesus makes of himself before God in the heavenly sanctuary. Christ waves the offering of his body and blood to the Father as a living sacrifice. Because it's the same priest making the offering (Jesus), the same victim (Jesus), and the same person to whom the offering is made (the Father), it's the same sacrifice. The only difference is that his sacrifice in heaven doesn't involve him shedding his blood and dying. It's offered in an unbloody way since the shedding of his blood was done "once for all" on the cross (Heb. 7:27).

COUNTER-CHALLENGE

Are you saying that the Mass contradicts what the Bible says about Jesus' sacrifice being offered "once for all," but Jesus' heavenly offering of his sacrifice to the Father doesn't?

AFTERTHOUGHT

Through the prophet Malachi, God prophesies: "For from the rising of the sun to its setting my name is great among the nations, and in every place incense is offered to my name, and a pure offering; for my name is great among the nations, says the Lord of hosts" (Mal. 1:11). What "pure offering" could be offered among all the nations in the days of the Messiah? In such days, there would be no other "pure offering" besides Christ's single sacrifice of his body and blood. So, if the "pure offering" is Christ's sacrifice, then we have a prophetic text of Gentile people all over the world offering Christ's sacrifice in the messianic age (today). That sounds a lot like the Mass. This interpretation of Malachi 1:11 is found in the *Didache* (14) and in the writings of some of the early Church Fathers, such as Justin Martyr[99] and Irenaeus of Lyons.[100]

"The Fruit of the Vine"

Mark 14:25 and the Real Presence

How can the Catholic Church teach that the Eucharist is the actual body and blood of Jesus when Jesus refers to his so-called blood as the "fruit of the vine"?

Catholics defend their belief in the Eucharist by appealing to Christ's words at the Last Supper. We argue that because Jesus said, "This is my body," and not, "This *represents* my body," he literally meant that bread becomes his body (and wine his blood).

Protestants,[101] however, sometimes respond: Ah, but Jesus couldn't have meant for the substance in the chalice to be his real blood because *after* what Catholics call the "words of consecration" he says, "I tell you I shall not drink again of *this fruit of the vine* until that day when I drink it new with you in my Father's kingdom" (Mark 14:25; Matt. 26:29). Why would Jesus call the substance in the chalice "this fruit of the vine" if it were actually his blood?

MEETING THE CHALLENGE

1. The challenge fails to consider that Luke records these words before the words of consecration.

Mark and Matthew have Jesus saying these words after Jesus says "This is my blood," but in Luke they come before:

> And he took a cup, and when he had given thanks he said, "Take this, and divide it among yourselves; for I tell you that from now on I shall not drink of the fruit of the vine until the kingdom of God comes" (Luke 22:17-18).

The words of consecration follow, perhaps in order to clarify the sequence in Mark and Matthew's account.

It was known in the first century that Mark did not write things in chronological order. A second-century Christian bishop named Papias records John the presbyter, an eyewitness of Jesus' ministry, as saying, "Mark, having become an interpreter of Peter, wrote down accurately, *though not in order*, whatsoever he remembered of the things said or done by Christ."[102] Luke tells us explicitly in the prologue to his Gospel that he set out "to write an *orderly* account" of the things accomplished among them, even though many before him, such as Mark, had already compiled such a narrative (Luke 1:1-3).

Therefore, it's reasonable to conclude that Luke diverts from Mark's order because he is clarifying Mark's placement of Jesus' statement. If so, this challenge loses all its force. But even if not, in Luke the order is reversed, weakening any argument based strictly on the order in Mark and Matthew.

2. It's possible that Jesus is using phenomenological language to describe his blood in the chalice.

Even if we concede for argument's sake that Jesus did use the "fruit of the vine" phrase after he said, "This is my blood," it wouldn't necessarily follow that he intended to attest that the substance was merely wine. That's because biblical authors often described things according to their appearance. Scholars call this *phenomenological* language.

We use it even today. For example, the weatherman says the sun will "rise" at six a.m. and "set" at seven p.m. Should we conclude that the weatherman is an advocate of geocentrism who believes that the sun moves up and down over the earth? Of course not! He's simply describing something according to the way we see it.

In the Bible, angels and even God are described according to how they are revealed to the senses. The book of Genesis describes the Lord and his angels as *men* since that is the form they took when they conversed with Abraham (Gen. 18:2; cf. 18:10, 19:1). Tobit does the same thing with reference to an angel in Tobit 5:2-4.

These authors were not trying to say that God and angels are *actually* men. They simply described phenomena in a common way as they were observed according to the senses. Similarly, the Bible often refers to death as "sleep." Take Job 3:11-13, for example. In his suffering, Job laments about not dying at birth because then he would be at rest: "Why did I not die at birth, come forth from the womb and expire? . . . For then I should have lain down and been quiet; I should have slept; then I should have been at rest."

Jesus refers to Lazarus's death as sleep. In John 11:11, Jesus says, "Our friend Lazarus has fallen asleep, but I go to awake him out of sleep." John tells us in verse 13, "Now Jesus had spoken of his death," and then in verse 14 Jesus tells the apostles explicitly, "Lazarus is dead."

Paul also employs the sleep language to refer to death. In 1 Thessalonians 4:15, Paul contrasts those "who are alive, [and] who are left until the coming of the Lord" with those "who have fallen asleep." Given the contrast with Christians who are *alive*, we know those "who have fallen asleep" refers to Christians who have died.

That the Bible uses sleep language to speak of death is perfectly reasonable given that when someone is dead it appears as if he's sleeping.

A similar line of exegesis can be applied to Mark and Matthew's record of Jesus' words at the Last Supper. It's perfectly reasonable for Jesus to employ the phenomenological language of "wine" even when referring to his precious blood since that is how it appears to the senses. The mere reference to "the fruit of the vine," therefore, doesn't *prove* that the substance in the chalice is wine.

3. Jesus could be describing the substance in the chalice according to its prior state.

It's common for a biblical author to describe something according to its prior state. For example, Eve is called Adam's bone (Gen. 1:23). Aaron's rod is said to have devoured the "rods" of the magicians even though they had become serpents (Exod. 7:12).

This idiom of describing something according to its prior state could explain why Jesus describes his blood as wine. He could simply be referring to it according to what it once was. St. Paul does the same thing when he refers to the Eucharist as "bread" (1 Cor. 11:26), even though we know that he believed it to be a literal participation in the body of Christ (1 Cor. 10:16).

4. There is mystery but not a disproof of Catholic belief.

Note that Jesus doesn't point to the chalice and say, "The substance in here is wine." The gist of his statement seems not to be about identifying the contents of the chalice but to prophesy that he would not drink of the "fruit of the vine" until the coming of the kingdom.

What this means is something of a mystery—especially since his death was less than a day away. Was he referring to the heavenly banquet (Isa. 25:6–8; Rev. 19:9)? It's possible, given that Jesus describes heaven as a banquet: "I tell you, many will come from East and West and sit at table with Abraham, Isaac, and Jacob in the kingdom of heaven" (Matt. 8:11).

Was he referring to the sour wine he would partake of while hanging on the cross (John 19:30)? That's also possible since it's the first time he drinks wine since his cryptic statement in the upper room.

Or it could refer to what St. John Chrysostom (c. 347–407) thought it referred to—Jesus' drinking wine with his disciples after his Resurrection. For Chrysostom, Jesus' talk about the kingdom refers to his Resurrection. And Jesus' talk about drinking wine "new" refers to drinking wine "after a new manner . . . no longer having a passible body, or needing food."[103]

Despite the mystery, the words don't disprove the Catholic belief about the Eucharist.

COUNTER-CHALLENGE

How can you be so sure that "fruit of the vine" in Matthew and Mark is mere wine because Jesus says it after consecration when Luke says that Jesus uttered these words before *consecration? Shouldn't we at least conclude that it's ambiguous and thus not a strong argument against belief in the Real Presence?*

AFTERTHOUGHT

Remember that Catholics don't deny that the Eucharist also has a "symbolic" value. The *Catechism* explains that the sacraments "confer the grace they signify" (1127). The visible sign of bread and wine *signifies* Jesus as our true food and true drink: "My flesh is food indeed and my blood is drink indeed" (John 6:55). Therefore, it's reasonable to refer to the Eucharist as bread and wine in a symbolic sense while at the same time affirming that they are Jesus' body and blood in reality.

"God Alone Can Forgive Sins"

Mark 2:7 (Matt. 9:6) and the Priest's Power to Forgive Sins

How can the Catholic Church teach that a priest can forgive sins when the Bible teaches that God alone forgive sins?

The Catholic Church teaches that priests can absolve sins. The *Catechism* teaches in paragraph 1495, "only priests who have received the faculty of absolving from the authority of the Church *can forgive sins* in the name of Christ" (emphasis added). Similarly, in 1463 the *Catechism* states that a priest has the power to "absolve from every sin."

For many Protestants[104] this is problematic because the Bible teaches that God alone forgives sins: "Who can forgive sins but God alone?" (Mark 2:7). Jesus, since he is God, has this power, as he claimed, "The Son of Man has authority on earth to forgive sins" (Matt. 9:6).

MEETING THE CHALLENGE

1. God can use humans as instruments to communicate blessings of which he alone is the source.

The Catholic Church doesn't believe that a priest can forgive sins by his own authority. This is why the *Catechism* teaches that a priest forgives sins "in the name of Christ" (1495). The Church also stresses that God alone has that *ability:* "Only God forgives sins" (CCC 1441).

Although the authority and the power to forgive sins belong only to God by nature, this doesn't mean that he can't let humans mediate that power as he does with other blessings.

Take physical healings, for example. Only God has the power by nature to perform a miracle. Yet he often involves human ministers when he performs a miracle, allowing them to mediate that power through their human actions (for example, Acts 3:6). God doesn't need human agents to perform healings, but he chooses to use them.

It is God who illuminates the mind to know truth, yet he chooses humans to mediate such illumination. He tells the apostles in Matthew 28:20, "Go therefore, and make disciples of all nations . . . teaching them to observe all that I have commanded you." God didn't need the apostles (or today's missionaries) to administer truth. He could have infused knowledge of truth into our minds like he did the angels. Yet he chose to do it through cooperation with humans.

The inspiration of Scripture is another example. God could have delivered an inspired holy book straight from heaven, but instead he chose to work through man to communicate his revelation to us. No Protestant would deny the inspiration of Scripture on the grounds that God alone has the power to reveal himself!

In all of these examples, God works *through* man to communicate his blessings. God alone is the source, but that doesn't prevent humans from being his instruments. To say then that God alone has the power to forgive sins by nature doesn't mean he can't work through his ordained ministers to forgive sins.

2. In the Old Testament, God willed to use ordained ministers to help reconcile penitents back to God.

The idea of God associating his ordained ministers with the forgiveness of sins is not foreign to the Bible. For example, we read in Leviticus 5:5-6,

> When a man is guilty in any of these [refusal to testify as a witness when adjured, contact with unclean thing or person, and rash oath], he shall confess the sin he has committed, and he shall bring his guilt offering to the LORD for the sin which he has committed, a female from the flock, a lamb or a goat, for a sin offering; and the priest shall make atonement for him for his sin.

A similar example is found in Numbers 15:27-28:

> If one person sins unwittingly, he shall offer a female goat a year old for a sin offering. And the priest shall make atonement before the LORD for the person who commits an error, when he sins unwittingly, to make atonement for him; and he shall be forgiven.

These examples in Scripture show that God involved ordained ministers in his forgiveness of people's sins. And if God willed to do this in the Old Covenant, it's reasonable to think he might do the same for his people in the New Covenant.

3. The Bible offers evidence that Jesus gave the apostles authority to forgive sins.

John records in John 20:20-23,

> Jesus said to them again, "Peace be with you. As the Father has sent me, even so I send you." And when he had said

this, he breathed on them, and said to them, "Receive the Holy Spirit. If you forgive the sins of any, they are forgiven; if you retain the sins of any, they are retained."

Since the apostles were given the authority to judge whether to forgive or not forgive ("retain") sins, penitents seeking forgiveness first would have to confess their sins and express their contrition.

Moreover, notice that Jesus says, "If *you* forgive . . . if *you* retain." He doesn't say, "If *God* forgives . . . if *God* retains." This is not to say that God doesn't forgive and retain. But it does indicate that Jesus gives his ministers discretion over forgiving and retaining since he emphasizes his ministers as the subject of action in the act of forgiving and retaining sins.

COUNTER-CHALLENGE

Can we say that no man can forgive sins when Jesus explicitly gives the apostles a share in his power to forgive sins?

AFTERTHOUGHT

Some Protestants argue that all Jesus means by "forgive" and "retain" is for his ministers to *tell people* that their sins are forgiven or retained based on how they respond to the gospel (see Luke 24:47). But telling someone to forgive is not the same thing as telling someone to preach. So this interpretation without any evidence forces the text to be taken in an unnatural sense.

"We Confess Our Sins Directly to God"

1 John 1:9 and Confession to a Priest

How can the Catholic Church teach that we need to confess our sins to a priest when John says that we need to confess our sins to *God* in order to be forgiven?

The *Catechism* identifies the "confession of sins to a priest" as an "essential element" of the sacrament of confession (1424). It goes on in paragraph 1456 that "all mortal sins of which penitents after a diligent self-examination are conscious must be recounted by them in confession."

But many Protestants object[105] since John tells us in 1 John 1:9, "If we confess our sins, he is faithful and just, and will forgive our sins and cleanse us from all unrighteousness." Since there is no mention here of any need for confession to an ordained minister, we should only confess our sins directly to God.

MEETING THE CHALLENGE

1. The instruction doesn't specify direct confession to God and, in fact, it fits with a Catholic view of confession.

Nowhere does the text say that we must confess *directly* to God alone. Anyone who makes this challenge is guilty of reading that idea into the text. In fact, John's instruction fits just as easily with the Catholic view that the confession of sins can be directed to God through the ministry of his ordained priests—with forgiveness received from him, as we saw, through that same ministry.

It could be read either way, and the immediate context doesn't suggest one reading or the other. However, when you take into consideration that the same author, John, records Jesus' instruction for the apostles to forgive and retain sins in John 20:23, it's reasonable to conclude that this is the sort of confession of sins that he would have in mind here in 1 John 1:9.

2. The Greek word for confess (*homologeō*) has a public connotation, which would suggest that the confession of sins that John speaks of is not merely a direct confession to God.

Over the course of time, the Church adopted the ordinary practice of private confession of sins to a priest. But originally, confession of sins was done publicly. And there are hints that suggest this is what John has in mind in 1 John 1:9.

Consider, first of all, that one of the meanings of *homologeō* is "to acknowledge something, ordinarily in public."[106] This is how John uses it in his writings.

For example, in John 1:20, he uses *homologeō* to describe how John the Baptist "confessed" to the Jewish leaders that he was not the Christ. In John 12:42, he uses the word to describe how some Jewish leaders, due to fear, weren't "confessing" aloud their internal belief in Jesus. John also uses *homologeō* in 1 John 4:3 and 2 John 1:7 in reference to non-Christians making promises, declarations, or confessions of belief and unbelief to other people.

Homologeō also takes on a public dimension in the wider context of Scripture where it's consistently used for public declarations. For example, Luke uses it in Acts 7:17 in reference to the promise that God "made" to Abraham. Matthew uses it in Matthew 7:23 to describe how Jesus will "say" to the damned, "I never knew you. Depart from me." Matthew uses it again in Matthew 10:32 when he records Jesus' teaching about those who go to heaven because they "acknowledge" him before men. Other passages where *homologeō* is used for public declarations are Matthew 14:7, Acts 23:8, and Hebrews 11:13.

If *homologeō* is used by John and within the wider context of Scripture to refer to public declarations, it's reasonable to conclude that when John uses it in 1 John 1:9 in reference to confessing sins he's not referring merely to private confession to God within one's heart but instead thinks of it as having a public dimension. And since John also told us that Christ's ministers have the authority to forgive and retain sin (John 2:23), it's reasonable to conclude that such ministers would have presided over such public confessions of sin and done what Christ commanded them to do: forgive and retain.

3. In Scripture, the confession of sins is a public affair.

In both the Old and New Testaments, confession of sins is ordinarily done in public. Consider, for example, Leviticus 5:5-6, which instructs the guilty man to "confess the sin he has committed" and "bring his guilt offering to the Lord for the sin which he has committed." The confession is tied to the public event of the sin offering performed by the priest at the temple.

We even see public confession of sins in the New Testament. For example, Matthew tells us in Matthew 3:5-6 that those who were baptized by John the Baptist in the Jordan were "confessing their sins." In Acts 19:18, after Paul exorcized a demon-possessed girl, many of the Ephesians "came confessing and divulging their practices." The Greek word here for *confessing* is *exomologeō*, which like *homologeō* has a public connotation: "to declare openly in acknowledgment."[107]

James 5:16 is another example. Here, James gives instruction for sinners to "confess your sins one to another," which in light of the previous verses (vv.14-15) involved the presbyters.

In light of the biblical precedent of public confessions, it's reasonable to conclude, along with nineteenth-century Anglican New Testament scholar Brooke Westcott, that John's phrase "confess your sins" means "not only acknowledge them, but acknowledge them openly in the face of men."[108] And as we saw above, it's reasonable to think that those ministers to whom Christ gave the authority to forgive and retain would have presided over such public confessions of sin, carrying out the commission that came with that authority.

COUNTER-CHALLENGE

If in the Bible the ordinary practice of confessing sins was a public affair, why doesn't your Church practice public confession? Wouldn't that be the more biblical thing to do?

AFTERTHOUGHT

The *Didache* describes the public dimension of the confession of sins: "Confess your sins in church, and do not go up to your prayer with an evil conscience. This is the way of life. . . . On the Lord's Day gather together, break bread, and give thanks, after confessing your transgressions so that your sacrifice may be pure."[109]

"We're All Priests"

1 Peter 2:9 and the Hierarchical/ Ministerial Priesthood

How can the Catholic Church teach that there is a ministerial priesthood when the Bible tells us that we're *all* priests?

Catholicism is a priestly religion. The *Catechism* teaches that there is a "ministerial or hierarchical priesthood of bishops and priests" at the service of God's people, and this priesthood is the "means by which Christ unceasingly builds up and leads his Church" (1547).

But for some Protestants[110] this contradicts what Peter teaches in 1 Peter 2:9, namely that *all* Christians are priests: "You are a chosen race, a royal priesthood, a holy nation." Like Martin Luther,[111] Protestants argue that if all believers are priests in Christ, the one priest, then there is no need for a ministerial priesthood.

MEETING THE CHALLENGE

1. The parallel that Peter makes with Exodus 19:6 supports the Catholic view of a ministerial priesthood.[112]

Everyone agrees that Peter's statement in 1 Peter 2:9 is an allusion to Exodus 19:6, which refers to Israel as "a kingdom of priests and a holy nation." Peter is obviously drawing a parallel between Israel and the Church.

But rather than disproving the Catholic position, this verse actually supports it. During the time of Exodus, the universal priesthood of the Israelites was merely one rank (the lowest rank) of priestly status among two others: the top level of Aaron the high priest and the middle level, which comprised his sons, Nadab, Abihu, Eleazar, and Ithamar, who served with Aaron (see Exodus 28 and Leviticus 8).

When we look in the New Testament, we discover a top level there, too: Jesus, our high priest (Heb. 3:1). We've already seen that the bottom rank consists of the body of Christian believers (1 Pet. 2:9) in a parallel with the universal priesthood of the Israelites. It makes biblical sense, therefore, that there would also be a New Testament parallel to the middle rank: ministers specially ordained to serve the people with Jesus just as Aaron's sons served with him.[113] This appeal to 1 Peter 2:9, then, only strengthens the Catholic position.

2. Jesus' command for his ministers to forgive sins in John 20:23 reveals that his ministers are *ministerial* priests over and above the common priesthood of believers.

Jesus tells his disciples, "If you forgive the sins of any, they are forgiven; if you retain the sins of any, they are retained" (John 20:23). Granting his disciples the power to forgive and retain sins is a clue that Jesus is making them ministerial priests.

We see this paradigm in the Old Testament. In Leviticus 5:5-6, the sinner had to present a lamb or a goat to the priests as a sin offering and confess his sin, then the priest offered the victim in atonement for the sin. The same practice is found in Numbers 15:27-28. The penitent presented his sin offering to the *priest*, and through the intercession of the priest the sin was atoned for. God didn't need to employ priests in this manner, but he willed to.

It is against this Old Testament backdrop that Jesus commands his disciples to forgive sins. If God administered the forgiveness of sins in the Old Testament with the *cooperation* of his ministerial priests, and Jesus, who is God incarnate, is giving his New Testament ministers *a share in his power* to actually forgive sins, then we can conclude that Jesus intends his ministers to be New Covenant ministerial priests.

3. **Jesus' instruction to "do this in remembrance of me" (Luke 22:19) at the Last Supper is evidence that Jesus intends the apostles to be his New Testament ministerial priests.**

Offering sacrifice is a duty that belongs to priests (Heb. 8:3). And because as all Christians belong to the universal priesthood of Christ (1 Pet. 2:9), Christians can offer their prayers and even their bodies as sacrifices to the Lord (Rom. 12:1).

But in the Old Testament, some sacrifices were offered only by a distinct class of priests (Lev. 9:7, 14:12). There is good reason to think that with his instruction to "do this in remembrance of me" Jesus is giving the apostles the duty to offer a sacrifice, thus making them a distinct class of *New* Testament priests.

The first thing to note is that Jesus' command is given privately in the upper room—there is no evidence that it's meant to apply to all believers. The apostles are being called to perform a duty that is distinctive of their Christian ministry.

With regard to the sacrificial nature of the instruction, we can look to two clues. The first is the command, "*Do this . . .*"

The Greek text says *touto poieite*. The verb *poieō* means "do" or "make." But as we saw earlier, in Scripture the word has sacrificial overtones. It's translated from the Septuagint as "offer"—in the sense of offering a sacrifice—in passages such as Exodus 29:38, Leviticus 9:7, and Psalm 66:15. Jesus' command, therefore, for the apostles to *touto poieite* suggests Jesus understands the Last Supper to be a sacrifice, and he is commanding the apostles to offer it as such.

A second clue is the word *remembrance*. The Greek *anamnēsis* has sacrificial meaning in both the Old and New Testaments. For example, in Numbers 10:10 of the Septuagint, the sacrifices of peace offerings are said to "serve you for remembrance [*anamnēsis*] before your God." *Anamnēsis* is also used in Hebrews 10:3 in reference to the sacrifices that serve as a "reminder" year after year. The usage of *anamnēsis*, therefore, also suggests that Jesus sees the Last Supper as a sacrifice, and he is commanding the apostles to offer it themselves.

Since, in the Bible, offering distinct sacrifices on behalf of God's people is a duty that belongs to ministerial priests, and Jesus is commanding the apostles to offer the Last Supper as a sacrifice that is distinctive of their ministry, it follows that the apostles are Jesus' New Testament ministerial priests.

4. There is evidence that Paul views his ministry as a priestly ministry distinct from the common priesthood.

The key text is Romans 15:15-16, where Paul writes,

> But on some points I have written to you very boldly by way of reminder, because of the grace given me by God to be a minister of Christ Jesus to the Gentiles in *the priestly service* of the gospel of God, so that the offering of the Gentiles may be acceptable, sanctified by the Holy Spirit.

Notice that Paul refers to his ministry as a "priestly service." The Greek word that Paul uses is *hierourgeō,* which is the verb form of the Greek word *hiereus.*

In the Bible, forms of *hiereus* are commonly used in reference to the Jewish priests of the Old Covenant. For example, Exodus 28 verses 1, 4, and 41 speak of the ordination of Aaron and his sons as "priests." If Paul sees his apostolic work specifically through the lens of the *priestly* work of the Old Testament, then he must recognize his apostolic office as a distinct priestly office over and above the common priesthood.

COUNTER-CHALLENGE

If Jesus gave the apostles priestly functions to perform, and Paul recognized his ministry as a priestly ministry, shouldn't all church leaders exercise priestly ministry? Wouldn't that be more consistent with the biblical paradigm for church leadership?

AFTERTHOUGHT

In about A.D. 215, St. Hippolytus of Rome affirmed the existence of a hierarchical/ministerial priesthood. He wrote, "When a deacon is to be ordained he is chosen after the fashion of those things said above, the bishop alone in like manner imposing his hands upon him as we have prescribed. In the ordaining of a deacon, this is the reason why the bishop alone is to impose his hands upon him: he is not ordained to the priesthood, but to serve the bishop and to fulfill the bishop's command. He has no part in the council of the clergy, but is to attend to his own duties and is to acquaint the bishop with such matter as are needful. He does not receive that Spirit which the presbytery possesses and in which the presbyters share. He receives only what is entrusted to him under the bishop."[114]

"Except for Unchastity"

Matthew 19:9 on Divorce and Remarriage

How can the Catholic Church teach that a person who divorces can't remarry when Jesus teaches that remarriage is permitted in the case of adultery?

The Church teaches that marriage is indissoluble. Thus the *Catechism* teaches that while spouses are living, a new marital union "cannot be recognized as valid, if the first marriage was" (1650). Those who attempt civil remarriage after divorce, therefore, "find themselves in a situation that objectively contravenes God's law." The Church bases this teaching on Jesus' words in Mark 10:11-12: "Whoever divorces his wife and marries another, commits adultery against her; and if she divorces her husband and marries another, she commits adultery."

But many Protestants[115] critique this teaching for not taking into consideration what Jesus says in Matthew 19:9: "Whoever divorces his wife, *except for unchastity*, and marries another, commits adultery; and he who marries a divorced woman, commits adultery." Since Jesus inserts the clause "except for unchastity," a man who divorced his wife and married another wouldn't be committing adultery if his wife were guilty of infidelity.

MEETING THE CHALLENGE

1. The Greek word for *unchastity* in this verse isn't part of the group of words that Matthew uses for adultery in his Gospel.

The Greek word *porneia*, translated as "unchastity" or sometimes "fornication" or "sexual immorality," is different from the Greek word for "adultery" (*moichaō*). In its broadest sense, *porneia* means unlawful sexual intercourse,[116] so it can include adultery, but Matthew never uses the word that way in his Gospel. Instead, he uses *moichaō* and related words.

For example, in the same verse of the *porneia* clause Matthew uses *moichaō* twice to refer specifically to adultery: "Whoever divorces his wife, except for unchastity, and marries another, commits adultery [*moichatai*]; and he who marries a divorced woman, commits adultery [*moichatai*]." In 5:27, Matthew uses *moicheuō* to refer to the exterior act of adultery, in 5:28 to broaden the concept of adultery to include lust, and in 5:32 in reference to the husband making his wife an "adulteress" by divorcing her.

If Matthew thought that Jesus was talking about adultery providing an exception to his teaching on divorce, why doesn't he use the word he always used for adultery? As Bible scholar John P. Meier argues, "[I]f Matthew wishes to name adultery as a reason for divorce, he would be almost forced to employ some form of *moicheia* [noun] to express the concept."[117]

Since Matthew doesn't use any form of the Greek word that he commonly uses for adultery, it's reasonable to conclude that Matthew doesn't think Jesus was referring to spousal infidelity when he spoke of "unchastity."

2. The reaction of the disciples to Jesus' teaching is unintelligible on the supposition that Jesus is allowing spousal infidelity to be grounds for divorce and remarriage.

After Jesus overturns the permissive teaching on divorce in the Mosaic Law, his disciples say, "If such is the case of a man with his wife, it is not expedient to marry" (Matt. 19:10). This suggests that Jesus was not providing a loophole for infidelity.

At the time of Jesus there were two rabbinic schools of thought as to what constituted legitimate grounds for divorce. The Hillel school, which followed the Jewish leader Hillel, believed that practically anything could be grounds for divorce. It could be something as simple as burnt food or a prettier woman.[118] The school of Shammai, on the other hand, believed that a more serious reason was necessary, something like adultery, or even immodest conduct shy of actual adultery.[119]

Given this background, the disciples' reaction that it would be better not to marry would be unintelligible if Jesus were allowing for divorce and remarriage, as the challenge suggests, in cases of adultery or sexual immorality. The disciples already were accustomed to divorce and remarriage, as the Hillel and Shammai schools attest. Their strong reaction suggests that they understood Jesus to be giving a new and different teaching.

3. **Jesus' own teaching indicates that he is distancing his view on divorce and remarriage from the prevailing views among first-century Jews, who saw adultery and other forms of spousal ifidelity as grounds for divorce and remarriage.**

Jesus' teaching about divorce and remarriage in verse 9 is part of his response to a question posed by the Pharisees: "Is it lawful to divorce one's wife for any cause?" (v.3). Notice the phrase, "for any cause." It seems the Pharisees were testing Jesus to see which school of thought he would side with, Hillel or Shammai.

But Jesus' response indicates that he sides with neither, for he appeals to God's original design for marriage, which didn't involve divorce and remarriage *at all*:

Have you not read that he who made them from the beginning made them male and female, and said, "For this reason a man shall leave his father and mother and be joined to his wife, and the two shall become one flesh"? So they are no longer two but one flesh. What therefore God has joined together, let not man put asunder (vv.4–6).

Jesus' appeal to God's original design, along with his words, "What therefore God had joined together, let not man put asunder" (v.6), proves that he sides with neither the Hillel nor the Shammai view on divorce and remarriage.

This context excludes the interpretation that *porneia* refers to adultery; in fact, it excludes reference to sexual immorality of *any* manner within marriage. For if Jesus intended the *porneia* clause to refer to any of these alternative interpretations, he would have been siding with either the Hillel or Shammai school. But Jesus didn't side with either of them. Instead, he gave a more radical teaching: that marriage is indissoluble. Therefore, we must conclude that Jesus didn't intend the *porneia* clause to refer to sexual immorality within the context of the marriage bond, whether adultery or some other kind of immoral conduct.

Jesus underscores his radical view by saying that no man can marry a divorced woman without committing adultery: "He who marries a divorced woman, commits adultery" (v.9; cf. Matt. 5:32). This implies that no deed for which the woman is divorced renders her free to marry another man, including adultery. Adultery, therefore, doesn't constitute grounds for divorce and remarriage in the mind of Jesus.

4. That the other New Testament writers never refer to an "unchastity clause" gives good reason to think that Jesus was not giving a loophole to permit divorce and remarriage.

Nowhere else outside of Matthew does the New Testament include this so-called adultery exception clause when it deals with divorce and remarriage (see Mark 10:11-12; Luke 16:18; Rom. 7:2-3; 1 Cor. 7:10-13) or otherwise refer to any exception to the indissolubility of marriage. This is noteworthy because the four other sources that deal with the issue of divorce are written for Greco-Roman audiences, among whom sexual immorality abounded. If anyone needed to know about an immorality loophole for divorce and remarriage, it was the Gentile audiences for whom Mark, Luke, and Paul wrote!

By itself this doesn't prove that there *isn't* a loophole to permit divorce and remarriage. But considering how big a deal it is, you would think there'd be some corroboration by other New Testament authors. Since there isn't, it is reasonable to conclude that whatever the exception clause means, it probably doesn't mean that infidelity severs the marriage bond.

In fact, in the seventh chapter of his first letter to the Corinthians, Paul seems to close the door to any exception to Jesus' prohibition of divorce and remarriage. In verse 10, he writes,

> To the married I give charge, *not I but the Lord*, that the wife should not separate from her husband (but if she does, let her remain single or else be reconciled to her husband)—and that the husband should not divorce his wife.

Paul gives only two options if a husband and wife separate: remain separated or get back together. Divorce and remarriage is not an option. And this, Paul claims, is the teaching of Jesus, not his own: "not I but the Lord" (v.10).

Paul distinguishes his own counsel from the Lord's in verses 12-13 when he gives instruction about what to do if one of the spouses is an unbeliever. He prefaces his remarks by saying, "To the rest I say, *not the Lord*."

According to Paul's inspired words, therefore, Jesus didn't allow for an exceptional case where a man could divorce his wife, marry another, and not be guilty of adultery.

5. There are good reasons to think that *porneia* instead refers to forms of sexual immorality that took place before or at the time of the attempted union, rendering it unlawful (invalid).

Porneia is used twenty-five times in the New Testament. For only two of these do scholars even suggest that it's used for adultery: the passages that include the debated *porneia* clause concerning divorce and remarriage (Matt. 5:32, 19:9). Every other time, *porneia* refers to some sort of sexual immorality *outside* the lawful bounds of marriage: fornication (Matt. 15:19; Mark 7:21; John 8:41; Gal. 5:19; Eph. 5:3; Col. 3:5; Rev. 17:2; Rev. 17:4, Rev. 19:2), incest (1 Cor. 5:1; Acts 15:20, 29; Acts 21:25), general sexual immorality (1 Cor. 6:13, 18, 1 Cor. 7:2; 2 Cor. 12:21; Rev. 2:21; Rev. 9:21; 1 Thess. 4:3), and metaphorical impure passions (Rev. 14:8; Rev. 18:3).

Since we know from above that *porneia* can't refer to adultery in Matthew 19:9, and every time *porneia* is used in the New Testament it refers to sexual immorality outside the boundaries of the marital bond, it's likely that the "*porneia* exception" in Matthew refers to sexual immorality that took place before and at the time of the attempted union, invalidating it.

We can support this interpretation by considering two things. First, it adequately explains why in these cases a man that puts away his wife and marries another doesn't commit adultery. If he was never in a lawful union to begin with, he would be free to marry. This is the basis for Catholic teaching on *annulments*: allowing remarriage of civilly divorced persons whose first "marriage" was judged not to have been valid.

That Matthew, who is writing to a Jewish audience, is the only Gospel that records this exception clause, also works in favor of this interpretation. The Jews understood that certain sexual relationships rendered a union unlawful, meaning null and void—such as relationships of close consanguinity and affinity (Lev. 18:1-20).

Only the Jewish community would know about the Levitical Law concerning unlawful unions, and thus only the Jewish community would raise the question about whether these unions are an exception to Jesus' teaching against divorce and remarriage.

Matthew's intention is to clarify for his Jewish audience that Jesus' prohibition of divorce doesn't apply to those unlawful unions contracted before Christian baptism because they weren't lawful to begin with. To use modern language, these unions would have been considered null and void and thus wouldn't fall under Jesus' prohibition of divorce and remarriage. Jesus was concerned with lawful marriages.[120]

COUNTER-CHALLENGE

Isn't it interesting that the dominant view among Christians throughout the history of Christianity, all the way back to St. Paul, was that Jesus didn't permit divorce and remarriage? Why should we go against historic Christianity on this point in favor of a view that only gained traction during the Reformation?

AFTERTHOUGHT

Another theory[121] suggests that *porneia* may refer to spousal infidelity before consummation. It was Jewish custom for a newly wedded couple to remain physically separate for some time until the husband prepared a place for his bride. Only after the husband had prepared a place for his bride would the couple consummate the marriage. This interval would have been the time period of Mary and Joseph's marriage in which Gabriel appeared to Mary (see Luke 1:27). This theory suggests that Jesus' reference to *porneia* in Matthew 19:9 refers to spousal infidelity during this time interval. In such a case the bond could be dissolved. This is consistent with Catholic teaching that consummation is a necessary condition for marriage to be indissoluble (CCC 2382).

This theory could also explain why Matthew was the only Gospel writer to include the clause. He is also the only one to record Joseph's decision to divorce Mary after discovering she was pregnant during the period of their betrothal. It's possible that Matthew includes the *porneia* clause to explain how Joseph could be a righteous man and yet decide to divorce his wife.

V

Mary

So far, we have dealt with challenges dealing mainly with authority and salvation. Although these topics are central to Christian faith, often the challenges that Protestants pose to Catholics begin with other topics. In my experience, one of those topics is *Mary*.

Sometimes it's her intercessory role that Protestants have a problem with. (We're going to deal with that issue in our next section.) But most often, Protestants object strongly to the beliefs that Mary was sinless and a perpetual virgin. In both cases, they will point to Bible verses that, in their eyes, clearly state the opposite of what Catholicism teaches. How can Catholics possibly accept them?

We can be sympathetic to their doubt because as Catholics we don't want to believe anything that contradicts the Bible either. So, like all the other challenges that we've looked at so far, these are worthy of consideration. We can't just dismiss them without giving them their due. But as we meet these challenges, we'll see that they fail to prove what they set out to prove. Scripture does not contradict Catholic Marian doctrine; for your Protestant friend, this may be a first step to coming to see how the two are in agreement.

"All Have Sinned"

Romans 3:23 and Mary's Freedom from Personal Sin

How can the Catholic Church teach that Mary was sinless throughout her life when the Bible proclaims that "all have sinned and fall short of the glory of God"?

The Church teaches that not only was Mary conceived without original sin but that she also remained free from personal sin throughout her life. The *Catechism* states: "Mary benefited first of all and uniquely from Christ's victory over sin: she was preserved from all stain of original sin and by a special grace of God committed no sin of any kind during her whole earthly life" (411).

If there is any Catholic doctrine that Protestants insist is unbiblical, it's this one. Paul writes in Romans 3:23, "[A]ll have sinned and fall short of the glory of God." If *all* have sinned and fallen short of God's glory, it's impossible for Mary to have been free from personal sin throughout her life.[122]

MEETING THE CHALLENGE

1. The use of the word *all* (Greek, *pas)* in Scripture doesn't preclude exceptions.

The Greek word *pas,* which is translated "all," has different applications. It can mean "every single one without exception." But it doesn't have to mean that. It can also be used in a more general way that doesn't preclude exceptions. These are examples of *hyperbole*: intentional exaggeration to make a point.

In Matthew 2:3, we read that "all Jerusalem," along with Herod, was troubled when they heard of the wise men from the East speak of the birth of the king of the Jews. Almost certainly this doesn't mean that *every single person* in Jerusalem without exception—man, woman, and child—was troubled. There must have been at least some who didn't have a clue about what was going on.

Similarly, Matthew says in Matthew 3:5-6 that "all Judea and all the region about Jordan" were baptized by John the Baptist. Does this mean that John baptized *every single person* in that region without exception? We know that's not the case because Luke tells us that some didn't get baptized (Luke 7:30).

Here are some more examples where "all" is used in a way that doesn't preclude exceptions.

- Matthew 4:24: "they brought him [Jesus] all the sick."
- Matthew 21:10: "all the city" was stirred, saying, "Who is this?"
- Matthew 27:25: "all the people" answered, "His blood be on us and on our children."

Paul also uses "all" in a non-absolute way. In Romans 3:10-12, just a few verses before the passage in question, he quotes Psalm 14:2-3: "None is righteous, no, not one; no one understands, no one seeks for God. All have turned aside, together they have gone wrong; no one does good, not even one."

But we know that the Psalmist doesn't intend *all* to be taken in an absolute sense without exception because a few verses later he speaks of a "generation of righteous" (v.5). If by quoting Psalm 14:2-3 Paul intended to say that all have fallen away in an absolute sense without exception, then he would have been misapplying the passage. But that's unlikely.

That the word *all* doesn't preclude exceptions, it allows for the possibility that Mary could be an exception to Paul's statement that "all have sinned and fall short of the glory of God."

2. Given that Paul is referring to personal sin, we know that there are exceptions to the statement "all have sinned."

Unborn babies can't sin.[123] Paul recognizes this in Romans 9:11. There he refers to Jacob and Esau in the womb and says, "They were not yet born and had done nothing either good or bad." Paul acknowledges that Jacob and Esau in the womb, and thus all babies by way of extension, can't sin. (Most Protestants would agree that people are incapable of personal sin until they have reached the age of reason.) According to Paul, therefore, we know that there are exceptions to the "all have sinned" norm that he speaks of in Romans 3:23.

Jesus is another example. He is fully man yet was free from sin (Heb. 4:15). Obviously, Jesus is an exception to the "all have sinned" norm.

So we see that there are many exceptions to the "all have sinned" norm, as most Protestants will agree. It's true that this doesn't *prove* that Mary was sinless, but it does meet the challenge that Mary *couldn't* be sinless because the Bible says that "all have sinned."

3. Paul's statement that "all have sinned" refers to sin being characteristic of both Jews and Gentiles.

The context in which Paul makes this statement concerns the New Testament truth that salvation is obtained apart from the Law of Moses. For example, Paul argues, "For no human being will be justified in his sight by works *of the law*" (v.20) since "the righteousness of God has been manifested *apart from law*" (v.21).

The thrust of Paul's message is that it doesn't matter if a person is a Jew or Gentile. Either way, he can obtain the "righteousness of God through faith in Jesus Christ for all who believe" (v.22a). This is why, just before speaking of the universal need for salvation ("all have sinned"—v.23), Paul writes in reference to Jews and Gentiles, "For there is no distinction" (v.22b). For Paul, such equality precludes him and the Jews from "boasting" (v.27) in their unique relationship with God through the law.

A few verses later, Paul gives further evidence for why no distinction is to be made between Jews and Gentiles:

> Is God the God of Jews only? Is he not the God of Gentiles also? Yes, of Gentiles also, since God is one; and he will justify the circumcised on the ground of their faith and the uncircumcised through their faith (vv.29-30).

If the whole context of Paul's statement that "all have sinned" is about the equal need for salvation among both Jews and Gentiles, and that no distinction is to be made between them, then we shouldn't take it as an absolute statement about the personal sinfulness of every human being that excludes all possible exceptions—like babies, Jesus, or Mary.

COUNTER-CHALLENGE

Why do you deny that Mary was an exception to a general rule but accept that there are other exceptions to it?

AFTERTHOUGHT

For positive evidence that suggests why Mary is an exception to the "all have sinned" teaching, see Tim Staples's book *Behold Your Mother: A Biblical and Historical Defense of the Marian Doctrines.*

"Mary Needed a Savior"

Luke 1:47 and Mary's Freedom from Original and Personal Sin

How can the Catholic Church teach that Mary was immaculately conceived when she calls God her "Savior"?

Besides Romans 3:23, there is another passage that some Protestants[124] think contradicts the Catholic belief of Mary's freedom from sin—both original and personal. In Luke 1:47, Mary says, "My spirit rejoices in God my *Savior.*" How can Mary acknowledge God as her savior if she never contracted original sin or committed personal sin? The fact that she admitted having a savior proves that she was a sinner.

MEETING THE CHALLENGE

1. The Catholic Church agrees that God is Mary's Savior—but in a unique way

In his 1987 encyclical *Redemptoris Mater,* Pope St. John Paul II reflects upon Mary's acknowledgment of God as her savior, saying, "In her exultation Mary confesses that she finds herself in the very heart of this fullness of Christ" (36). In defining the Immaculate Conception, Pope Pius IX acknowledged that Christ was Mary's Savior, stating, "In view of the merits of Jesus Christ, the Savior of the human race,

[Mary] was preserved free from all stain of original sin."[125]

The *Catechism* affirms this teaching in paragraph 492:

> The "splendor of an entirely unique holiness" by which Mary is "enriched from the first instant of her conception" comes wholly from Christ: she is "redeemed, in a more exalted fashion, by reason of the merits of her son.

The *Catechism* also recognizes Christ as Mary's Savior with regard to her freedom from personal sin:

> Mary benefited first of all and uniquely from Christ's victory over sin: she was preserved from all stain of original sin and by a special grace of God *committed no sin of any kind during her whole earthly life* (411, emphasis added).

But what is the "exalted" and "unique" way by which Mary was saved (rescued from original and personal sin)? First, it is "in view of" the merits of Jesus' death on the cross. Unlike we who are saved by the application of graces of a *past* event, Mary was saved by the application of graces of a *future* event.

Likewise, whereas we're saved in the sense of being *liberated* from original and personal sin—after the fact—Mary was saved by being *preserved* from original and personal sin before the fact.

Suppose we're walking along a path in the woods and I suddenly fall into a covered-up pit that a hunter dug to trap animals. I cry out for help, and you pull me out with a rope. You *saved* me from the pit.

Now, consider another scenario where we're walking along the path and you happen to notice the covered pit and you immediately stop me from walking over it. You *saved* me from the pit just as much by preventing me from falling into it just as much as you did by pulling me out of it.

Similarly, the Catholic Church teaches that rather than God saving Mary after contracting the stain of original sin and falling into personal sin, God saved her by preserving her from such defilement. Therefore, God is just as much Mary's savior as he is for all those whom he redeems from sin.

A Protestant may object, "You're just making up this preservation view of salvation to fit your theology. The Bible doesn't speak of salvation in this way."

But the Bible, in fact, does speak of salvation as preservation. Consider, for example, Jude 24-25:

> Now to him *who is able to keep you from falling* and to present you without blemish before the presence of his glory with rejoicing, to the only God, our Savior through Jesus Christ our Lord, be glory, majesty, dominion, and authority, before all time and now and forever.

If the Bible views salvation not only as liberation but also preservation, then the idea that Mary was saved by way of preservation is consistent with the Bible.

This doesn't *prove* that Mary was preserved free from the defilement of original and personal sin. But it does show that Luke 1:47 can't be used as evidence that she wasn't.

COUNTER-CHALLENGE

Doesn't preservation from sin by God's special grace count as being "saved" just as much as restoration after falling into sin?

AFTERTHOUGHT

If St. John the Baptist could be "filled with the Holy Spirit, even from his mother's womb" (Luke 1:15), it would not be beyond the pale to say that Mary was preserved free from all stain of original sin at the moment of her conception.

"The Lord's Brothers"

Matthew 13:55 and Mary's Perpetual Virginity

How can the Catholic Church teach that Mary was a perpetual virgin when the Bible says that Jesus had brothers?

The Church professes Mary's "real and Perpetual Virginity" (CCC 499) and bases this profession in part on the liturgy of the Church, which celebrates her as the "*Aeiparthenos,* the ever-Virgin."

Like Mary's freedom from sin, this is a Catholic doctrine that many Protestants[126] see as contradicting the plain sense of Scripture. One passage they often turn to is Matthew 13:55 where Matthew records the crowds saying in reference to Jesus, "Is not this the carpenter's son? Is not his mother called Mary? And are not his *brethren* James and Joseph and Simon and Judas?"

Protestants who appeal to this passage argue that the Greek word for "brethren," *adelphoi* (plural form of *adelphos*), means biological brothers. If Jesus had biological brothers, then Mary couldn't have remained a virgin.

MEETING THE CHALLENGE

1. The Greek word *adelphos* has a range of meaning wider than "biological brother."

In both the Septuagint (Greek Old Testament) and the New Testament, *adelphos* is used for relationships that extend beyond biological brotherhood. The most famous example is in the Septuagint, which describes Lot as Abraham's *adelphos* (Gen. 14:14, 16). Here *adelphos* translates the Hebrew word *'āḥ*, which means *brother*. But we know that Lot wasn't Abraham's blood brother because Genesis 14:12 tells us that Lot was the son of Abraham's brother—that is, his nephew.

Other examples in the Septuagint include 1 Chronicles 23:22, Tobit 7:2-4, and Genesis 29:15. In these cases, *adelphos* is used not in reference to blood brothers but to kinsmen of some other sort. And in 1 Chronicles 23:22 and Genesis 29:15, *adelphos* again is used to translate the Hebrew word *'āḥ*.

When it comes to Jesus, for starters we should remember that he didn't have any *full* brothers since Joseph was not his biological father (Matt. 1:18; Luke 1:26-35). As such, to speak of James, Joseph, Simon, and Jude as the "brothers" of Jesus is already not to use the term in the most common sense (a male sibling who has the same mother and father). At most, they could only be half-brothers.

And the New Testament is the same as the Old when it comes to using *adelphos* to refer to relationships other than blood-brotherhood. For example, in Matthew 23:8 Jesus tells his disciples that they are all "brothers." And Ananias calls Saul "Brother Saul" in Acts 9:17.

So given the wide range of meaning for *adelphos* in both the Greek Old Testament and the New Testament, it's ineffective to argue that Mary couldn't have remained a virgin because the Bible says Jesus had "brothers." The term may have been used in a different sense as it is elsewhere in the Bible. More information would be needed to determine how it's being used.

2. There are other scriptural texts suggesting that the "brothers" of Jesus were not biological brothers.

First, it seems from Paul's letter to the Galatians that the "James" whom Matthew lists as a "brother" of Jesus is an apostle. Concerning his trip to Jerusalem to visit Cephas, Paul writes, "But I saw none of the other apostles except James, the Lord's brother" (Gal. 1:19). There are only two among the Twelve apostles named James, and neither one of them is the son of Joseph ("James of Zebedee" and "James of Alpheus"—Matthew 10:2-3).[127]

Furthermore, two of the four "brothers" of Jesus—James and Joseph—are identified in Matthew 27:56 as sons of *another* Mary. Matthew writes concerning the women at the cross, "There were also many women there . . . among whom were Mary Magdalene, and Mary the mother of James and Joseph, and the mother of the sons of Zebedee."

The mention of James and Joseph together seems to indicate that these are the same men referred to as Jesus' "brothers" in Matthew 13:55. But if these men were Jesus' blood brothers, why would Matthew call this Mary "the mother of James and Joseph" and not "the mother of Jesus"? Elsewhere in Scripture, Mary is always identified by her relationship to Jesus (John 2:1,3; Acts 1:14).

Therefore, if James and Joseph in Matthew 27:56 are the same two brothers mentioned in Matthew 13:55, we can conclude that James and Joseph are sons of *another* Mary, not Mary the mother of Jesus.

3. There is positive evidence that Mary remained a virgin.

One example is Jesus' act of giving his mother over to John's care in his last moments before death. John records,

> When Jesus saw his mother, and the disciple whom he loved standing near, he said to his mother, "Woman,

behold, your son!" Then he said to the disciple, "Behold, your Mother!" And from that hour the disciple took her to his own home" (John 19:26-27).

The early Church saw it this way, too. In his *De Virginitate,* Athanasius (296-373) argues, "If [Mary] had other children, the Savior would not have ignored them and entrusted his mother to someone else; nor would she have become someone else's mother."[128]

Hilary of Poitiers (c. 310-367) argued along the same lines when he commented on the "brothers of the Lord" mentioned in Matthew's Gospel:

> If these were Mary's sons, instead of children that Joseph had fathered during a previous marriage, then, at the moment of the Passion, Mary never would have been given the apostle John as his mother . . . For the Lord, to help her face her solitude, left her, in his disciple, the love of a son.[129]

Given that Jesus entrusts Mary to an outsider instead of to one of the "brethren" listed in Matthew 13:55, it's likely that these "brethren" weren't Mary's biological children. (Hilary speculates that they may have been Joseph's, which is another possibility.)

There are biblical reasons to think that Mary didn't have other children because she had intended to remain a virgin her entire life. One reason is Mary's question to the angel Gabriel, "How shall this be, seeing I know not a man?" (Luke 1:34, KJV).

In Scripture, the term *know* (Greek, *ginōskō*) commonly refers to sexual relations. (For example, Matthew 1:25 reads, Joseph "knew [*eginōsken*] her not until she had borne a son.") Luke 1:27 has already told us that Mary was "betrothed" to

Joseph (which in ancient Jewish culture was the equivalent of legal marriage). So Mary's question suggests that Gabriel's appearance occurs during the interim period between betrothal and consummation.

The angel tells Mary that she will conceive a child, but Mary seems puzzled as to how that could possibly happen. Why would Mary inquire as to *how* she was going to conceive a child if she were in a normal, soon-to-be-consummated marriage with Joseph? Surely she was aware that normal marriages involve sexual intercourse that results in children.

That Mary asks such a question suggests that she wasn't planning on a normal marriage that involved sexual intercourse. This is why Gabriel's response explains the miraculous nature of the conception that will take place: "The Holy Spirit will come upon you, and the power of the Most High will overshadow you" (Luke 1:35).

The idea of having a vow of virginity within marriage would not have been totally out of bounds for the ancient Jews. In Numbers 30, we find instructions given for a woman still living in her father's house (vv.3-5)—a married woman (vv.6-8) and a widowed or divorced woman (v. 13)—concerning her oath to "afflict herself." According to Torah scholar Jacob Milgrom, this is an idiom among ancient Jews that refers to fasting and refraining from sexual intercourse.[130] And as the context bears out, in the case of the married woman her vow remained if the husband did not object.

So if Mary had made such a vow after their betrothal, and Joseph didn't object, then the instructions in Numbers chapter thirty would provide a historical basis for such a situation. And even if Mary made the vow *before* betrothal, the instructions would still provide a historical context that would make her vow intelligible.

COUNTER-CHALLENGE

If a biblical word has a wide range of meanings, shouldn't we figure out how it's being used before we draw theological conclusions?

AFTERTHOUGHT

Some Catholics have suggested that the "brothers" of Jesus may have been his cousins, to which Protestants may respond that there is a different Greek word for cousin, *anepsios* (Col. 4:10)—and Matthew doesn't use it. But we note that New Testament authors often preserved certain Hebraic expressions or forms of speech in their Greek text even when the Greek language provided them the means to communicate the meaning of the Hebraic expressions. For example, the Hebraic expression, "I love one and hate the other" has the meaning of, "I love one more than the other." Yet the Hebraic expression is preserved in Greek in both Romans 9:13 and Luke 14:26. We have to be careful to make conclusions based solely on the Greek word in use since there may be a Hebraic meaning that underlies it.

"He Knew Her Not . . . *Until*"

Matthew 1:25 and Mary's Perpetual Virginity

How can the Catholic Church teach that Mary was a perpetual virgin when the Bible says that Mary was a virgin only "until" Jesus was born?

For many Protestants,[131] the Catholic Church's teaching on Mary's "real and Perpetual Virginity" (CCC 499) is at odds with Matthew 1:25, which reads, "[Joseph] knew her [Mary] not until she had borne a son; and he called his name Jesus." Matthew's use of the word "until" (Greek—*heōs*) tells us that Mary was a virgin only up to the time of Jesus' birth and that thereafter Joseph began to have sexual relations with Mary.

MEETING THE CHALLENGE

1. Even in English, the word *until* doesn't necessarily indicate a subsequent change.

The challenge assumes that the word *until* necessarily indicates change in the future when a select period of time is complete. For example, if I tell my wife that I'll be speaking at an event until eight o'clock in the evening, the implication is that after eight I will not be speaking anymore.

But the word doesn't *always* indicate change. It can also be used to indicate only an existing state up to a point, without any reference to what occurs afterward. For example, I may say to a friend, "Be safe, until I see you again." By this I don't mean that after I see him again I expect him to begin behaving unsafely.

2. The Bible uses *heōs* to indicate a select period of time without reference to change in the future.

Both the Old and New Testaments give examples of this. Consider Deuteronomy 34:6, which speaks of Moses' burial place: "No man knows the place of his burial to this day." "To" is a translation of the Greek *heōs* in the Septuagint. And we still don't know where Moses was buried.

2 Samuel 6:23 is another example. We read that Saul's daughter Michal "had no child to [*heōs*] the day of her death." Obviously, this doesn't mean that Michal's childless state changed *after* the day of her death. It only means that she went throughout her life without having any children.

This is a common usage of *heōs* in the New Testament, too. Here are some examples from Paul's writings:

- 1 Timothy 4:13: "Till [*heōs*] I come, attend unto reading, to exhortation, and to doctrine."

- 1 Corinthians 1:8: "Our Lord Jesus Christ, who will sustain you to [*heōs*] the end, guiltless in the day of our Lord Jesus Christ."

- 2 Corinthians 3:15: "To [*heōs*] this day whenever Moses is read a veil lies over their minds."

Further commentary is unnecessary. It's obvious upon reading these examples that Paul doesn't use *heōs* to suggest a subsequent change.

Matthew uses *heōs* in this way in his Gospel. For example, in Matthew 13:33, Jesus compares the kingdom of heaven to the leaven that a woman takes and hides in three measures of flour, "till it was all leavened." By using *heōs*, Matthew doesn't mean that the leaven was taken *out* of the flour once it was leavened.

Another example is Matthew 10:23: "For truly, I say to you, you will not have gone through all the towns of Israel, before [*heōs*] the Son of man comes." In this verse, *heōs* is rendered "before" in most English translations, not "until." (No one thinks Jesus is saying that when he returns the apostles will then go through all the towns of Israel.) And that's the point—Matthew sometimes uses *heōs* to mean "up to the time of" without implying a subsequent change. So we can read Matthew 1:25 in the same way.

Given this common usage of *heōs* in both the Old and New Testaments, it's reasonable to suggest that Matthew *could* be employing *heōs* only to refer the period of time before Jesus' birth without any reference to what happened after. The only way to know is to look at the context.

3. **The context suggests that Matthew's point is that Joseph and Mary had no sexual relations prior to Jesus' birth. Whether they had sexual relations afterward is a separate question that Matthew's language does not settle for us.**

Matthew states his primary interest in verse 18: "Now the birth of Jesus Christ took place in this way." The *birth* of Christ is Matthew's concern, not what came after.

Matthew even explicitly tells us which period of time in Mary and Joseph's relationship he's focusing on: "*Before they came together*, she was found to be with child of the Holy Spirit" (Matt. 1:19). He then reiterates the virginal conception two more times—when he records Gabriel's words, "that which is conceived in her is of the Holy Spirit" (v.20) and when he quotes Isaiah 7:14, "Behold, a virgin shall conceive and bear a son" (v.23).

Since the immediate context bears on the period of time *before* Jesus' birth, we have good reason to think that this is what Matthew was interested in, not what happened after Jesus' birth. Matthew is trying to persuade his audience that Jesus' conception and birth were miraculous, not to tell us what Mary did afterward.

COUNTER-CHALLENGE

Would you agree that when we read Scripture we should consider all the meanings of a word instead of just the meanings that support our own view?

AFTERTHOUGHT

Some Protestants[132] may argue that unlike the passages listed in this chapter, which use *heōs* by itself, Matthew 1:25 uses the phrase *heōs hou*, which they say indicates a difference in meaning. Yet Matthew's use of *hou* ("that") merely points to the particular moment when Jesus was born—"until that time." The phrase "until she bore a son" means exactly the same thing as "until *that* she bore a son." Moreover, we see the same construction in Acts 25:21: *heōs hou* is used to describe how Paul was to be kept in custody "until" Festus sent him to Caesar. But we know that Paul was *kept* in custody after being sent in transit to Caesar (Acts 27:1) and even after his arrival in Rome (Acts 28:16, 20).[133]

"'Queen of Heaven' Condemned"

Jeremiah 7:18 and Mary's Queenship

How can the Catholic Church teach that Mary is the queen of heaven when the Bible condemns the worship of a pagan queen of heaven?

In 1954, Pope Pius XII issued the encyclical *Ad Caeli Reginam*, in which he consistently refers to Mary as the "queen of heaven." But for some Protestants,[134] this is problematic because the Bible explicitly condemns practices that involve a "queen of heaven":

> Do you not see what they are doing in the cities of Judah and in the streets of Jerusalem? The children gather wood, the fathers kindle fire, and the women knead dough, to make cakes for the queen of heaven; and they pour out drink offerings to other gods, to provoke me to anger (Jer. 7:17–18).

They say that not only is calling Mary "queen of heaven" equivalent to worshipping her as a goddess but that Scripture explicitly tells us that the title is evil.

MEETING THE CHALLENGE

1. Jeremiah is not condemning the idea of a "queen of heaven" but the worshipping of a pagan goddess that took place in the streets of Jerusalem hundreds of years before the time of Christ.

It's unclear exactly which pagan goddess Jeremiah was referring to—the nearby ancient world had many of them. Regardless, Jeremiah is condemning a particular act of worship of such a deity. The Jews were burning incense and pouring out libations to this "queen of heaven"—as they were doing for other deities (Jer. 7:18; 44:15). This infidelity on the part of his people provokes God's anger and wrath to be poured out on the "cities of Judah" and the "streets of Jerusalem" (Jer. 7:17, 20).

But in calling Mary "queen of heaven," the Catholic Church isn't worshipping Mary as a deity in place of the one God. Instead, it is honoring her for the exalted place she holds among all creatures by virtue of being the Mother of the Savior. And this idea of giving honor is definitely biblical.

For example, Paul instructs us to give "double honor" to "elders who rule well" in the Church (1 Tim. 5:17). Also, concerning those who are "over [us] in the Lord," Paul tells us that we need to "esteem [them] very highly" (1 Thess. 5:12-13). The Psalmist even speaks of certain members of God's family being "praised . . . forever and ever," with their name being "celebrated in all generations" (Ps. 45:17).

Because the Catholic Church believes Mary is the most exalted member of God's family, more worthy of honor even than elders and rulers in the Lord, it gives to her the highest honor possible for a creature. And since this honor is given to her as a creature and not a goddess, the condemnation in Jeremiah 7:18 doesn't apply.

2. Just because the phrase "queen of heaven" was used for a pagan goddess doesn't mean that it can't have a legitimate use.

The challenge assumes that the mere use of queenly language for a pagan goddess precludes the possibility of using such language for Mary. But this simply doesn't follow.

Consider, for example, that other religions have holy books. Other religions also have sons of deities, like Apollo (son of Zeus and Hera) and Horus (from Isis and Osiris), along with kings that rule the heavens.

Does this mean that we must stop calling the Bible a holy book? Must a Christian no longer refer to Jesus as the "Son of God" (Mark 1:1) or God as "king of heaven" (Dan. 4:37)? Of course not!

Similarly, just because a pagan goddess was referred to as "queen of heaven," it doesn't follow that we can't refer to Mary with the same title.

3. There is positive evidence for Mary's queenly role.

Mary's queenship is based on her son, Jesus, being the true king of Israel (Luke 1:32; John 1:49, etc.) and the universal heavenly king, who sits "on his throne" (Rev. 3:21) in heaven with his Father. That Mary is queen in virtue of being the mother of king Jesus follows from the role of queenship in ancient Israel.

Hints of this are found throughout the Old Testament. For example, we're told in 1 King 2:19 that Solomon "rose to meet [Bethsheba, mother of Solomon]," "bowed down to her," and then "had a seat brought for [her]" in order that she may "[sit] on [the] right" of his throne.

Other examples refer to the "queen mother" explicitly:

- 2 Chronicles 15:16: "Even Maacah, his mother, King Asa removed from being queen mother [Hebrew, *gebirāh*] because she had made an abominable image for Asherah."

- Jeremiah 13:18: "Say to the king and the queen mother [*gebirāh*]: 'Take a lowly seat, for your beautiful crown has come down from your head.'"

Someone might object that the above passages refer to wicked queen mothers. But there have been wicked kings, too, and that doesn't stop us from referring to Jesus as king. Moreover, these Old Testament passages show that the mother of the king had a queenly role, which Mary fulfills in the New Testament.

Given this background knowledge of the "queen mother" in the Davidic kingdom and given our knowledge that Jesus is the new Davidic king, it's reasonable to conclude that Mary is the new "queen mother" in the restored Davidic kingdom, the Church. And since Jesus rules as king in heaven, and Mary is in heaven with him, then we rightly call her by the title "queen of heaven."

COUNTER-CHALLENGE

Just because a bad, counterfeit thing exists, does that mean a good, authentic thing doesn't?

AFTERTHOUGHT

John seems to describe Mary as the queen mother in Revelation 12 when he speaks of "a woman . . . with a crown of twelve stars" (v.1) who brings forth "a male child, one who is to rule all the nations with a rod of iron" (v.5). Obviously, the child is Jesus. But the language of ruling with "a rod of iron" bespeaks his royal authority as the messianic king (see Ps. 2). If Jesus is described as the messianic king within the context of being born of a woman crowned with stars, and Mary is the one who gives birth to this messianic king, it follows that Mary is being described as the new "queen mother."

VI

The Saints

After Mary, the Catholic doctrine of the intercession of the saints may elicit more challenges from Protestants than any other topic. These tend to be of two types.

Some challenges are based on the idea that it's not appropriate for Christians to request the saints to pray for them. Either it takes away from the uniqueness of Jesus' mediation or God outright forbids it as an abomination. Other challenges are more practical. Some Protestants may think that, in principle, requesting the saints to pray for us could be appropriate, but it's just futile to do so because the souls in heaven aren't able to intercede for us.

Recognizing these distinct challenges is important. In our conversations, if we know what the obstacle is, we can focus our time and attention in making our answer.

In either case, the motivation behind these challenges is understandable. We don't want to do anything that contradicts the Bible or takes away from Jesus. Nor do we want to engage in pointless piety.

But as we meet these challenges, we'll see that these motivations are simply mistaken when it comes to our Catholic beliefs about the saints and their intercession. These beliefs are scriptural and they give great honor to Jesus and his saving work.

"One Mediator"

1 Timothy 2:5 and the Intercession of the Saints

How can the Catholic Church teach that the saints in heaven intercede for us when the Bible teaches that Jesus is the "one mediator between God and man"?

The Church teaches that "we can and should ask [the saints] to intercede for us and for the whole world" (CCC 2683). But for many Protestants,[135] this is a hard teaching to accept since Paul explicitly teaches in 1 Timothy 2:5 that there is "one mediator between God and men, the man Christ Jesus." (*Mediation* and *intercession* mean the same thing.)

Doesn't the Catholic practice of requesting the saints' intercession usurp or take away from the unique mediation of Christ? So Catholics need to stop praying to the saints if they want to be faithful to God's word.

MEETING THE CHALLENGE

1. **The logic embedded in this challenge requires us to deny *all* forms of Christian intercession.**

The challenge operates on the assumption that to ask the saints to pray for us takes away from Christ's unique mediation. But this line of reasoning contradicts Christian teaching and practice since it belongs to the Christian life to ask for the intercession of other Christians.

Even the context of the passage in question proves this. In verse 1, Paul encourages Christian intercession: "I urge that supplications, prayers, *intercessions*, and thanksgivings be made for all men." Then, in verse four, he says that such prayers and intercessions are "acceptable in the sight of God our Savior." Other such passages include Romans 15:30, 2 Corinthians 1:10, and Colossians 1:4, 9-10.[136]

If asking for the intercession of Christians in heaven (the saints) took away from Christ's unique mediation, as the challenge suggests, then what is Paul doing encouraging us to request prayers from Christians on earth? Wouldn't that, too, detract from Christ's unique mediation? No Christian wants to affirm that conclusion. Most Protestants, like Catholics, pray for and request prayers from their fellow Christians all the time. This biblical practice doesn't conflict with Christ's role as a unique mediator, and neither does requesting prayers from the saints in heaven.

2. As the God-man, Jesus' mediation is unique, but this doesn't mean he can't share that ministry with others.

Jesus is our unique "teacher" (Greek, *didaskalos*—Matt. 23:8), yet there are many who participate in his teaching ministry (Eph. 4:11; James 3:1). Jesus is our one "high priest" (Heb. 3:1), yet we're all priests inasmuch as we are Christians (1 Pet. 2:5, 9).

The same principle could apply to the intercession of the saints. Of course, Jesus is the one mediator, and he "always lives to make intercession" (Heb. 7:25). But that doesn't mean he couldn't share that intercessory role with his saints.

In fact, we know that he *does* share that intercessory role with at least some of his saints: the Christians here on earth (*saints* is a common word used for all Christians in the New Testament—see 2 Cor. 1:1; Eph. 1:1; Phil. 1:1). Paul urges Timothy that "intercessions . . . be made for all men" (1 Tim. 2:1). Therefore, it's at least possible that Jesus could share his intercessory ministry with Christians in heaven, too.

3. The saints participate in Christ's unique mediation because they're members of the Mystical Body of Christ.

In his first letter to the Corinthians, Paul teaches, "For by one Spirit we were all baptized into one body" (v.13), which he identifies as "the body of Christ" (v.27). Christians are united with each other in the body by virtue of their union with the head, Jesus. This union with Christ enables the intercessory prayer of Christians to bring about effects in the lives of other members in the body.

Viewed this way, we see that intercessory prayer of one member of Christ's mystical body for another no more takes away from Christ's unique mediation than my nervous system aiding my fingers to type takes away from the life that is uniquely mine. It is only *because* of my life that the different members of my natural body can aid each other for a proper functioning of the whole.

Similarly, it's because of Christ the head that different members of his body can intercede for one another. Rather than detracting from the head, the intercession among members of his body manifests its glory.

The saints in heaven are still members of Christ's mystical body. We know this because Paul teaches in Romans 8:35-39 that death is among his list of things that cannot separate us from "the love of God which is in Christ Jesus."

And the saints are not just average members of Christ's body—they are "the spirits of just men made perfect" (Heb. 12:23). This matters because James tells us that "the prayer of a righteous man avails much" (James 5:16). Since the saints in heaven are *perfected* in righteousness, their prayers will bear much fruit.

COUNTER-CHALLENGE

When you ask your pastor to pray for you, does that take away from Christ's unique mediation?

AFTERTHOUGHT

Revelation 5:8 reveals twenty-four elders surrounding the throne of the lamb in heaven offering up the prayers of Christians on earth in the form of incense. If that is what the Christians in heaven are doing, it's reasonable for we Christians on earth to make our requests known to them.

"Invoking the Dead Is an Abomination"

Deuteronomy 18:10-12 and Intercession of the Saints

How can the Catholic Church teach that we should ask the saints to intercede for us when the Bible forbids communicating with the dead?

The Catholic practice of invoking the saints to pray for us seems to contradict God's prohibition of necromancy in Deuteronomy 18:10–12:

> There shall not be found among you any one who burns his son or his daughter as an offering, anyone who practices divination, a soothsayer, or an augur, or a sorcerer, or a charmer, or a medium, or a wizard, or a necromancer. For whoever does these things is an abomination to the LORD; and because of these abominable practices the LORD your God is driving them out before you.

For some Protestants,[137] it couldn't be clearer: the Bible explicitly rules out the Catholic practice of praying to the saints. It's not only unbiblical, it is "abominable."

MEETING THE CHALLENGE

1. Deuteronomy 18:10-12 is not condemning communication with the dead but the practice of conjuring the spirits of the dead in order to gain secret knowledge.

The dictionary defines *necromancy* as "conjuration of the spirits of the dead for purposes of magically revealing the future or influencing the course of events."[138] The term comes from two Greek words: *nekros* ("dead person") and *manteia* ("oracle," "divination").

There are at least two reasons we know that eliciting secret knowledge from the dead is what Deuteronomy 18:10-12 has in mind. First, the text also forbids "divination" and seeking a "medium," a "sorcerer," and a "wizard," all of which have to do with an attempt to gain secret knowledge—knowledge beyond ordinary human intelligence. The Hebrew biblical phrase *doresh'el-ha-metim*, which is translated as "necromancer," literally means "an inquirer of the dead."[139]

The second reason is the subsequent instructions that Moses gives concerning a coming prophet. In verse 15, Moses says, "The Lord your God will raise up for you a prophet like me from among you, from your brethren—*him* you shall heed." In other words, there is no need to go to mediums, sorcerers, wizards, and necromancers to gain knowledge because God will send a prophet of his own.

God then speaks through Moses and says, "I will put my words in his mouth, and he shall speak to them all that I command him" (v.18). As for the prophet who presumes to speak in God's name without God's command or the prophet who speaks in "the name of other gods," God says that prophet "shall die" (v.20).

Since the context is about looking to God's prophet and not to mediums, sorcerers, wizards, and necromancers, it's clear that the prohibition has to do with seeking secret knowledge apart from God. And since conjuring up the dead (necromancy) is one way of doing that, God forbids it.

2. **The Catholic practice of invoking the saints to pray for us isn't necromancy.**

Asking saints to pray for us is an entirely different thing from necromancy. The Church doesn't teach that we are to invoke the saints to gain secret knowledge—in fact, this is condemned in CCC 2116. Rather, we're *giving information to the dead* by making our requests known to a departed soul.

Nor does the Catholic Church teach that we conjure the saints' spirits when we invoke their prayers. In fact, the same *Catechism* passage also explicitly affirms the Bible's condemnation of such a practice.

Since the Catholic practice of requesting the saints to pray for us is not a form of necromancy, then it doesn't fall under the prohibition in Deuteronomy 18:10-12.

COUNTER-CHALLENGE

Can the biblical prohibition of necromancy apply to a practice that doesn't fit the definition of necromancy? Shouldn't we be careful to use words correctly?

AFTERTHOUGHT

Many Protestants further appeal to 1 Samuel 28:8-19 where Saul conjures Samuel's spirit through a medium to elicit knowledge about the impending battle with the Philistines. But, once again, there is an essential difference between conjuring spirits to elicit secret knowledge about the future and invoking the saints to pray for us.

"The Dead Know Nothing"

Ecclesiastes 9:5,10 and Intercession of the Saints

How can the Church teach that the saints can pray for us when Ecclesiastes says they have no knowledge in the afterlife?

The last two challenges had to do with whether or not requesting the saints' prayers was appropriate Christian practice. Some Protestants, however, might concede that in principle such requests aren't offensive to God but still object that the practice is inconsistent with what the Bible teaches.

For example, some Christians both within and outside mainstream Protestantism[140] appeal to Ecclesiastes 9:5, where the author writes, "For the living know that they will die, but the dead know nothing." Just a few verses later in that same chapter, the author asserts again, "There is no work or thought or knowledge or wisdom in Sheol, to which you are going" (v.10). If the dead "know nothing," so it's argued, and there is "no thought or knowledge" in the afterlife, then wouldn't it be futile to request the saints to pray for us?

MEETING THE CHALLENGE

1. The author is not intending to make an assertion about the nature of the afterlife. He is trying to make sense of death from an earthly perspective.

In the beginning verses of the chapter, the author makes it clear that death is his main topic:

> But all this I laid to heart, examining it all, how the righteous and the wise and their deeds are in the hand of God; whether it is love or hate man does not know. Everything before them is vanity, since *one fate comes to all*, to the righteous and the wicked, to the good and the evil, to the clean and the unclean, to him who sacrifices and him who does not sacrifice. As is the good man, so is the sinner; and he who swears is as he who shuns an oath. This is an evil in all that is done under the sun, *that one fate comes to all*; also the hearts of men are full of evil, and madness is in their hearts while they live, and after that *they go to the dead*. But he who is joined with all the living has hope, for a living dog is better than a dead lion. For the living know that *they will die*, but the dead know nothing, and they have no more reward; but the memory of them is lost. Their love and their hate and their envy have already perished, and they have no more for ever any share in all that is done under the sun (Eccl. 9:1-6).

The author also is making the point that from his earthly perspective ("under the sun") living is better than dying. Note the following statements: "he who is joined with all the living has hope, for a living dog is better than a dead lion" (v.4) and "they have no more for ever any share in all that is done under the sun" (v.6).

Within this context, the author says, "The dead know nothing, and they have no more reward" (v.5). He's not trying to give a definitive teaching about the afterlife but is simply saying that life "under the sun" is better than death. That's what you would expect him to think when all he has to work with is his earthly perspective—a perspective from which we can't be certain about the conscious activity of souls in the afterlife. Divine revelation is required for knowledge of such things.

2. **Given that souls in heaven possess the beatific vision, we have good reason to think that they would be conscious of our requests made to them**

Consider, for example, what John tells us in 1 John 3:2: "Beloved, we are God's children now; it does not yet appear what we shall be, but we know that when he appears *we shall be like him*, for we shall see him as he is."

John recognizes that our status in heaven will be far beyond what we can imagine. Our natures will be elevated to a state that will "be like him [God]" since we will "see him [God] as he is." If the saints are elevated to such a state in heaven, then we have good reason to think that they can be aware of the requests that we make to them.

Furthermore, in many instances the Bible speaks of us being transformed to be like Christ (Rom. 8:29; 1 Cor. 15:49-52; 2 Cor. 3:18; 2 Pet. 1:4; 1 John 3:2). And we know that transformation will be complete in heaven.

The book of Hebrews tells us that Christ, as priest of the heavenly temple, "always lives to make intercession" (Heb. 7:25). If Christ always lives to make intercession for Christians on earth, and the saints are going to be perfectly like Christ, it's at least reasonable to think that the saints would be doing what Christ does—namely, interceding for Christians on earth. And since Christ's intercession involves knowledge of Christians on earth, it's reasonable to infer that such knowledge would be shared with the saints who participate in that intercession.

3. **There is clear and convincing evidence in both the Old and New Testaments that there is consciousness in the afterlife.**

Let's start with the Old Testament, in particular its prohibition against consulting a necromancer: "There shall not be found among you . . . a necromancer" (Deut. 18:11). A necromancer is someone who conjures up spirits in order to gain hidden or secret knowledge beyond ordinary human intelligence.

This prohibition against necromancy would be unintelligible unless it were believed that souls in the afterlife were conscious. Why would someone try to conjure the dead to gain secret knowledge if such spirits were unconscious? That doesn't make sense.

Indeed, it was the belief that the souls of the dead were conscious that led Saul to consult the "medium at Endor" and request of her to conjure the spirit of Samuel (1 Samuel 28). We're told that Samuel communicated with Saul (vv.15-19). How could Samuel communicate with Saul if Saul were unconscious?

The New Testament gives even clearer and more convincing evidence. In his parable of Lazarus and the rich man (Luke 16:19-31), Jesus depicts all three characters—the rich man, Lazarus, and Abraham—as conscious in the intermediate state between death and resurrection.

And we have good reason to think that such consciousness in the afterlife is a reality because Jesus' parables often teach us about real things such as kings, fathers, sons, banquets, vineyards, death, judgment, reward, and punishment. If we can affirm these things to be real in Jesus' parables, then it's reasonable to conclude that consciousness after death is a real thing, too.

Perhaps the clearest evidence for consciousness in the afterlife is found in the book of Revelation. Several times John describes human souls in heaven in a way that suggests they know what's going on here on earth. Consider, for example, Revelation 5:8:

And when he had taken the scroll, the four living creatures and the twenty-four elders fell down before the
Lamb, each holding a harp, and with golden bowls full of
incense, which are the prayers of the saints.

The "twenty-four elders" represent human souls, perhaps
deceased leaders of both the old and new covenants (twelve
patriarchs and twelve apostles). That they are human souls
becomes evident in light of the different creatures extending
out from the throne of the Lamb in concentric circles.

The four living creatures, which are angels, constitute
the first circle (Rev. 4:6). The twenty-four elders make up
the second (Rev. 4:4). Outside the circle of the twenty-four
elders, we're told there is a multitude of angels, "numbering
myriads of myriads and thousands of thousands" (Rev. 5:11).
Beyond this large number of angels, there exists "a great
multitude which no man could number, from every nation,
from all tribes and peoples and tongues, standing before the
throne and before the Lamb, clothed in white robes, with
palm branches in their hands" (Rev. 7:9).

That the multitude is from every nation, tribe, and peoples
suggests that it consists of humans and not angels. And since
the multitude is identified as "standing before the throne and
before the Lamb," we know they are in heaven because the
throne of God and the Lamb exists in heaven and not on earth.

Moreover, we know this great multitude consists of human souls in heaven because verse 17 of the same chapter tells
us that they "shall hunger no more, neither thirst any more."
Then, in verse 19, we read, "God will wipe away every tear
from their eyes." To no longer hunger, thirst, and have sorrow
is not characteristic of earthly life but only the life in heaven.

How can we know that the elders are human souls? Notice the pattern: the four angels, the twenty-four elders, a

multitude of angels, and a multitude of human souls. There seems to be a comparison of rank between the two angelic groups and the other two groups. The four angels are higher in rank than the multitude of angels, and the twenty-four elders are higher in rank than the multitude of peoples.

If the comparison of rank is angel to angel for the first and third concentric circles, and we know that the fourth circle to which the second group is compared consists of human souls, then it's reasonable to conclude that the second concentric circle of creatures, the twenty-four elders, are human souls. It makes sense that there would be a comparison of rank between two groups of angels and two groups of human souls.

In Revelation 5:8, John tells us that twenty-four elders are offering bowls of incense, which the context reveals are the prayers of Christians on earth. How can these elders, human souls, be engaging in intercessory prayer for Christians on earth if they aren't conscious?

Revelation 6:9 is another example. When the fifth seal is opened, John sees under the altar the souls "who had been slain for the word of God," and they cry out, "O Sovereign Lord, holy and true, how long before thou wilt judge and avenge our blood on those who dwell upon the earth?" Notice that the martyrs are fully aware that their enemies are still living on earth, something not possible if they were unconscious.

Another example is Revelation 7:13-14, where an "elder" tells John whom the ones "clothed in white robes" are: "These are they who have come out of the great tribulation; they have washed their robes and made them white in the blood of the Lamb." This elder had knowledge that these Christians were martyrs and was aware of the tribulation that they suffered while on earth.

In Revelation 19:1-4, we read about a "great multitude" singing praises to God for judging "the harlot" and avenging "the blood of his servants." When John introduces this great multitude in Revelation 7:9 standing before the throne and before the Lamb, he specifies that the multitude is "from every nation, from all tribes and peoples and tongues." Therefore, the great multitude that John sees singing praises to God consists of (very conscious) human souls.

All of the above passages strongly suggest that human souls in heaven are aware of God's dealings with mankind on earth, both friend and foe alike.

COUNTER-CHALLENGE

Shouldn't we allow New Testament revelation to fill in the gaps about the afterlife where Old Testament revelation is lacking?

AFTERTHOUGHT

Other examples of consciousness in the afterlife can be taken from Peter and Paul's epistles. Consider, for example, 1 Peter 3:19 where Peter informs us that after death Jesus "went and preached to the spirits in prison." Such preaching would be futile if these spirits couldn't know what Jesus was preaching to them. 2 Corinthians 5:8 is a good example from Paul: "We would rather be away from the body and at home with the Lord." Why would Paul desire a state of existence without knowledge (the afterlife) over a state of existence with knowledge (this life)? If there were no knowledge in the afterlife, then Paul's desire would be unintelligible.

"God Alone Knows Our Hearts"

2 Chronicles 6:30 and the Intercession of the Saints

How can the Catholic Church say that the saints in heaven are aware of our interior thoughts when the Bible clearly says that *God alone* knows the hearts of men?

The Catholic practice of invoking the intercession of the saints assumes that the souls in heaven can know prayers we make in our interior thoughts. But for many Protestants, both classic and contemporary,[141] this is a problem because it attributes to the saints a power that the Bible says belongs to God alone. 2 Chronicles 6:30 reads as follows:

> [T]hen hear thou from heaven thy dwelling place, and forgive, and render to each whose heart thou knowest, according to all his ways (for thou, thou only, knowest the hearts of the children of men).

If the Bible says that *only* God knows the hearts of men, then the saints can't hear our mental requests for intercession.

MEETING THE CHALLENGE

1. There is no reason why God can't reveal his knowledge of our interior thoughts to others.

Here is how St. Thomas Aquinas responded to the above challenge in his *Summa Theologiae*:

> God alone of himself knows the thoughts of the heart: yet others know them, insofar as these are revealed to them, either by their vision of the Word [Second Person of the Trinity] or by any other means.[142]

Notice how Aquinas articulates the difference between how God knows the thoughts of men and how the saints in heaven know the thoughts of men. God alone knows "of himself," whereas the saints know "by their vision of the Word or by any other means."

God knows the interior movements of man's heart and mind *by nature*. In other words, he has this knowledge by virtue of being God. He alone can know the interior thoughts of men in *this way*. But it's not a problem for God to *reveal* this knowledge to others, such as the saints in heaven, by whatever means he wills.

Some Protestants might counter that for saints to receive that knowledge of the interior thoughts of many people at the same time requires *omniscience*, which only God possesses.

But omniscience, which is full knowledge of all things including the divine essence, isn't the same as knowing a finite number of thoughts at the same time. So it's not necessary for the saints in heaven to be truly omniscient to know simultaneously the interior prayer requests of Christians on earth. Therefore, it follows that God can communicate this kind of knowledge to rational creatures. According to

Aquinas, God does this by giving a "created light of glory" that is "received into [the] created intellect."[143]

Because this "created light of glory" is *created*, it's not infinite by nature and doesn't require infinite power to comprehend or act upon. Therefore, it's not impossible for God to give it to a human or angelic intellect in order to know the interior prayer requests of human beings—even many simultaneously—and respond to them.

2. There is evidence in Scripture that God *does* reveal his knowledge of the interior thoughts of men to others.

Consider, for example, the Old Testament story in Daniel 2 involving Joseph and his interpretation of King Nebuchadnezzar's dream. According to the narrative, Nebuchadnezzar had a troubling dream and asked his sorcerers and wise men to interpret it.

But Nebuchadnezzar made it more difficult by demanding his wise men first to *tell* him his dream, something the wise men recognized only the gods could do: "The thing that the king asks is difficult, and none can show it to the king except the gods, whose dwelling is not with flesh" (Dan. 2:11). All of the wise men failed to fulfill the king's request.

We then read in verse 19 that "the mystery was revealed to Daniel in a vision of the night." Afterward, Daniel was able to articulate the dream (and then interpret it) for Nebuchadnezzar. In other words, God *revealed to him the interior thoughts of a man*. If God can reveal knowledge of Nebuchadnezzar's dream to Daniel, surely he can reveal to the saints in heaven the interior prayer requests of Christians on earth.

Revelation 5:8 serves as an example in the New Testament where God reveals the interior thoughts of men to created intellects, particularly to souls in heaven. Recall that John sees "twenty-four elders" along with the "four living creatures" prostrating themselves "before the Lamb, each holding a harp, and with golden bowls full of incense, which are the prayers of the saints."

As we saw in the previous challenge, the "twenty-four elders" are representative of human souls. And they are cognitively aware of *multiple* prayers even though they don't have physical ears.

COUNTER-CHALLENGE

If the Bible shows that God can and does communicate people's interior thoughts to others, why can't he let the saints know our interior prayers? Does he not have the power to do this?

AFTERTHOUGHT

Paul provides a helpful principle for meeting this challenge: in this world we know only partly what we will know fully in heaven. He writes to the Corinthians, "For now we see in a mirror dimly, but then face to face. Now I know in part; then I shall understand fully, even as I have been fully understood" (1 Cor. 13:12). Thus, it's at least reasonable to think that the things that souls in heaven know and the manner in which they know them will be greater than here on earth.

"*We* Are the Saints"

Colossians 1:2 and Canonized Saints

How can the Catholic Church call only a select few Christians "saints" when the Bible says that *all* Christians are saints?

In the section where it defines the "veneration of saints," the *Catechism* teaches that those Christians who led lives of "prayer and self-denial in giving witness to Christ" have their virtues publicly recognized and proclaimed when they are canonized "as saints." It also teaches in paragraph 2683 that the Church recognizes "as saints" those witnesses "who have preceded us into the kingdom."

For some Protestants,[144] though, the Catholic custom of reserving the term *saints* for souls in heaven is yet another unbiblical practice. Consider, for example, what Paul says in Colossians 1:2: "To the *saints* and faithful brethren in Christ at Colossae: Grace to you and peace from God our Father." This is just one example among many where the New Testament refers to *all* Christians as "saints." If the Bible says that we're all saints, Catholics shouldn't reserve the title for a select few.

MEETING THE CHALLENGE

1. The Greek word for *saint* (*hagios*) is used to refer to many different kinds of people in the Bible, which means there is no definite biblical way the term *must* be used.

The Greek word *hagios* means "sanctified," "set apart," or "holy." It's used in a variety of ways when it refers to people in the Bible—both the Greek version of the Old Testament (the Septuagint) and the New Testament:[145]

- Christians on earth are "saints" (2 Cor. 1:1; Eph. 1:1; Phil. 1:1; Rev. 5:8).

- The Israelites are "holy" (Lev. 20:26) and, therefore, are called "saints" (Ps. 34:9; Dan. 7:18, 8:24).

- Angels are called "holy ones" (Ps. 89:6; Dan. 4:13, 17, 23, 8:13).

- A person is called "holy" or "saint" (Isa. 4:3-4; Matt. 27:52-53).

- Jesus is the ""Holy One" of God (Mark 1:24; Luke 4:34; John 6:67-69).

- God is the "Holy One of Israel" (Ps. 71:22, 78:41, 89:18; Isa. 1:4; Jer. 50:29).

That there is no single biblical use of the term *hagios* gives Catholics some freedom to decide how they want to use the term.

2. The Catholic Church recognizes that it's legitimate to use the term to refer to all baptized Christians.

In his General Audience on August 16, 1989, Pope St. John Paul II affirmed the use of *saint* in reference to Christians on earth. After surveying some passages in the Bible where living Christians are called saints, he said, "All these cases refer to Christians, or to the faithful, that is, to the brethren who have received the Holy Spirit."[146]

The *Catechism* affirms this custom in paragraph 1475:

In the communion of saints, a perennial link of charity exists between the faithful who have already reached their heavenly home, those who are expiating their sins in purgatory *and those who are still pilgrims on earth.* Between them there is, too, an abundant exchange of all good things (emphasis added).

Notice that Christians who are "still on earth" are part of the communion of *saints.* The *Catechism* makes this point even clearer in paragraph 948:

After confessing "the holy Catholic Church," the Apostles' Creed adds "the communion of saints." In a certain sense this article is a further explanation of the preceding: "What is the Church if not the assembly of all the saints?" The communion of saints is the Church. . . . The term "communion of saints" therefore has two closely linked meanings: communion in holy things (*sancta*)" and "among holy persons (*sancti*)."

Sanctus is the Latin term from which we derive the English word *saint.* It means "holy one" and is the equivalent of the Greek *hagios.* Since all baptized Christians are "holy persons" (*sancti*), set apart unto the Lord, it follows that all baptized Christians are "saints." This is why the Church affirms that the term can be used even for a Christian on this side of the veil.

But in a narrower and more formal way, the Catholic Church also uses the word to refer to those individual Christians who are perfected in the heavenly kingdom. So why is that?

3. **It's reasonable for the Church to use the term *saint* as a title of honor for those Christians in heaven because of their perfected state.**

Because the blessed in heaven are perfected in righteousness, they are "saints" in the fullest sense of the term. They are *completely* holy, perfected by God and separated unto him. Unlike us, their saintliness is not mixed with sin and disordered inclinations.

Our saintly status is a share in part of the saintly status of those in heaven. This seems to be how Paul describes it just a few verses after the passage in question: "Giving thanks to the Father, who has qualified us *to share* in the inheritance of the saints in light" (Col. 1:12).

The Greek word for "share" in this verse is *meris*, which literally means "part or portion." It can mean to take part in the same amount, but it can also mean to take part in partially, as opposed to possessing in full. For example, Paul writes in 2 Corinthians 1:13-14, "I hope you will understand fully, as you have understood in part [Greek, *merous*], that you can be proud of us as we can be of you, on the day of the Lord Jesus."

Just as here on earth, we only know in *part* but will know in *full* at the end of time, so too we share in part in the inheritance of the saints who dwell in heaven. Because of this difference and the unique status that the "saints in light" have, it's fitting that Catholics honor them with the title *saint*.

COUNTER-CHALLENGE

Given how saintly the blessed in heaven are, wouldn't it be more fitting to reserve the word saint *for them? This would at least remind us of the saintly perfection that we should be striving for.*

AFTERTHOUGHT

The *Catechism* articulates beautifully the relationship between what we believe about holy things and the way we pray: "*Sancta sanctis!* ("God's holy gifts for God's holy people") is proclaimed by the celebrant in most Eastern liturgies during the elevation of the holy gifts before the distribution of Communion. The faithful (*sancti*) are fed by Christ's holy body and blood (*sancta*)" (948).

VII

The Last Things

Eschatology is the study of the Last Things: death, judgment, heaven, and hell. There's not much that orthodox Catholics and Protestants disagree on concerning death, heaven, and hell; when it comes to *judgment*, however, there are some differences. And this, of course, gives rise to Protestant challenges.

For example, the Catholic Church teaches that if a person is not perfectly purified at the time of death, his soul will have to undergo a final purification after death before entrance into the glory of heaven. The Church gives the name *purgatory* to such purification. But for some Protestants, the Bible doesn't allow for any interim period between death and glory.

Other disagreements are related to what Scripture teaches about the end times. Will there be a "Rapture"? Will Christ physically reign on earth for a thousand years before his Second Coming? Protestants can't see how Catholic teaching on these matters coheres with Scripture.

But in meeting these challenges and others, it will be clear that any lack of coherence between the Bible and Catholic belief is only apparent. It all comes down to reading Scripture the right way.

"Today You Will Be with Me"

Luke 23:43 and Purgatory

How can the Catholic Church teach that purgatory is a state after death before entering heaven when Jesus promises that the good thief would be with him in heaven *on that day*?

The Church teaches those "who die in God's grace and friendship, but still imperfectly purified . . . undergo purification, so as to achieve the holiness necessary to enter the joy of heaven" (CCC 1030). That which is purified is the "unhealthy attachment to creatures," and thus frees one from "what is called the 'temporal punishment' of sin" (CCC 1472). The Church gives the name *purgatory* to this "final purification of the elect" (CCC 1031).

A great many Protestants[147] don't like this idea of a state of purification before entrance into heaven. And they think they have a clear biblical prooftext against it: the promise of eternal life that Jesus makes to the good thief on the cross in Luke 23:43: "Truly, I say to you, today you will be with me in paradise."

If the good thief was going to be with Jesus in heaven *that day*, how could the Catholic Church teach that there is an intermediate state of purification before entering into heaven?

MEETING THE CHALLENGE

1. The "paradise" that Jesus refers to is possibly not heaven.

The challenge assumes that the "paradise" Jesus speaks of is heaven. But that is not *necessarily* true. "Paradise" (Greek, *paradeisos*) could be referring to the "dwelling place of the righteous dead in a state of blessedness,"[148] which at the time of Jesus' crucifixion wasn't heaven because Jesus had not yet ascended. Such a place was instead the "prison" to which Jesus went after his death in order to preach to the spirits held there (1 Pet. 3:19).

So on *that day,* Jesus may have been promising to be with the good thief in the abode of the dead, not heaven. In that case, this verse does not rule out the good thief's (or anyone else's) need for final purification before entrance into heaven.

2. Purgation is not necessarily an enduring process but could be instantaneous.

The challenge assumes that purgation is a process that takes time. But the Church has never defined the exact nature of the duration of the final purification of purgatory.

The common understanding in the Tradition of the Church is that it is a process with a duration of time. But it could be something akin to an instantaneous purgation, something much like the instantaneous change that we will undergo when we receive our resurrected glorified bodies. As Paul writes, "[W]e shall all be changed, in a moment, in the twinkling of an eye, at the last trumpet" (1 Cor. 15:22).

In fact, Pope Benedict XVI, as Cardinal Joseph Ratzinger, proposed a view of purgatory along these lines in his book *Eschatology*:

The transforming "moment" of this encounter cannot be quantified by the measurements of earthly time . . . trying to qualify it as of "short" or "long" duration on the basis of temporal measurements derived from physics would be naive and unproductive. The "temporal measure" of this encounter lies in the unsoundable depths of existence, in a passing-over where we are burned ere we are transformed. To measure such *Existenzzeit*, such an "existential time," in terms of the time of this world would be to ignore the specificity of the human spirit in its simultaneous relationship with, and differentiation from, the world.[149]

Then, in his encyclical *Spe Salvi,* he said the same thing: "It is clear that we cannot calculate the "duration" of this transforming burning in terms of the chronological measurements of this world" (47).

So even if Jesus were referring to heaven, and the good thief received it on *that day*, it still wouldn't follow that the good thief didn't have to go through a final purification. He could have experienced a purgation that was not defined in ordinary terms of duration and still entered heaven on that same day.

3. There is ambiguity as to what Jesus meant by "today."[150]

The challenge assumes that "today" refers to the time when the good thief will be with Jesus in paradise. And this is due to the punctuation in the English translation: "Truly, I say to you, *today* you will be with me in paradise."

But there are no punctuations in the original Greek. So the passage could be read as, "Truly, I say to you *today*, you will be with me in paradise." On this reading, "today" doesn't refer to when the good thief will be with Jesus in paradise but to when Jesus *tells* the good thief that he will be with him in paradise.

There's a parallel construction in Deuteronomy 30:18, where Moses says to the Israelites, "I declare to you this day, that you shall perish." In the text it's unclear whether Moses intends "this day" to refer to when he's making his declaration or to when the Israelites will perish. The placement of the comma in the English translation, unlike in Luke 23:43, suggests the former (as does the fact that the Israelites did *not* perish that day).

The redundant mention of "this day" could also be meant to increase the gravity of his pronouncement. Moses could be saying, "I'm telling you *today* [meaning, this is important] that you will perish [at some point in the future]." In English we also sometimes stress the importance of something by noting the immediate time, for example by saying, "I'm telling you *now*."

Likewise, Jesus may have been telling the good thief, "I say to you *today* [this is important] that you will be with me in paradise [at some point in the future]." Without commas to aid our understanding of the Greek, there's no way to know for sure.

Since there is ambiguity in Luke 23:43 as to what Jesus means by "today," this passage can't be used to undermine the Catholic belief in purgatory.

4. Even if we concede that the good thief didn't have to undergo a final purification in purgatory, the challenge only proves that *he* didn't have to endure purgatory. It doesn't prove that *no one* has to undergo final purification.

The Catholic Church recognizes that *not all* souls have to undergo the final purification of purgatory. Notice in the above quote from paragraph 1030 in the *Catechism* that purgatory is *only* for "those who die in God's grace and friendship, but *still imperfectly purified.*" The implication is that there are some who could die in God's grace and friendship *perfectly* purified and so would not need a final purification.

The *Catechism* teaches this explicitly in paragraph 1472: "A conversion which proceeds from a fervent charity can attain the complete purification of the sinner in such a way that no punishment would remain." Again in paragraph 1022 when referring to a soul's "entrance into the blessedness of heaven," the *Catechism* teaches it will enter either "through a purification or *immediately*" (emphasis added).

Purgatory is for souls to satisfy the need for temporal punishment due for sins. It's possible that the good thief may have done this through the fervor of conversion and suffering of crucifixion and would have had no need for purgatory. That's a legitimate position for Catholics.

COUNTER-CHALLENGE

Would you agree that before we try to show how a doctrine contradicts the Bible we should make sure that we correctly understand what that doctrine entails?

AFTERTHOUGHT

In his encyclical *Spe Salvi*, Benedict XVI suggests that purgatory may very well be the soul's experience of the particular judgment, which is an encounter with Jesus (47). As such, if the good thief experienced the final purification he still would have been with Jesus on *that day*.

"At Home with the Lord"

2 Corinthians 5:8 and Purgatory

How can the Catholic Church teach that there is an intermediate state after death like purgatory when the Bible says that the only place for a Christian to be (besides this life) is heaven?

Referring to a soul's "entrance into the blessedness of heaven," the *Catechism* teaches that it will enter either "through a purification or immediately" (1022). This presupposes that it's possible for a soul to die in God's friendship but not yet be present with the Lord in heaven.

Some Protestants[151] view Paul's teaching in 2 Corinthians 5:6-8 as contradicting this belief. Paul writes,

> So we are always of good courage; we know that while we are at home in the body we are away from the Lord . . . and we would rather be away from the body and at home with the Lord.

Since the Bible says that for a Christian to be "away from the body" is to be "at home with the Lord," there can't be any intermediate state in the afterlife.

MEETING THE CHALLENGE

1. Paul doesn't say what the challenge assumes he says.

Protestants who appeal to this passage often fail to realize that Paul doesn't say that "to be away from the Lord *is* to be at home with the Lord." Paul simply says, "While we are at home in the body we are away from the Lord" and that "we would rather be away from the body and at home with the Lord."

Protestants may reply that although Paul doesn't exactly *say* what the challenge claims, that's what he *means*. Are they right? Does the logic follow? Does the statement, "We would rather be away from the body and at home with the Lord" mean the same as, "To be absent from the body is to be at home with the Lord"?

Suppose I'm at work and I'm wishing that I could instead be away from work and at home. Can we conclude from this that if I'm away from work I must automatically be at home?

Doesn't seem like it. I could be away from work, eating lunch at McDonald's. I could be away from work on my *way* home but sitting in traffic. So it's fallacious to conclude from this verse that once away from the body a Christian must immediately be present with the Lord.

2. Even if we concede the interpretation of 2 Corinthians 5:8 that the challenge asserts, it still doesn't rule out purgatory.

But let's assume for argument's sake that the interpretation this challenge offers of 2 Corinthians 5:8 is true and that to be away from the body *is* to be immediately present with the Lord. That still wouldn't pose a threat to purgatory.

First, this is so because the challenge assumes that purgatory involves a period of time (during which we are "away from the body" but not "with the Lord"). But as we've seen, the Catholic Church has never defined the precise nature of the duration of purgatory. We simply don't know what the experience of time is beyond this life. If purgatory did not involve a duration of time as we know it, it would be perfectly compatible with the challenge's interpretation of this verse.

A second reason is that the challenge assumes purgatory is a state of existence *away* from the Lord. But as we have also seen, purgatory could very well be that encounter with the Lord that we experience in our particular judgment as we "appear before the judgment seat of Christ" (2 Cor. 5:10). This makes sense because Paul describes the soul's judgment as being one of a purifying fire (1 Cor. 3:11-15). It makes sense for God's *presence*, not his absence, to be part of our soul's purification.

COUNTER-CHALLENGE

Shouldn't you make sure that the Bible passage you use to challenge a Catholic belief actually says what you think it says?

AFTERTHOUGHT

The early Christian writer Tertullian (c. A.D. 160-220) affirms the existence of a state after death before entering heaven when he writes, "Inasmuch as we understand the prison pointed out in the Gospel to be Hades [Matt. 5:25], and as we also interpret the uttermost farthing to mean the very smallest offense which has to be recompensed there before the resurrection, no one will hesitate to believe that the soul undergoes in Hades some compensatory discipline, without prejudice to the full process of the resurrection."[152]

"Caught Up with the Lord in the Air"

1 Thessalonians 4:15-17 and the Rapture

How can the Catholic Church teach that faithful Christians will experience the final trial when the Bible teaches that Christians will be raptured before such a time?

The *Catechism* says that that the Church "must pass through a final trial that will shake the faith of many believers" and such a persecution will "unveil the 'mystery of iniquity' in the form of a religious deception offering men an apparent solution to their problems at the price of apostasy from the truth." And this religious deception will be "that of the Antichrist" (675).

But some Protestants[153] believe that the Bible teaches otherwise, that Christians will not experience the persecution of the Antichrist but will be snatched up by the Lord prior to it. This is a doctrine known as the *pre-tribulation Rapture*.

The passage they often appeal to is 1 Thessalonians 4:15–17, which reads,

> For this we declare to you by the word of the Lord, that we who are alive, who are left until the coming of the Lord, shall not precede those who have fallen asleep. For

the Lord himself will descend from heaven with a cry of command, with the archangel's call, and with the sound of the trumpet of God. And the dead in Christ will rise first; then we who are alive, who are left, shall be caught up together with them in the clouds to meet the Lord in the air; and so we shall always be with the Lord.

Protestants argue that Paul can't be talking about the Second Coming here because Jesus only comes part-way down and then goes back up. Moreover, because no judgment of the nations is mentioned like we see in Matthew 25:31–46 and Revelation 20, it must be referring to the "Rapture."

MEETING THE CHALLENGE

1. **The challenge misreads the text as a *partial* coming-from and return back to heaven.**

Verse fifteen reads that the Lord will "descend from heaven with a cry of command." But nowhere does Paul actually say that Jesus *returns* to heaven. If Jesus' descent is definitive, it's not a partial coming like the pre-tribulation Rapture requires it to be.

But what are we to make of Paul's description that the saints who are alive will be "caught up . . . to meet the Lord in the air"? A possible interpretation is that Paul is describing how Christians will meet the Lord in the air to escort him in a way that is analogous to the ancient custom of citizens ushering in important visitors.

It was common for citizens to meet an illustrious person (such as dignitary or victorious military leader) and his entourage outside the walls of their city and accompany him back in. This was a way for people to honor the visitor and take part in the celebration of the visitor's coming.

We see an example of this in Acts 28:14-15 where the brethren at Rome went out of the city to meet Paul as he approached: "And so we came to Rome. And the brethren there, when they heard of us, came as far as the Forum of Appius and Three Taverns to meet us." This ancient custom also explains why the crowds go out to meet Jesus on Palm Sunday and usher him into Jerusalem (see Matt. 21:1-17).

So for Paul, those who are alive at the Second Coming will do for our blessed Lord what the ancients did for their dignitaries: they will be caught up in the air to meet the approaching king, Jesus, and escort him as he "descend[s] from heaven with a cry of command" (1 Thess. 4:16).

2. The details of the passage reveal that Paul is talking about the final coming of Jesus at the end of time.

Notice that it's not just the living who are caught up with the Lord but also the dead in Christ: "And the dead in Christ will rise first" (v.16). That Paul speaks of the resurrection of the dead tells us that he's referring to the *end of time.*

We know this for several reasons. First, Paul states in 1 Corinthians 15 that the end happens in tandem with the resurrection of the dead:

> For as in Adam all die, so also in Christ shall all be made alive. But each in his own order: Christ the first fruits, then at his coming those who belong to Christ. *Then comes the end,* when he delivers the kingdom to God the Father after destroying every rule and every authority and power (1 Cor. 15:22-24).

If Paul viewed the resurrection of the dead as occurring in tandem with the end of time, and if he speaks of the resurrection of the dead in tandem with Christ's coming in

1 Thessalonians 4:15-17, it follows that Christ's coming in those verses is his coming *at the end of time* and not the beginning of a pre-tribulation Rapture.

A second reason we know Paul is talking about the end of time is because when he speaks about the "coming of the Lord" in 2 Thessalonians he says that the Antichrist and his reign of evil must precede it:

> Now concerning the coming of our Lord Jesus Christ and our assembling to meet him, we beg you, brethren, not to be quickly shaken in mind or excited, either by spirit or by word, or by letter purporting to be from us, to the effect that the day of the Lord has come. Let no one deceive you in any way; for that day will not come, unless the rebellion comes first, and the man of lawlessness is revealed, the son of perdition, who opposes and exalts himself against every so-called god or object of worship, so that he takes his seat in the temple of God, proclaiming himself to be God. Do you not remember that when I was still with you I told you this? And you know what is restraining him now so that he may be revealed in his time. For the mystery of lawlessness is already at work; only he who now restrains it will do so until he is out of the way. And then the lawless one will be revealed, and the Lord Jesus will slay him with the breath of his mouth and destroy him by his appearing and his coming (2 Thess. 2:1-8).

It's clear that Paul is connecting the "coming of our Lord" here in 2 Thessalonians and the "coming of the Lord" in 1 Thessalonians 4:15 because he speaks of "our assembling to meet him."

So if the "coming of the Lord" in 1 Thessalonians 4:15-17 must be preceded by the Antichrist and his reign of evil, those verses can't be referring to a pre-tribulation Rapture. Rather, they must refer to our Lord's coming at the end of time when he vanquishes all evil and condemns those "who did not believe the truth but had pleasure in unrighteousness" (2 Thess. 2:12).

A final clue for this being the final day of judgment is the fact that the Lord will descend with "the sound of the trumpet of God" (v.16). Paul speaks of the same trumpet when he describes the resurrection of the dead at the end of time:

> Lo! I tell you a mystery. We shall not all sleep, but we shall all be changed, in a moment, in the twinkling of an eye, at the last trumpet. For the trumpet will sound, and the dead will be raised imperishable, and we shall be changed. For this perishable nature must put on the imperishable, and this mortal nature must put on immortality (1 Cor. 15:51-53).

Since in Paul's mind the trumpet is associated with the resurrection of the dead at the end of time, and he speaks of it when describing the "coming of the Lord" in 1 Thessalonians 4:15-17, we can conclude that the "coming of the Lord" that Paul writes of in 1 Thessalonians 4:15-17 is the final coming at the end of time.

COUNTER-CHALLENGE

How can a text be used to support an idea when the text never mentions that idea?

AFTERTHOUGHT

The Rapture is often portrayed as a "secret coming" of Jesus. But in 1 Thessalonians 4:15-17, Paul describes Christ's coming with "the sound of the trumpet of God." There is nothing secret about descending with the sound of a trumpet!

"A Thousand-Year Reign"

Revelation 20:3 and the Millennial Reign of Christ

How can the Catholic Church reject the idea that Christ will reign on earth for a thousand years when the Bible says that he will?

In 1944, during the reign of Pope Pius XII, the Supreme Sacred Congregation of the Holy Office was asked whether it could be safely taught that Christ would come visibly to rule over this world before the Final Judgment. Its response:

> In recent times on several occasions this Supreme Sacred Congregation of the Holy Office has been asked what must be thought of the system of mitigated Millenarianism, which teaches, for example, that Christ the Lord before the Final Judgment, whether or not preceded by the resurrection of the many just, will come visibly to rule over this world. The answer is: The system of mitigated Millenarianism cannot be taught safely.[154]

But for some Protestants,[155] this contradicts the Bible since Revelation 20 teaches that the saints will "[reign] with Christ a thousand years," a time during which the devil is bound (v.2) and after which the devil will be loosed only to be defeated by Christ at the Final Judgment (vv.7-14).

MEETING THE CHALLENGE

1. There is good reason to interpret the thousand years as symbolic.

The first problem with this challenge is that the number 1,000 is often used in the Bible as a stock number indicating a large amount or a long time and is not meant to be taken literally. For example, in Psalm 50:10 we're told that God owns "the cattle on a thousand hills." The Psalmist is not intending to say that God doesn't own the cattle on all the rest of the hills in the world.

Another example is 1 Chronicles 16:15, which reads, "He is mindful of his covenant forever, of the word that he commanded, for a thousand generations." Obviously, the author does not intend "a thousand generations" to be taken literally, since he just said that God is mindful of his covenant "forever." "A thousand generations" is just another way of saying that God is *always* mindful of his covenant.

The number 1,000 is likewise symbolically used for a large amount of years in 2 Peter 3:8: "one day with the Lord is a thousand years, and a thousand years as one day."

What the above passages tell us is that the mere reference to a thousand years doesn't prove one way or the other if it's literal. We have to look at the context to determine how it's being used. And when we do that for the passage in question, it becomes clear that the thousand years is symbolic.

Consider, for example, how John says Satan will be bound with a chain. How can a chain literally hold a nonphysical spirit? Also, we're told that Satan will be thrown into a pit and kept there for the thousand years. Once again, how can pure spirit be bound to a physical pit? What sort of seal would be required to keep a purely spiritual being in a single spatial location? If the details that make up the context of the thousand years are highly symbolic, then it's reasonable to conclude that the thousand years is symbolic as well.

2. The contextual details of the passage suggest that the thousand years overlaps with the ministry of Jesus and the Church age.

Take, for example, John's description of Satan being bound during the thousand years and later being loosed.

During the time of Jesus' ministry, it's implied that Satan is active. Jesus hints at this in Matthew 12:29: "How can one enter a strong man's house and plunder his goods, unless he first binds the strong man?" The strong man that is bound is Satan. Jesus is the one doing the plundering.[156]

How does Jesus plunder the goods of Satan? For starters, he exorcises demons. There are seven non-overlapping accounts of exorcisms performed by Jesus in the synoptic Gospels.[157] Luke 10:17-18 tells us that the demons were subject to Christ's *disciples* in his name, and Jesus informs his disciples that he had seen Satan "fall like lightning from heaven."

Jesus also binds Satan and plunders his goods with his death on the cross. Prior to Jesus' death, the human race was under the dominion of Satan. But Christ broke that dominion and redeemed the human race with the cross. Inasmuch as Satan no longer has dominion over the human race, Christ has bound him in a sense.

Jesus' initial interference with Satan's activity gives way to a fuller binding with the spread of the gospel during the Church age. The gospel enlightens people and impedes the devil's efforts to deceive. Paul hints at this in Acts 17:30 when he speaks of "the times of ignorance" that "God overlooked," which for Paul was the time prior to the advent of Christ. The "times of ignorance" are no more because the gospel is preached. Satan is restrained in his power to deceive.

This fits John's description of how Satan is thrown into the pit "that he should deceive the nations no more, till the thousand years were ended" (v.3). St. Augustine interpreted the text in the same way:

> It was for the purpose of binding this strong man [the devil] that John, in the Apocalypse [book of Revelation], saw "an angel coming down from heaven . . . who bound [the ancient serpent] for a thousand years." The angel, that is, checked and repressed his power to seduce and possess those destined to be set free.[158]

In order for Christ's gospel to move forward in the world, there must be some sense in which Satan is bound in a way different from before. The symbolic millennium of the Church age might not be so "golden" when compared with the glories of the age to come, but it is a time when the gospel has spread to all corners of the earth. It truly is the fulfillment of what the prophet Isaiah foretold: "For the earth shall be full of the knowledge of the LORD as the waters cover the sea" (Isa. 11:9; Hab. 2:14).

Another detail worthy of note is how the saints, who are identified as "priests," reign with Christ during the thousand years:

> Blessed and holy is he who shares in the first resurrection! Over such the second death has no power, but they shall be priests of God and of Christ, and they shall reign with him a thousand years (Rev. 20:6).

This fits the description of Christians as a "kingdom" and "priests" in the new song sung by the heavenly host:

Thou wast slain and by thy blood didst ransom men for God from every tribe and tongue and people and nation, and hast made them a kingdom and priests to our God, and they shall reign on earth (Rev. 5:10).

In the same vein, in 1 Peter 2:9 Peter refers to the Christian community as a "royal priesthood."

Given the symbolic nature of the thousand years and the parallels between what John describes in the heavenly vision and the characteristics of the Church age, it's reasonable to conclude that the thousand years refers to the Church age—in which Christ bound Satan by his ministry and sacrifice and the gospel spread over all the world—and not to a literal millennium where Christ reigns physically on earth before the Final Judgment.

COUNTER-CHALLENGE

In a biblical book of prophecy that relies heavily on symbols and frequently uses numbers in a symbolic way, does it make more sense to interpret a number literally or symbolically?

AFTERTHOUGHT

St. Thomas Aquinas also interpreted the thousand years as referring to the Church age: "And by the thousand years one understands the whole time of the Church in which the martyrs as well as the other saints reign with Christ, both in the present Church which is called the kingdom of God, and also—as far as souls are concerned—in the heavenly country: for 'the thousand' means perfection, since it is the cube whose root is ten, which also usually signifies perfection."[159]

VIII

Catholic Life & Practice

All the challenges we've examined have to do with Catholic doctrinal beliefs. But Protestants also raise biblical objections to Catholic *practice*. They latch on to Catholic rules, disciplines, and habits of prayer that they think contradict scriptural example and thus reveal Catholicism to be a false, unbiblical religion.

A big one is clerical celibacy. Doesn't it fly in the face of Paul's express instructions? Worse, based on their reading of this text, it's motivated by "deceitful spirits" and it promotes "doctrines of demons."

We agree that no Christian should be promoting demonic doctrines! But as we'll see, that is not what Catholics do.

Other practices that Protestants challenge include calling priests Father, doing penance, setting out religious rules, repetitious prayers, the use of religious statues, and more.

For Catholics who interact with Protestants, it's almost impossible to not be challenged with at least one, if not all, of these objections. They stand as real obstacles keeping Protestants from embracing the truth of Catholicism. So even though they don't have to do with doctrine, it's just as important to meet these challenges skillfully.

"Doctrines of Demons"

1 Timothy 4:1-3 and Celibacy and Abstinence from Food

How can the Catholic Church mandate celibacy for its clergy and abstinence from foods during Lent when the Bible calls forbidding of marriage and consumption of certain foods as "doctrines of demons"?

Catholicism is well-known for its celibate clergy, at least in the Latin Church (CCC 1599), and for mandating periods of fasting and abstinence from certain foods at different times of the year (CCC 2043).

For some Protestants,[160] these Catholic precepts fall under what Paul calls "doctrines of demons":

> Now the Spirit expressly says that in later times some will depart from the Faith by giving heed to deceitful spirits and doctrines of demons, through the pretensions of liars whose consciences are seared, who forbid marriage and enjoin abstinence from foods which God created to be received with thanksgiving by those who believe and know the truth (1 Tim. 4:1-3).

To them, the Bible clearly says that mandating the Catholic practices of clerical celibacy and abstinence from food are not just wrong but demonic.

MEETING THE CHALLENGE

1. We know that Paul is not against celibacy because he strongly encourages it and gives instructions for governing the practice in the early Church.

There are several reasons Paul can't be condemning celibacy in an absolute sense in these verses. The first is that in the next chapter he gives Timothy instructions on proper implementation of celibacy regarding "enrolled" widows:

> Let a widow be enrolled if she is not less than sixty years of age, having been the wife of one husband . . . well attested for her good deeds. . . . But refuse to enroll younger widows; for when they grow wanton against Christ they desire to marry, and so they incur condemnation for having violated their first pledge (1 Tim. 5:9-11).

Notice Paul's instruction about the younger widow incurring "condemnation" for marrying again and "having violated her first pledge." This seems to contradict Paul's permission for a widow to remarry in Romans 7:2-3,

> A married woman is bound by law to her husband as long as he lives. . . . But if her husband dies she is free from that law, and if she remarries another man she is not an adulteress."

Why is it that the widow in Romans 7 can remarry without violating her first pledge and incurring condemnation but the widow in 1 Timothy 5 can't?

The answer is that the "first pledge" doesn't refer to previous wedding vows. Rather, it refers to the vow that a widow took to be "enrolled" in the first century order of widows that Paul is speaking about in 1 Timothy 5. Paul's support for those vows shows that he was not against celibacy, or even enforcing vows of celibacy.

A second reason we know Paul is not condemning celibacy is because he strongly encourages it himself! For example, in 2 Timothy 2:4 he recommends that "a good soldier of Christ Jesus" shouldn't get "entangled in civilian pursuits," which includes things like marriage and a family.

In 1 Corinthians 7:8, he encourages the unmarried and the widows to "remain single" as he does: "To the unmarried and the widows I say that it is well for them to remain single as I do." In subsequent verses, he gives further instruction on the importance of celibacy (vv.32-38), saying that one who chooses such a life "will do better" (v.38). If Paul himself practiced celibacy and recommended to others to practice it, obviously he is not opposed to celibacy.

Finally, Paul can't be condemning celibacy because to do so would contradict Jesus, who encourages celibacy in Matthew 19.

After Jesus' strong rejection of divorce and remarriage in verse 9, the apostles respond, "If such is the case of a man with his wife, it is not expedient to marry" (v.10). Jesus then says,

> Not all men can receive this saying, but only those to whom it is given. For there are eunuchs who have been so from birth, and there are eunuchs who have been made eunuchs by men, and there are eunuchs who have made themselves eunuchs for the sake of the kingdom of heaven. He who is able to receive this, let him receive it (vv.11-12).

Notice that Jesus' teaching about eunuchs for the kingdom is in response to the apostles' statement about not marrying. For Jesus, to be a eunuch for the kingdom is to be celibate for the kingdom, something that he affirms at least for those who are able to live such a lifestyle. Lest we say Paul is contradicting Jesus, we must say that Paul has no problem with celibacy.

2. **Paul explicitly states that he is willing to abstain from some foods out of charity for those who are weaker in faith.**

In 1 Corinthians 8, Paul gives counsel to the Corinthians concerning their liberty with regard to food offered to idols: "Food will not commend us to God. We are no worse off if we do not eat, and no better off if we do" (v.8). Even though they have such freedom, Paul warns them to "take care lest this liberty of yours somehow become a stumbling block to the weak" (v.9).

The "weak" that Paul has in mind are those who, "accustomed to idols, eat food as really offered to an idol; and their conscience, being weak, is defiled" (v.7). For Paul, these people might be encouraged to worship idols if they saw Christians eating foods offered to idols at the idol's temple. He writes,

> For if any one sees you, a man of knowledge, at table in an idol's temple, might he not be encouraged, if his conscience is weak, to eat food offered to idols? And so by your knowledge this weak man is destroyed, the brother for whom Christ died. Thus, sinning against your brethren and wounding their conscience when it is weak, you sin against Christ (vv.10–12).

In order to avoid leading into sin those who are weak in faith, Paul concludes,

> Therefore, if food is a cause of my brother's falling, I will never eat meat, lest I cause my brother to fall (v.13).

Paul, therefore, is not against abstinence from food in some situations.

3. Paul is condemning those who forbid marriage and certain foods in an *absolute* sense. And since the Catholic Church does not do this, the challenge has no force.

So Paul was not against celibacy and not against encouraging abstinence from certain foods. And what about "doctrines of demons"?

What Paul is actually condemning in these verses is the idea that *nobody* should marry and the idea that everyone should *always* abstain from certain foods. The immediate context of the passage in question suggests as much.

[They] forbid marriage and enjoin abstinence from foods *which God created to be received with thanksgiving* by those who believe and know the truth. For *everything created by God is good*, and nothing is to be rejected if it is received with thanksgiving (1 Tim. 4:3-4).

Notice Paul's counter to those who forbade marriage and foods: such things are *created by God* and *are good*. Paul would have no need to emphasize this unless the early Christians were being tempted to believe that such things were not created by God and were not good.

It's unclear which group was promoting these beliefs. It could have been early Gnostics, who believed that the material world came from an evil god and that a good god created the world of pure spirit. Consequently, they believed that we must rid ourselves of the influence of matter as much as possible.

This is why the Gnostics forbade marriage because it involved the fleshly activity of propagating the species. This is also why they had strict food laws since the needs of the body had to be suppressed as much as possible.

Paul also could be referring to some heretical Jewish group since there were Jewish groups in the first century that practiced celibacy and extreme forms of abstinence, such as the Essenes.

Regardless of the identity of the group, it's clear that Paul is only condemning the forbidding of marriage and certain foods in an *absolute* sense because both marriage and food are from God and thus good. This condemnation finds no target in Catholic teaching.

The Catholic Church doesn't stipulate clerical and religious celibacy because marriage is bad. Nor does it make disciplinary laws concerning abstinence from foods because certain foods are evil.

In its practice of celibacy, the Church simply follows the wisdom of Jesus and Paul mentioned above. Celibacy for the kingdom anticipates in this life the life to come since there will be no marriage in the new heaven and new earth: "For in the resurrection they neither marry nor are given in marriage, but are like angels in heaven" (Matt. 22:30).

There are even practical benefits to celibacy. Paul writes,

> I want you to be free from anxieties. The unmarried man is anxious about the affairs of the Lord, how to please the Lord; but the married man is anxious about worldly affairs, how to please his wife, and his interests are divided (1 Cor. 7:32-34).

Some Protestants might object that the Catholic Church's precept concerning celibacy is not a recommendation but a *prohibition*. But this is not true. The Church doesn't prohibit anyone from marrying. The Church simply says that anyone who desires to receive holy orders or enter into a religious order must take a vow of celibacy.[161] Such a person is entirely free to choose to take the vow or not.

As the *Catechism* states, "Only on candidates who are *ready to embrace celibacy freely* and who publicly *manifest their intention* of staying celibate" (1599) can the sacrament of holy orders be conferred. As to the requirement of the vow itself, it's no different from the binding vow of the "enrolled" widow spoken of in 1 Timothy 5.

Concerning its fasting precepts, the Catholic Church is simply following the example of Jesus in the wilderness (Luke 4:2-4) and his teaching in the Sermon on the Mount (Matt. 6:16-18). It also follows in the footsteps of Paul, who didn't take any food or drink for three days after his encounter with the risen Jesus (Acts 9:9).

Moreover, the Catholic Church recognizes the spiritual benefits of fasting. When exercised in a sacrificial spirit, the hunger for food is a helpful reminder that we hunger for God. This hunger in turn reminds us that only in God can the deepest longings of our hearts be fulfilled. It also proves that we are not slaves to our bodily passions and are able to govern them with reason. Paul affirms this when he writes, "I pommel my body and subdue it, lest after preaching to others I myself should be disqualified" (1 Cor. 9:27).

COUNTER-CHALLENGE

If a practice isn't obviously immoral, shouldn't we consider the reasons for it before condemning it?

AFTERTHOUGHT

It's possible that Paul is alluding to Gnosticism in 1 Timothy 6:20 where he writes, "O Timothy, guard what has been entrusted to you. Avoid the godless chatter and contradictions of what is falsely called knowledge." The Greek word for "knowledge" here is *gnōsis*, from which we derive *Gnostic*.

"Call No Man Father"

Matthew 23:9 and the Catholic Priesthood

How can Catholics call their priests "Father" when Jesus says explicitly, "Call no man father on earth"?

There is not much that needs to be said by way of introduction for this challenge. Catholics call their priests "Father." Jesus says, "Call no man father on earth." It's as simple as that. The contradiction is evident, right?[162]

MEETING THE CHALLENGE

1. The Bible approvingly uses the term *father* for individuals other than God. Therefore, Jesus can't be restricting the use of the term to God alone in an absolute sense.

The Bible uses *father* to refer to biological fathers, which Protestants don't deny. Paul quotes the fourth commandment in Ephesians 6:2: "Honor your father and your mother."

Paul refers to himself as a spiritual "father" in 1 Corinthians 4:15: "For though you have countless guides in Christ, you do not have many fathers. For I became your father in Christ Jesus through the gospel." If Matthew 23:9 forbade calling any man "father," then Paul would be disobeying Jesus' express command. But Paul's words in 1

Corinthians 4:15 are divinely inspired and, therefore, can't contradict what Jesus says.

It's also not uncommon in the New Testament for Christ's ministers to view themselves as spiritual fathers, showing that taking the *role* of father is also not off-limits.[163] Paul calls the Galatians his "little children" (Gal. 4:19). He also views Timothy (1 Cor. 4:17; 1 Tim. 1:2, 18; 2 Tim. 1:2, 2:1), Titus (Titus 1:4), and Onesimus (Philem. 10) as his spiritual sons. Peter calls Mark "my son" (1 Pet.5:13), and John, like Paul, refers to his audience as "my little children" (1 John 2:1; 3 John 4).

Here are a few other examples where *father* is used for people other than God in respectful and reverential ways:

- Abraham (Luke 16:24; Acts 7:2; Rom. 4:12; James 2:21)
- Isaac (Rom. 9:10)
- Jacob (John 4:12)
- David (Acts 4:25)
- The Jewish elders (Acts 7:2)
- Older Christian men (1 John 2:13-14)

A Protestant may object that Abraham, Isaac, Jacob, and David are not men "on earth" and thus can't be used in response to the challenge. But the Jewish elders and older Christian men *were* individuals on earth.

Lest we say that the Holy Spirit is contradicting himself and that the early Christian leaders directly disobeyed a command of the Lord, we must conclude that Jesus' command to "call no man father on earth" doesn't forbid calling *anyone* "father" other than God. There must be something else going on.

2. **The principle of this challenge leads to absurdities when it's applied to other things Jesus says in the immediate context.**

Before Jesus gives the instruction to "call no man father on earth," he gives the same sort of instruction concerning calling men "rabbi": "But you are not to be called rabbi, for you have one teacher [Greek, *didaskalos*], and you are all brethren" (Matt. 23:8). John tells us in John 1:38 that *rabbi* means "teacher" (*didaskalos*).

If we were to follow the logic of this challenge from Matthew 23:9, we would have to conclude that we cannot call another person "teacher" either since Jesus is our one teacher. But several times the Bible uses *didaskalos* for people other than Jesus:

- 1 Timothy 2:7: "For this I was appointed a preacher and apostle (I am telling the truth, I am not lying), a teacher [*didaskalos*] of the Gentiles in faith and truth."

- 1 Corinthians 12:28: "And God has appointed in the Church first apostles, second prophets, third teachers [*didaskalous*]."

- James 3:1: "Let not many of you become teachers [*didaskaloi*], my brethren, for you know that we who teach shall be judged with greater strictness."

As with Paul's use of *father* to describe himself, here we must conclude that Paul and James under the inspiration of the Holy Spirit were not disobeying Jesus' instruction when they referred to *teachers* other than God.

3. **Jesus is using hyperbole to indict the scribes and Pharisees for their pride.**

Since the Bible elsewhere uses *teacher* and *father* for persons other than God, it's likely that instead of forbidding those words in an absolute sense, Jesus is using *hyperbole* (exaggeration to make a point)—as when he commands to gouge out our eye or cut off our hand if one of them causes us to sin (Matt. 18:8-9).

The purpose of this hyperbole in Matthew 23:8-9 is to indict the religious leaders for the disordered love they had for their roles of leadership, a disordered love that apparently led them to hold in contempt those they were appointed to lead. There are two clues that suggest this.

First, in the verses preceding the teaching in question, Jesus says that the Pharisees "love the place of honor at feasts and the best seats in the synagogues" (v.6) and that they love "salutations in the market places, and being called rabbi by men" (v.7). Then, immediately following the teaching in question, Jesus pronounces a series of "woes" to the Pharisees for their hypocrisy (vv.13-36).

The second clue is found in verse 8 where Jesus emphasizes equality, saying, "You are all brethren." This is not to say that all members of God's family have equal roles. But it is to remind the religious leaders that before God they are equal in dignity with their brethren. Their leadership roles don't make them any better than others insofar as they are all God's children.

The Pharisees had allowed pride to well up in their souls with the honorific titles of *rabbi* and *father*. Consequently, they began to have a disordered love for their superior roles, puffing up their self-importance and forgetting that their worth came from God, who is our ultimate Father and Teacher. It's for this reason that Jesus rebukes them and puts them in their place, employing hyperbole to drive home his point that they need to be more humble and recognize that their leadership roles don't make them better than others.

Moreover, Jesus is teaching us not to confuse the unique role of teacher that Christ has—which is ultimate and permanent—with the role of teacher that anyone else has on earth, which is conditional and temporary. Likewise, we must avoid confusing the fatherhood that God has—which is absolute and not dependent on anything else—with the conditional fatherhood that anyone has on earth, whether biological or spiritual, which depends on God's fatherhood.[164]

As we've seen, God has given the role of teaching and fatherhood to people. And since he has chosen to do so, he's not going to have a problem with our recognizing that truth by calling those people "teacher" and "father." God is all in favor of us acknowledging his truth.

COUNTER-CHALLENGE

Was Paul disobeying Jesus when in an inspired letter he called himself "father"? Or is it possible that Jesus wasn't speaking in a strictly literal way?

AFTERTHOUGHT

Scripture provides a key to understanding the spiritual role of fatherhood that religious leaders possess. Paul writes, "For this cause I bow my knees to the Father [Greek, *patera*] of our Lord Jesus Christ, of whom all paternity [Greek, *patria*, "family" or "fatherhood"] in heaven and earth is named" (Eph. 3:15, Douay-Rheims). Paul's point is that all fatherhood, whether biological or spiritual, *participates* in the one unique fatherhood of God and establishes it on earth.

"It Is Finished"

John 19:30, Redemption, and Penance

How can the Catholic Church teach that we must do penance when Jesus said from the cross, "It is finished"?

The Catholic Church teaches that when a sinner is raised up from sin, he "must still recover his full spiritual health by doing something more to make amends for the sin" (CCC 1459). And whatever a Christian does to make amends, such as offering prayers after the sacrament of confession or abstaining from foods on certain days throughout the year, is what the *Catechism* calls "penance."

For some Protestants,[165] such a belief undermines the sufficiency of Christ's death on the cross. They often appeal to Jesus' words uttered on the cross in John 19:30, "It is finished"—taking Jesus to mean that his salvific work was complete and *nothing else* needed to be done for us to be saved. Therefore, for the Catholic Church to teach that we must do "something more" like penance when we're forgiven of our sins implies that Christ's death on the cross wasn't enough to save us.

MEETING THE CHALLENGE

1. What Jesus says is "finished" is his earthly mission and/or the redemption of the human race, neither of which excludes penance as a legitimate Christian practice.

Jesus' statement can be read in two ways. First, he may be simply referring to the completed work of his earthly ministry. On Holy Thursday, the night before his crucifixion, Jesus speaks of his accomplished work in his high-priestly prayer to the Father:

> I glorified you on earth, having accomplished the work which you gave me to do; and now, Father, glorify me in your own presence with the glory which I had with you before the world was made (John 17:4-5).

Given that Jesus prays this prayer the night before his crucifixion, and it's John who records this prayer in which Jesus speaks of *completing* his work, it's reasonable to conclude that Jesus is referring to this accomplished work on *earth* when he says, "It is finished." Using this interpretation, penance is in no way excluded.

A second possible reading is that it could refer to the completed action whereby the human race is reunited back to God and saving grace is made available for all humanity. This is what John refers to in 1 John 2:1-2:

> We have an advocate with the Father, Jesus Christ the righteous; and he is the expiation for our sins, and not for ours only but also for the sins of the whole world.

The Church affirms that this aspect of Christ's redemptive work was sufficient (CCC 616, 1708). But penance applies to something else.

Paragraph 1459 in the *Catechism* (quoted above) makes clear the twofold purpose of penance. First, it's ordered to making "amends for" a person's sins (1459). Second, it's ordered to remedying the "disorders sin has caused," identified as "injuries [to] the sinner himself, as well as his relationships with God and neighbor."

Penance atones for the damage done by past, already forgiven sins and is meant to help the sinner "recover his full spiritual health." In doing so, it helps the sinner be configured more to Christ (CCC 1460).

When seen in this light, penance doesn't apply to the redemption of the human race and the grace of salvation that remits the *eternal* consequences of sin, which is "finished." The person who performs penance is presumed to have already received the fruits of the sufficient work of Christ on the cross—namely, saving grace—since penance refers to works done after a sin is forgiven. We do penance not to add to Christ's saving work but to make up for temporal consequences of sin and become more spiritually healthy.

Therefore, whether we embrace one or both of the above interpretations, neither one precludes penance.

2. The New Testament reveals that penance is a part of the Christian life.

Consider, for example, Hebrews 12:6, 10:

> The Lord disciplines him whom he loves, and chastises every son whom he receives . . . [He] disciplines us for our good, that we may share his holiness.

Notice that God chastises "every son whom he receives"—that's to say, God disciplines *Christians*. But being chastised involves some sort of suffering for bad behavior. The Greek word used here, a form of *mastigoō,* literally means to "lash," "whip," "flog," or "scourge" *for the sake of punishment.* Therefore, God wills for suffering to be a way to amend for sins, which is the essence of penance.

The author of Hebrews also tells us that such suffering is "for our good, that we may share his holiness." So God doesn't punish his children merely to reform external behavior but to conform us to *his holiness*. He chastises us so that we may become holy like him.

According to the Bible then, embracing suffering for sins in order to be sanctified (penance) and the sufficient work of Christ on the cross are not mutually exclusive.

Another example in the New Testament where God bestows a form of punishment for past sins comes from Jesus himself. Consider his teaching in Luke 12:47–48:

> And that servant who knew his master's will, but did not make ready or act according to his will, shall receive a severe beating. But he who did not know, and did what deserved a beating, shall receive a light beating.

Notice that the master still disciplines the servant who did what was wrong without full culpability.

Now, as every parent knows, discipline not only involves inflicting some form of suffering for the wrong done but also making the offender *do* something to make up for what he did. For example, a father might demand that his son do extra chores around the house in order to make up for hitting a baseball into the neighbor's window.

The New Testament reveals this part of discipline for sin as well. For example, Jesus says in Matthew 6:16–18,

> And when you fast, do not look dismal, like the hypocrites, for they disfigure their faces that their fasting may be seen by men. Truly, I say to you, they have received their reward. But when you fast, anoint your head and wash your face, that your fasting may not be seen by men

but by your Father who is in secret; and your Father who sees in secret will reward you.

Notice that Jesus doesn't say, "*If* you fast" but "*when* you fast." This implies that fasting is something that Jesus intends his disciples to do. Jesus also teaches in Mark 2:20, "The days will come, when the bridegroom is taken away from them, and then *they will fast* in that day."

The Jews practiced fasting as a form of penance (see Joel 2:12; 2 Chron. 20:3-4; Ezra 8:21-23; Dan. 9:3; 1 Kgs. 21:27-29). In this context, Jesus' instructions to his disciples to fast are instructions to perform acts of penance.

Since the New Testament teaches Christians to do penance, it follows that penance doesn't contradict Jesus' statement on the cross, "It is finished."

3. The Bible teaches about making atonement for temporal consequences of sin and being made holy through the process of sanctification.

Recall from above that the twofold purpose of penance is to atone for past forgiven sins and to help the sinner "recover his full spiritual health."

This definition of penance is consistent with the Bible's teaching on acts that atone for sin and the process of being made holy by God's grace (what both Catholics and Protestants call "sanctification"). Let's consider the former first: acts that atone for sin.

- Matthew 6:16-18: "And when you fast, do not look dismal, like the hypocrites . . . But when you fast, anoint your head and wash your face, that your fasting may not be seen by men but by your Father who is in secret." (Recall that fasting is a penitential act that atones for past sins.)

- Proverbs 16:6: "By *loyalty and faithfulness* iniquity is atoned for."
- 1 Peter 4:8: "Above all hold unfailing your *love for one another*, since love *covers a multitude of sins*."

The atoning character of these acts can't refer to the atonement that Christ made for the eternal consequences of sin (all the fasting, loyalty, and love in the world couldn't get us to heaven without Christ's sacrifice). Therefore, it must be referring to atonement for the *temporal* consequences of sin.

If the biblical doctrine that certain acts can atone for the temporal consequences of sin doesn't undermine the sufficiency of Jesus' death on the cross, and penance is the doctrine that a person can make atonement for the temporal consequences of sin, it follows that penance is a doctrine that doesn't undermine the sufficiency of Jesus' death on the cross.

Let's now consider sanctification:

- 2 Corinthians 7:1: "Since we have these promises, beloved, let us cleanse ourselves from every defilement of body and spirit, and *make holiness perfect* in the fear of God."
- James 1:2-4: "Count it all joy, my brethren, when you meet various trials, for you know that the testing of your faith produces steadfastness. And let steadfastness have its full effect, *that you may be perfect and complete*, lacking in nothing."

- Philippians 2:12: "Therefore, my beloved, as you have always obeyed, so now, not only as in my presence but much more in my absence, *work out your own salvation* with fear and trembling."

From these passages, it's clear that in the Christian life there is more we must do after being initially saved by the completed work of Christ on the cross. That something more is sanctification.

So given our definition of penance and the biblical foundation for that definition, it follows that penance is one of the ways by which we can be sanctified. And since sanctification doesn't undermine the sufficiency of Jesus' death on the cross, then penance doesn't undermine the sufficiency of Jesus' death on the cross.

COUNTER-CHALLENGE

Does "It is finished" mean there's nothing else for us to do in our journey of salvation?

AFTERTHOUGHT

Paul's writes in Colossians 1:24: "Now I rejoice in my sufferings for your sake, and in my flesh I complete what is lacking in Christ's afflictions for the sake of his body, that is, the church." Notice that on the surface it seems that Paul is denying the sufficiency of Christ's death on the cross as if it wasn't enough to redeem the human race and remit the eternal consequences of sin. But obviously he doesn't mean that. He must be referring instead to the *application* of graces (for salvation or sanctification) merited by Christ's afflictions to individual members of the body. Just as we must understand Paul's language in this case with greater nuance, so too must we consider with greater nuance the Catholic teaching on penance.

"Yoke of Slavery"

Galatians 5:1 and Catholic Rules

How can the Catholic Church have so many rules when the Bible says that we are set free in Christ and no longer are subject to a yoke of slavery?

It's no secret that the Catholic Church has rules. Catholics are obliged to attend Mass every Sunday and on every holy day of obligation. We have to fast and abstain on Ash Wednesday and Good Friday and abstain from meats on Fridays during Lent. We *have* to confess our serious sins at least once a year, and so on.

Some Protestants have a problem with this since they tend to associate rules with the kind of vain, works-based religion that Christ has done away with. A favorite passage of those who make this challenge is Galatians 5:1 where Paul writes, "For freedom Christ has set us free; stand fast therefore, and do not submit again to a yoke of slavery." Martin Luther appealed to this very verse to make the same challenge. [166] In making all its rules, is the Catholic Church not submitting Christians to a yoke of slavery?

MEETING THE CHALLENGE

1. The yoke of slavery that Paul is talking about is the yoke of the Mosaic Law, not laws in general.

Paul makes it clear within the context that he's talking about the Mosaic Law. For example, in the verses immediately preceding the passage in question, Paul draws a contrast between Sarah and Isaac, who were free, and Hagar and Ishmael, who were slaves:

> Now we, brethren, like Isaac, are children of promise. But as at that time he who was born according to the flesh persecuted him who was born according to the Spirit, so it is now. But what does the Scripture say? "Cast out the slave and her son; for the son of the slave shall not inherit with the son of the free woman." So, brethren, we are not children of the slave but of the free woman (Gal. 4:28-31).

For Paul, Sarah and Isaac represent the New Covenant because it's through Isaac that God fulfills his promise for Abraham's seed to bless the world. Hagar and Ishmael represent the Old Covenant, which for Paul was a yoke of slavery like Hagar and Ishmael bore.

Another contextual detail that shows Paul has the Old Law in mind is found in the subsequent verses of the passage in question. He writes,

> Now I, Paul, say to you that if you receive circumcision, Christ will be of no advantage to you. I testify again to every man who receives circumcision that he is bound to keep the whole law. You are severed from Christ, you who would be justified by the law; you have fallen away from grace. For through the Spirit, by faith, we wait for the hope of righteousness. For in Christ Jesus neither circumcision nor uncircumcision is of any avail, but faith working through love (Gal. 5:2-6).

Notice that circumcision, which is an example *par excellence* of a precept from the Mosaic Law, is the focus of the passage. This is a clue that it's the "rules" associated with the *Mosaic Law* or "works of the law" (Gal. 2:16) that Paul is calling the "yoke of slavery," not rules in general.

2. All communities and families need rules; Christianity is no different.

Virtually all Protestants agree that rules can serve a good purpose. Nations and communities need laws. Sports need rules and referees to enforce them. Households have family rules for how children should behave. You can't just do whatever you want in a family if you want peaceful coexistence.

If rules are good for family life, especially in a home where parents love their kids and one another, then they are good for the Church—since the Church is the family of God. Paul writes in 1 Timothy 3:15,

> If I am delayed, you may know how one ought to behave in the *household of God*, which is the church of the living God, the pillar and bulwark of the truth.

If God's Church is his household, then it's reasonable for him to have rules to govern its members for the sake of maintaining peace and order within it. God's family rules also help keep his children spiritually safe.

The household rules of the Catholic Church are also designed to draw us into deeper relationship with God. In this respect, they do not bind us but *free* us. Just as knowledge of the law of gravity is necessary for man to learn to fly, the Church's laws are a foundation from which we can spiritually soar.

The Church's rule to abstain from meat on Fridays during Lent is a great example of this. When the precept is kept in a sacrificial spirit, the hunger for meat is a helpful reminder that we hunger for God. And such hunger in turn motivates us to seek union with God, in which we find true happiness.

Of course, Protestant communities aren't strangers to rules and laws. For example, many say that a person has to be fully immersed in water for his baptism to be valid. Some forbid the drinking of alcoholic beverages.

Other examples involve the governance of marriage. Many Protestant groups require that spouses profess their vows in the presence of witnesses. Most have the precept that divorce and remarriage is permitted only on the condition that a spouse has committed adultery.

If Protestant communities have these sorts of rules or laws, then wouldn't they be subject to this challenge as well?

3. The New Testament gives evidence that rules were a part of the Christian life in the early Church.

Let's start with Jesus. In Matthew 28:19, Jesus stipulates that the nations would be made disciples through baptism. So baptism is a New Covenant precept or rule, if you will.

Another is the celebration of the Eucharist. Jesus commands the apostles in Luke 22:19 to offer the Last Supper as a memorial offering: "Do this in remembrance of me."

In his Sermon on the Mount, Jesus reveals his intention that rules would be a part of the Christian life. For example, he gives us a variety of ethical precepts:

- Our righteousness must exceed that of the scribes and the Pharisees (Matt. 5:20).

- We must not be angry with our brother nor insult him (Matt. 5:22).

- We must reconcile with our brother before we offer our gifts at the altar (Matt. 5:23).
- We must not look at others lustfully in our hearts (Matt. 5:28).

These are just a sample of the ethical rules that Jesus intends Christians to live by.

Jesus also intends certain pious actions to be part of the Christian life: almsgiving (Matt. 6:2-4), prayer (Matt. 6:5-15), and fasting (Matt. 6:16-18). He even gives instructions (rules) on how those who disobey the judgment of the Church are to be dealt with: "If he refuses to listen even to the church, let him be to you as a Gentile and a tax collector" (Matt. 18:17).

Paul follows suit, stipulating a number of rules to govern the local churches. For example, he instructs the Corinthians to keep the feast of the new Passover, which is the Eucharist (1 Cor. 5:8). He even gives instructions concerning the reception of the Eucharist:

> Whoever, therefore, eats the bread or drinks the cup of the Lord in an unworthy manner will be guilty of profaning the body and blood of the Lord. Let a man examine himself, and so eat of the bread and drink of the cup. For anyone who eats and drinks without discerning the body eats and drinks judgment upon himself (1 Cor. 11:27-29).

We saw earlier that Paul lays down certain rules concerning proper implementation of consecrated celibacy with regard to "enrolled" widows in 1 Timothy 5:9-11. He instructs the Thessalonians in 2 Thessalonians 2:15 to "hold to the traditions which you were taught by us, either by word of mouth or by letter." In 1 Corinthians 14, Paul gives rules to govern the Corinthians and their practice of speaking in "tongues" as they gather in church.

Even on a more general level, Paul teaches that there is a "law of Christ" that Christians are subject to. For example, he writes in 1 Corinthians 9:21, "To those outside the law I became as one outside the law—not being without law toward God but under *the law of Christ*—that I might win those outside the law." Paul also speaks of Christ's law in Galatians 6:2, giving the rule that we must "bear one another's burdens, and so fulfill the law of Christ."

4. How many rules are too many?[167]

Most Protestants will probably concede that at least *some* rules can be part of the Christian life, especially in light of the evidence presented above. But they still might reject the *amount* of rules in the Catholic Church.

But how do we know what amount of rules is too many? What's the magic number of rules that a church should have? The Bible doesn't say. Whatever number someone comes up with, it would be completely arbitrary—whatever *feels* right. But Christians of all kinds have different feelings, and their different churches have varying numbers of rules.

And despite the charge that Catholicism has too many rules, in truth it has relatively few when compared to other groups of comparable size. For example, the United States has around 325 million citizens. The 2012 edition of its federal legislation, the United States Code, totals 45,000 pages in thirty-four volumes. By comparison, a standard English edition of the *Code of Canon Law*, which is the main legal text for the large majority of the Church's one billion members, totals a little more than *500* pages in a single volume.

Moreover, the minimum requirements for a Catholic are relatively few. For example, Catholics are expected to know and observe the Ten Commandments, follow the five precepts of the Church (CCC 2041-2043), and be familiar with the proper preparation required for receiving the sacraments, particularly penance and the Eucharist.

Of course, being a Catholic is not about just meeting the minimum requirements of the law. There is much more that a Catholic should know in order to have a committed relationship with Jesus. Love demands more than the minimum. But at least we can see that the general "rules" for an individual Catholic in his ordinary experience are relatively few, and they pertain to things reasonable for a religion, such as worship and morality.

Finally, we can also point out that not only is the Church's code of laws relatively short, but many of those laws apply to specific situations that an ordinary Catholic rarely—or never—encounters. So only a fraction of them impact his daily life. As for the rest, Catholics can be instructed on the "dos and don'ts" as the situation arises.

COUNTER-CHALLENGE

Isn't it unreasonable to think that no rules are binding just because the Bible says that some rules aren't binding?

AFTERTHOUGHT

The Council of Jerusalem in Acts 15 is a good example of the Church's not having an aversion to rules. The council fathers stipulated four rules that were to be binding on the new Gentile converts: "For it has seemed good to the Holy Spirit and to us to lay upon you no greater burden than these necessary things: that you abstain from what has been sacrificed to idols and from blood and from what is strangled and from unchastity. If you keep yourselves from these, you will do well. Farewell" (vv.28-29).

"Vain Repetitions"

Matthew 6:7 and the Rosary

How can the Catholic Church teach that the rosary is a legitimate prayer when the Bible forbids repetitious prayer?

The rosary is a popular Catholic devotion that the *Catechism* endorses as a "form of piety" that expresses the "religious sense of the Christian people" (1674). But for many Protestants,[168] the rosary with its repetition of the *Hail Mary* prayer contradicts Jesus' command to "Use no vain repetitions as the heathens do" (Matt. 6:7; KJV). It would seem that the Catholic practice of praying the rosary is a direct violation of Jesus' command.

MEETING THE CHALLENGE

1. Jesus wasn't condemning prayers that involve repetition but rather the idea that the quantity of prayer determines its efficacy.

The Greek word translated "vain repetition" is a form of *battalogeō*, which can mean to speak in a stammering way, saying the same words over and over again without thinking.[169] But it can also mean "to use many words, to speak for a long time."[170] So it can connote either mindless repetition or quantity. Which meaning does Jesus have in mind?

The context reveals that Jesus has the *quantity* of prayers in mind. For example, Jesus says in verse 7, "For they [the Gentiles] think that they will be heard *for their many words*" as if their many words could wear down the gods in order to get what they wanted. This is the mentality of prayer that Jesus is telling his disciples to avoid—the mentality that sheer volume of words ensures that God hears us.

This explains why Jesus says in verse 8, "Don't be like them, for your Father knows what you need before you ask him." The implication is that it's futile to think a bunch of words is needed for God to hear a prayer because he already knows it.

So Jesus is not concerned with repetition simply. He's concerned with the idea that simply multiplying words makes prayers efficacious.

2. The rosary is not meant to gain favors from God due to the *amount* of prayers repeated.

According to the *Catechism*, the rosary is an "epitome of the whole gospel" (971). It is meant to focus our hearts and minds on the mysteries of Christ's life, mysteries such as his conception in Mary's womb at the Annunciation, his birth in Bethlehem, his baptism and preaching ministry, his glorious Resurrection, and his ascension into heaven.

Meditating on these mysteries is meant to give us a deeper knowledge of Christ and draw us into a deeper communion with him so that we can be more conformed to him. And we include Mary in that meditation because her soul "magnifies the Lord" (Luke 1:46). The rosary, therefore, is a way to meditate on Christ in order to foster a greater love for him. The repetition of prayers serves that meditation—and that's a biblical thing.

3. The Bible affirms prayers that involve repetition.

We can start with Jesus himself. Notice that right after Jesus condemns the "vain repetitions" of the Gentiles, he commands the apostles, "Pray like this . . . Our Father who art in heaven." Does Jesus intend for us to only say it once? Are we forbidden to repeat the Lord's Prayer? Most Protestants have said it many times; perhaps they say it more than once a day.

Another example is Jesus' prayer in the garden of Gethsemane: "Father . . . remove this cup . . . not what I will, but what you will" (Mark 14:36). Mark tells us that Jesus prayed this multiple times: "And again he went away and prayed, saying the same words" (14:39). Surely, Jesus wouldn't be violating his own command not to pray with "vain repetitions."

We also have an example from the "four living creatures" (angels) that John sees in heaven: "*Day and night they never cease* to sing, Holy, holy, holy, is the Lord God Almighty" (Rev. 4:8). If any prayer involves repetition, it's this one!

The Psalms even give us forms of prayer that involve repetition. Consider, for example, Psalm 136. Its refrain, "for his steadfast love endures forever," occurs twenty-six times. Must we say that the Holy Spirit (the third person of the Trinity) who inspired the Psalmist to write this, is at odds with Jesus (the second person of the Trinity)?

Since the Bible affirms prayers that involve repetition, we can conclude that the repetition in the rosary does not violate Christ's words.

COUNTER-CHALLENGE

Why should we think that a condemnation of useless repetition is a condemnation of any repetition? Couldn't there be repetitious prayer that is heartfelt and helps us love God more?

AFTERTHOUGHT

One of the benefits of praying the rosary is that it protects us from focusing our prayer too much on what we want and need. Praying for our needs is a good thing, but it shouldn't be the only thing we pray about. The rosary helps us to focus on what should be the first object of prayer: Jesus.

"Wine Is a Mocker"

Amos 6:6 (Isaiah 5:11; Prov.20:1) and Drinking Alcohol

How can the Catholic Church permit the drinking of alcoholic beverages when the Bible forbids drinking wine or strong drink and says that those who do drink are not wise?

Catholic moral teaching does not forbid the consumption of alcohol. For some Protestants,[171] this goes against the Bible. For example, Isaiah 5:11 reads, "Woe to those who rise early in the morning, that they may run after strong drink." The prophet Amos pronounces a woe on those who "drink wine in bowls" (6:6). Proverbs 20:1 says, "Wine is a mocker, strong drink a brawler; and whoever is led astray by it is not wise."

Considering these passages, permitting the drinking of alcoholic beverages is a tradition of men that nullifies the word of God.

MEETING THE CHALLENGE

1. We know that these verses don't forbid the consumption of alcohol in an absolute sense because other verses affirm it.

One example is found in Deuteronomy 14. In verses 22–24, Moses instructs the Israelites about their obligation to tithe and informs them that if they are too far away from where they are to bring their crop, they are to "turn it into money" and "spend the money for whatever [they] desire, oxen, or sheep, or wine or strong drink, whatever your appetite craves; and you shall eat there before the Lord your God and rejoice, you and your household" (v26).

The Hebrew word used here for "strong drink" is *shekar,* and is used for beverages that contain alcohol, having the potential to intoxicate.[172] If alcoholic beverages were forbidden absolutely, as the challenge asserts, then Moses would be giving the Israelites permission to do something that's immoral.

Here are some other pro-wine passages:

- Genesis 14:18: "And Melchizedek king of Salem brought out bread and wine."
- Ecclesiastes 10:19: "Bread is made for laughter, and wine gladdens life."
- Psalm 104:15: "Thou dost cause the grass to grow for the cattle, and plants for man to cultivate, that he may bring forth food from the earth, and wine to gladden the heart of man."
- 1 Timothy 5:23: "No longer drink only water, but use a little wine for the sake of your stomach and your frequent ailments."

Some Protestants try to get around passages like these by arguing that the wine spoken of was diluted enough with water to exclude fear of excess and intoxication.[173] It's true that wine was often mixed with water. But if it were diluted to the point where intoxication wasn't possible, then no sense could be made of the many warnings about *drunkenness* (1 Cor. 6:9; Gal. 5:21; Eph. 5:18; Prov. 20:1; 23:21; Hab. 2:15). There would be no need for such warnings if the Jews and the early Christians only partook of non-intoxicating wine.[174]

2. Jesus was favorable to wine in his ministry.

We know that Jesus drank wine; in fact, he drank it enough that some people accused him of drunkenness: "The Son of Man has come eating and drinking; and you say, 'Behold, a glutton and a drunkard, a friend of tax collectors and sinners!'" (Luke 7:34). For him to be charged with being a drunkard, he must have drunk the kind of wine that has the potential to intoxicate.

One of Jesus' first miracles involved changing about 150 gallons of water into alcoholic wine (John 2:6) in response to the wedding party's dilemma of exhausting the original supply of wine (John 2:3). And we know that the wine Jesus produced was the alcoholic kind because the steward complimented the groom, saying, "Every man serves the good wine first; and when men have drunk freely, then the poor wine; but you have kept the good wine until now" (John 2:10). The "good wine" refers to high-quality wine that has the potential to impair man's ability to discern between good and inferior grades of wine. That's the kind of wine that Jesus changed water into.

3. The passages used to challenge the Catholic view of wine don't actually say what the challenge seeks to prove.

Take Isaiah 5:11, for example. The prophet doesn't pronounce a "woe" on someone who *partakes* of "strong drink" but on those who "rise early in the morning, that they may *run after* strong drink," and "tarry late into the evening till wine *inflames* them." The condemnation is directed to *excessive indulgence* in the strong drink, not all kinds of drinking.

Amos 6:6 doesn't condemn the mere partaking of "wine in bowls" either. If it did, we'd have to say that Scripture also condemns anointing with oil since Amos applies the same woe to those who "anoint themselves with the finest oils." But we know this isn't what Amos is saying because anointing was an accepted practice in the Old Testament, such as when the prophet Samuel anointed David with a horn of oil (1 Sam. 16:13).

The woe that Amos pronounces is actually intended for those who engage in celebratory behavior (drinking wine and anointing self with oil) "but are not grieved over the ruin of Joseph." (The "ruin of Joseph" may refer to the corruption of the Northern Kingdom of Israel.[175]) For Amos, the Israelites should be doing penance to mourn Israel's sins, not celebrating and being "at ease in Zion" (Amos 6:1).

Proverbs 20:1 warns against the type of behaviors that an overindulgence in strong drink can lead to and the negative effects that its misuse can have on someone: "Wine is a mocker, strong drink a brawler; and whoever is led astray by it is not wise." Being "led astray" by alcoholic drink is not the same as drinking alcohol. The Catholic Church recognizes this distinction, and Scripture also condemns excessive drinking as immoral (CCC 2290).

COUNTER-CHALLENGE
Isn't there a difference between use and misuse?

AFTERTHOUGHT
Some Protestants will argue that consuming "strong drink" is *only* for the purpose of relieving pain in extreme circumstances, as shown in Proverbs 31:6: "Give strong drink to him who is perishing." But in light of Deuteronomy 14:26, we know that God permits the consumption of "strong drink" even as a general beverage.

"No Graven Images"

Exodus 20:4-6 and Statues

How can the Catholic Church approve of religious statues when the Bible forbids having graven images?

Catholics are known for putting statues and images in their churches and using them in their private devotions. The *Catechism* affirms such devotions, calling the "honor paid to sacred images" a "respectful veneration" (2132).

But for many Protestants[176] this is problematic, biblically speaking. God commands in Exodus 20:4-5,

> You shall not make for yourself a graven image, or any likeness of anything that is in heaven above, or that is in the earth beneath, or that is in the water under the earth; you shall not bow down to them or serve them; for I the LORD your God am a jealous God.

God says, "No graven images," yet the Catholic Church has images all over the place. God says, "Don't bow down to images," but the Catholic Church encourages such acts of piety. These Catholic practices contradict God's word.

MEETING THE CHALLENGE

1. In these verses, God can't be condemning religious statues and images because elsewhere he explicitly commands making them.[177]

Consider, for example, the two gold cherubim (cast sculptures of angels) that God commanded to be put on the lid of the Ark of the Covenant (Exod. 25:18-20). God also instructed that cherubim be woven into the curtains of the tabernacle (Exod. 26:1).

When God gave instructions for building the temple during the reign of King Solomon, he commanded that two fifteen-foot tall cherubim statues be placed in the holy of holies (1 Kings 6:23-28) and that "figures of cherubim" be carved into the walls and doors of the temple (1 Kings 6:29). Later, in 1 Kings 9:3, we read that God approved of such things, saying to Solomon, "I have consecrated this house which you have built, and put my name there forever; my eyes and my heart will be there for all time." God's blessing on the temple is certain evidence that he doesn't oppose having statues and sacred images in places of worship.

Another example where God commanded the making of a statue is in Numbers 21:6-9. The Israelites were suffering from venomous snakebites; in order to heal them, God instructed Moses to construct a bronze serpent and set it on a pole so that those who were bitten could look upon it and be healed (Num. 21:6-9). God did later command that the bronze serpent be destroyed but only because the Israelites started worshipping it as a god (2 Kings 18:4).

2. What God's commandment forbids is the making of idols.

The context bears this out. Consider the prohibition that precedes it: "You shall have no other gods before me" (v.3).

Then after the passage in question, we read, "You shall not bow down to them or *serve* them; for I the Lord your God am a jealous God." Given this contextual prohibition of idolatry, it's reasonable to conclude that God's command not to make "graven images" refers to making images to be worshipped as deities or idols.

Accordingly, we note that every time the Hebrew word for "graven images" (*pesel*) is used in the Old Testament it's used in reference to *idols* or the *images of idols*. For example, the prophet Isaiah warns, "All who make idols [*pesel*] are nothing, and the things they delight in do not profit; their witnesses neither see nor know, that they may be put to shame" (44:9). Other examples include but are not limited to Isaiah 40:19; 17; 45:20; Jeremiah 10:14; 51:17; and Habakkuk 2:18.

Since making idols is what this commandment forbids, the Catholic custom of using statues and images for religious purposes doesn't contradict it because Catholics don't use statues and sacred images as idols. The whole of paragraph 2132 (referenced above) states the following:

> The Christian veneration of images is not contrary to the first commandment which proscribes idols. Indeed, "the honor rendered to an image passes to its prototype," and "whoever venerates an image venerates the person portrayed in it." The honor paid to sacred images is a "respectful veneration," not the adoration due to God alone.

Catholics don't treat statues or the people whom the statues represent as gods. As such, the biblical prohibition of idolatry doesn't apply.

This challenge from modern Evangelicals shows that there's nothing new under the sun. The Catholic Church dealt with this sort of objection all the way back in the eighth century when it condemned the heresy of *iconoclasm* at the Second Council of Nicaea (787). Iconoclasm was the belief that all religious images are superstitious. In response to this heresy, the council declared that religious images were worthy of veneration and that any respect shown to a religious image is really respect given to the person it represents.

In having images or statues of Jesus, angels, Mary, and the saints in its places of worship, the Catholic Church is following the Old Testament precedent of incorporating images of heavenly inhabitants that serve as reminders of who is present with us when we approach God in liturgical worship.

The representations of the cherubim in the Old Testament served as reminders that they were heavenly inhabitants present with God. Since humans have been admitted into heaven (Rev. 5:8; 6:9; 7:14-17), it's reasonable to employ representations of them, too.

What about pious acts directed to the statues, such as bowing? Doesn't Exodus 20:4 prohibit "bowing" before graven images? Yes, the Bible forbids bowing before *idols*. It doesn't forbid the physical act of bowing before something or someone when that something or someone is not an idol.

For example, Solomon was not guilty of idolatry when he bowed before his mother in 1 Kings 2:19. It was simply a gesture of honor given her as queen mother. Jesus himself says in Revelation 3:9 that he will make "those of the synagogue of Satan" "bow down" before the feet of the Christians in Philadelphia. If bowing before another were in and of itself an act of worship, Jesus would be causing idolatry. But that's absurd.

So pious acts and postures can be legitimate when directed to the person that a statue or picture represents if the action is not used as a sign of the adoration or worship that is due to God alone. And such honor for the saints is their due because of what God has done for them. Jesus says, "If any one serves me, the Father will honor him" (John 12:26). The saints in heaven, whom our statues represent, have served and do continue to serve Jesus. As such, the Father honors them. And if the Father honors them, we can too.

COUNTER-CHALLENGE

Are all religious images idols? How can you know which are and which aren't?

AFTERTHOUGHT

Among some Christian communities, the commandment not to make "graven images" is listed as the second of the Ten Commandments. This differs from the Catholic numbering of the Ten Commandments. But seeing the prohibition to make "graven images" as part of God's overall prohibition of idolatry provides an explanation for why the Catholic Church doesn't consider it a separate commandment.

After the Challenge

There are many more Bible-based Protestant challenges to Catholic teaching, enough to fill up another book or two! And, of course, there is the whole project of making a positive case for the Catholic faith using biblical evidence.

So by no means is this book the end of the story. There is much more work to be done. But the book does serve several important ends for both Catholics and Protestants.

Every Bible passage in this book that a Protestant thinks contradicts a particular Catholic teaching is at the same time used by Protestants to support their own belief. That being the case, meeting these challenges and offering counter-challenges can have a twofold effect on Protestants.

First, it gives Protestants occasion to reconsider beliefs that contradict Catholic teaching and the Bible passages that they use to support them. If a Protestant realizes that the passages he commonly uses to ground his beliefs don't succeed in doing so, he may begin to question his beliefs, especially since he operates on *sola scriptura*. Without Sacred Tradition to instruct him, he would have no reason to embrace those particular beliefs if the Bible didn't teach them clearly.

Of course, he may turn to other biblical passages apart from the ones covered in this book. But for the first time, he may wrestle with the question of whether he is interpreting *those* passages correctly. If he was wrong with the passages covered in this book, he may be wrong about others.

As Catholics, we don't want Protestants to doubt their beliefs just to make them squirm. Instead, we hope that exposing the weakness of their arguments against Catholicism will prepare a way for them to investigate and ultimately embrace the fullness of the Faith.

The second effect of meeting these challenges, therefore, is providing Protestants an encounter with positive biblical evidence for Catholic teaching. Given Protestants' love for God's word, this can make Catholicism seem biblically tenable or even attractive for the first time. They may wonder if other Catholic beliefs have a biblical basis, too. And as many Protestant converts to Catholicism will tell you, this curiosity can lead someday to crossing the Tiber.

What now of Catholics? What happens after the challenges are met?

First, meeting these challenges strengthens our own faith, reminding us that our beliefs don't "make void the word of God" (Mark 7:13). We take greater pride in and ownership of the teachings we learn to defend, and we have greater confidence that other teachings are true and defensible, too.

Meeting challenges also breeds confidence. Too often, we don't engage Protestants about the biblical foundations of our faith because we think Protestants know more about the Bible than we do. In learning how to meet challenges, we're less afraid of being stumped.

Finally, we also learn that meeting challenges to Catholicism made by our Protestant brothers and sisters is not contrary to a spirit of Christian love but an example of it.

Dialoguing with Protestants to persuade them that Catholicism coheres with the Bible is no different from the approach Paul took in Thessalonica where he "argued with [Jews] from the scriptures, explaining and proving that it was necessary for the Christ to suffer and to rise from the dead" (Acts 17:2-3). Just as Paul set out to persuade Jews by using the authority they recognized, so too we must set out to persuade Protestants with Sacred Scripture.

Since Protestants value the Bible so highly, exposing misinterpretations of it is truly an act of love. The essence of love is to will the good of the other. The truth is a good for human beings, and Protestants seek it in Scripture above all places. Therefore, to share biblical truth with them is a supreme act of love. Any time we set out to meet a Protestant challenge, we must look through this lens of love.

And ultimately, meeting the Protestant challenge is an act of love toward God. It shows that we care enough about the gift of his revelation to get it right.

Karlo Broussard is a staff apologist and speaker for Catholic Answers. He travels the country giving talks on apologetics, biblical studies, theology, and philosophy, is a regular guest on the radio program *Catholic Answers Live*, and is the author of *Prepare the Way: Overcoming Obstacles to God, the Gospel, and the Church*. A native of Southern Louisiana, Karlo now resides in Southern California with his wife and five children.

You can book Karlo for a speaking event by contacting Catholic Answers at 619-387-7200. You can also view Karlo's videos at KarloBroussard.com.

Endnotes

1   See Norman L. Geisler and Ralph E. MacKenzie, *Roman Catholics and Evangelicals: Agreements and Differences* (Grand Rapids, MI: Baker Academic, 1995), 208–209, 284–285; Normal L. Geisler and Joshua M. Betancourt, *Is Rome the True Church? A Consideration of the Roman Catholic Claim* (Wheaton, IL: Crossway Books, 2008), 79; Kenneth J. Colins and Jerry L. Walls, *Roman But Not Catholic: What Remains at Stake 500 Years after the Reformation* (Ada, MI: Baker Academic, 2017), 214, footnote: 68.

2   See James White, *The Roman Catholic Controversy* (Minneapolis, MN: Bethany House Publishers, 1996), 112.

3   This line of argument is taken from Scott Butler, Norman Dahlgren, and David Hess, *Jesus, Peter and the Keys* (Santa Barbara, CA: Queenship Publishing, 1996), 96–97.

4   For a similar argument, see Hugh Pope, "The Papacy in the New Testament" in Cuthbert Lattey, S.J., *The Papacy* (Cambridge, England: W. Heffer and Sons, 1924), 23.

5   See 1 Corinthians 8:8–9 where Paul gives permission to eat meat offered to idols.

6   Johannes P. Louw and Eugene A. Nida, *Greek-English Lexicon of the New Testament: Based on Semantic Domains*, 2nd ed., Vol. 1 (New York: United Bible Societies, 1996), 364. Electronic edition, 31.1.

7   See Loraine Boettner, *Roman Catholicism* (Phillipsburg, NJ: Presbyterian and Reformed Publishing Company, 1962), 106; Steve Urick, *Major Cults and False World Religions: What Every Person Needs to Know* (Bloomington, IN: Authorhouse, 2014), 219; "What is the Rock in Matthew 16:18?", www.gotquestions.org.

8   For a Protestant who agrees with this line of argument, see D.A. Carson, "Matthew," in *The Expositor's Bible Commentary: Matthew, Mark, Luke*, Vol. 8, ed. Frank E. Gaebelein (Grand Rapids: Zondervan, 1984), 368.

9   See Jimmy Akin, *A Daily Defense: 365 Days (Plus One) to Becoming a Better Apologist* (El Cajon, CA: Catholic Answers Press, 2016), 186.

10 See R.T. Kendall *The Parables of Jesus: A Guide to Understanding and Applying the Stories Jesus Told* (Grand Rapids: Chosen Books, 2006), 144; Norman L. Geisler and Ralph E. MacKenzie, *Roman Catholics and Evangelicals*, 211.

11 Louw and Nida, *Greek-English Lexicon of the New Testament: Based on Semantic Domains*, 765.

12 See Barclay M. Newman Jr., *A Concise Greek-English dictionary of the New Testament* (Stuttgart, Germany: Deutsche Bibelgesellschaft, United Bible Societies, 1993), 176.

13 Louw and Nida, *Greek-English lexicon of the New Testament*, 507.

14 W.F. Albright and C.S. Mann, *The Anchor Bible: Matthew* (New York: Doubleday, 1971) 195. Cited in Steve Ray, *Upon This Rock: St. Peter and the Primacy of Rome in Scripture and the Early Church* (San Francisco: Ignatisu Press, 1999), 34.

15 This Bible passage doesn't seem to be used on a scholarly level to challenge the Catholic belief in a hierarchical Church. But, due to its popularity in conversations with Protestants, I included it in this book.

16 See Kaufmann Kohler, "Binding and Loosing," *Jewish Encyclopedia*, www.jewishencyclopedia.com.

17 See Kaufmann Kohler, "Binding and Loosing." See also Flavius Josephus, *The Jewish War* 1.111.

18 John MacEvilly, *An Exposition of the Gospels of Matthew and Mark*, 4th ed. (New York: Benziger Brothers, 1898), 331.

19   A Protestant might respond that scholars believe Matthew 18:20 to be a composition of independent sayings given by Jesus on different occasions, which Matthew put together into one narrative. Therefore, an appeal to context in order to explain verse 20 doesn't hold water. It's true that scholars have said this, and good arguments have been given for its plausibility. But all this shows is that we can't *restrict* the meaning of the "two or three gathered" in verse 20 to the above interpretation. Given that verse 20 may have been an independent saying, we have to consider the possibility that it could refer to Christians in general. But even if we grant this, it still doesn't prove what the challenge asserts it does, because we know from verse 17 that the Church exercises judicial authority inasmuch as it binds and looses, which implies that the Church is not *merely* an invisible community of believers.

20   See Kenneth J. Colins and Jerry L. Walls, *Roman But Not Catholic: What Remains at Stake 500 Years after the Reformation* (Ada, MI: Baker Academic, 2017), 88.

21   Barclay M. Newman, *A Concise Greek-English dictionary of the New Testament*, 156.

22   I am grateful to Jimmy Akin for his research on this point. See Jimmy Akin, *A Daily Defense*, 301.

23   Ignatius of Antioch, *The Epistle of Ignatius to the Trallians*, in *The Apostolic Fathers with Justin Martyr and Irenaeus*, Vol. 1, eds. A. Roberts, J. Donaldson, & A. C. Coxe (Buffalo, NY: Christian Literature Company, 1885), 67.

24   See Eric Svendson, *Evangelical Answers: A Critique of Current Roman Catholic Apologists* (Lidenhurst, New York: Reformation Press, 1999), 46–47; John R. Waiss and James G. McCarthy, *Letters between a Catholic and an Evangelical: From Debate to Dialogue on the Issues That Separate Us* (Eugene, OR: Harvest House Publishers, 2003), 121; Kenneth J. Colins and Jerry L. Walls, Roman but not Catholic, 87.

25   See Adam Murrell, *Essential Church History: And the Doctrinal Significance of the Past* (Eugene OR: Wipf and Stock, 2009), 109.

26   KH. Rengstorf, "Korban" in *Theological Dictionary of the New Testament: Abridged in One Volume*, ed. G. Kittle et al. (Grand Rapids: Wm. B. Eerdmans, 1985), 459.

27   See Flavius Josephus, *The Jewish War* 2.9.4.

28   Trent Horn, *The Case for Catholicism: Answers to Classic and Contemporary Protestant Objections* (San Franciso: Ignatius, 2017), 41.

29   Protestant Adam Murrell writes, "Unless tradition is also *theopnuestos* it cannot be equal to the rest of the Word of God. For there can only be one ultimate authority and that is why the evangelical's supreme authority is, without question or reservation, the God-breathed Scriptures and nothing more." Adam Murrell, *Essential Church History*, 109.

30   James White, *Answers to Catholic Claims* (Southbridge: Crowne Publications, 1990), 42. See also Kenneth Samples, *A World of Difference: Putting Christian Truth-Claims to the Worldview Test* (Grand Rapids: Baker Books, 2007), 121.

31   William Arndt et al., *A Greek-English Lexicon of the New Testament and Other Early Christian Literature* (Chicago: University of Chicago Press, 2000), 136.

32   Ibid., 346.

33   Louw and Nida, *Greek-English lexicon of the New Testament*, 624.

34   J.N.D. Kelly, *Pastoral Epistles* (New York: Bloomsbury Academic, 2001), 202.

35   Jimmy Akin, *A Daily Defense*, 176.

36   See W. Robert Godfrey, "What Do We Mean By Sola Scriptura," in *Sola Scriptura: The Protestant Position on the Bible*, ed. Don Kistler (Morgan, PA: Soli Deo Gloria Publications, 1995), 24; Matthew Barrett, *God's Word Alone: The Authority of Scripture* (Grand Rapids: Zondervan, 2016), 341.

37 See David Peterson, *The Acts of the Apostles* (Grand Rapids: Wm. B. Eerdmans, 2009), 484; Barclay M. Newman, *A Concise Greek-English dictionary of the New Testament*, 75; Electronic edition.

38 See William J. Larkin, *Acts, Cornerstone Biblical Commentary*, Vol. 12 (Carol Stream, IL: Tyndale House Publishing, 2006), 540.

39 See Ron Rhodes, *Reasoning from the Scriptures with Catholics* (Eugene, OR: Harvest House Publishing, 2000) 63; Matthew Barrett, *God's Word Alone*, 326; Norman L. Geisler and Ralph E. MacKenzie, *Roman Catholics and Evangelicals*, 186.

40 See Ron Rhodes, *Reasoning from the Scriptures with Catholics*, 63.

41 Fee, Gordon D., *The First Epistle to the Corinthians*, The New International Commentary on the New Testament (Grand Rapids, MI: Wm. B. Eerdmans Publishing Co., 1987), 167–170.

42 For more information concerning this interpretive options, see Joseph A. Fitzmyer, *First Corinthians: A New Translation with Introduction and Commentary*, vol. 32, Anchor Yale Bible (New Haven; London: Yale University Press, 2008), 215–216; See also Gordon, *The First Epistle to the Corinthians*, 167–170.

43 *Commentary on 1 Corinthians* 4:6. Available at http://biblehub.com/commentaries/calvin/1_corinthians/4.htm.

44 Esther 10:4–16:24; Daniel 3:24–90; Daniel 13; Daniel 14.

45 See Philip Kayser, *The Canon of Scripture: A Presuppositional Study* (Omaha, NE: Biblical Blueprints, 2018), Chapter 4.

46 J.N.D. Kelly, *Early Christian Doctrines*, 5th ed. (New York: Bloomsbury, 1977), 55.

47 Louw and Nida, *Greek-English Lexicon of the New Testament*, 60.

48 See also: http://jimmyakin.com/deuterocanonical-references-in-the-new-testament.

49 See James G. McCarthy, *The Gospel According to Rome: Comparing Catholic Tradition and the Word of God* (Eugene, OR: Harvest House Publishers, 1995), 338; Ron Rhodes, *Reasoning from the Scriptures with Catholics*, 39.

50 See James White, *The God Who Justifies: The Doctrine of Justification* (Minneapolis, MN: Bethany House, 2001), 89.

51 *The Lexham English Bible*, 3rd ed., eds. W.H. Harris, III, E. Ritzema, R. Brannan, D. Mangum, J. Dunham, J.A. Reimer, and M. Wierenga (Bellingham, WA: Lexham Press, 2013).

52 See M.S. Heiser and V.M. Setterholm, *Glossary of Morpho-Syntactic Database Terminology* (Bellingham, WA: Lexham Press, 2013).

53 *The Lexham Analytical Lexicon to the Greek New Testament* (Logos Bible Software, 2011).

54 See Jimmy Akin, "Faith and Works," September 1, 1999, www.catholic.com.

55 See Jimmy Akin, "Whose Righteousness was Reckoned?" January 3, 2018, www.catholic.com.

56 Council of Trent, *Decree on Original Sin* 5

57 Council of Trent, *Canons on Justification*, Canon 24

58 See James White, *The God Who Justifies*, 325; Carl J. Broggi, "The Importance of the Reformation," in *How Do We Know the Bible is True?*, vol. 2 eds., Ken Ham and Bodie Hodge (Green Forest, AR: Master Books, 2012), 224.

59 This argument is taken from Trent Horn, *The Case for Catholicism*, 235. See also Jimmy Akin, *A Daily Defense*, 278.

60 Jimmy Akin, *A Daily Defense*, 278.

61 Council of Trent, *Decree on Justification* 10.

62 See R.C. Sproul, *Faith Alone: The Evangelical Doctrine of Justification* (Grand Rapids, MI:

Baker Books, 1995), 194, 202; James White, *The Roman Catholic Controversy*, 148–149.

63 See Waiss and McCarthy, *Letters Between a Catholic and an Evangelical*, 163; Geisler and MacKenzie, *Roman Catholics and Evangelicals*, 231.

64 See Waiss and McCarthy, *Letters Between a Catholic and an Evangelical*, 381; Norm Geisler, "A Moderate Calvinist View," in *Four Views on Eternal Security*, ed. J Matthew Pinson (Grand Rapids: Zondervan, 2002), 71.

65 See Dale Moody, *The Word of Truth: A Summary of Christian Doctrine Based on Biblical Revelation* (Grand Rapids: Wm. B. Eerdmans, 1981), 357.

66 See Todd Baker, *Exodus from Rome: A Biblical and Historical Critique of Roman Catholicism* (Bloomington, IN: iUniverse, 2014), 331; David N. Steele, Curtis C. Thomas, and Roger Nicole, *The Five Points of Calvinism: Defined, Defended and Documented* (Philadelphia, PA: The Presbyterian & Reformed Publishing Co., 1963), 57–59; Steven J. Cole, "Total Forgiveness," August 1, 2004, www.fcfonline.org; John Piper, "Perfected for All Time by a Single Offering," February 16, 1997, www.desiringgod.org.

67 Other Christian groups that don't believe in eternal security include Lutherans, Methodists, Pentecostals, and many Anglicans.

68 A talent of silver was equivalent to 6,000 denarii. One denarius was an acceptable day's wage for a laborer. 10,000 talents, therefore, would have been equivalent to six million denarii, which tallies to just over 164,000 years of daily wages. See R.T. France, *The Gospel of Matthew*, The New International Commentary on the New Testament (Grand Rapids, MI: Wm. B. Eerdmans Publication Co., 2007), 706.

69 R.T. France, *The Gospel of Matthew*, 706.

70 See William Arndt et al., *A Greek-English Lexicon of the New Testament and Other Early Christian Literature*, 996.

71 This response assumes that a Protestant is using Hebrews 10:14 to refer to an individual who has already been initially saved. A Protestant could read "those who are being sanctified" to refer to those who are initially becoming members of the Christian community through the spread of the Gospel, and it's those to whom the ongoing application of Christ's merits are applied. In other words, on this reading the ongoing application of Christ's merits applies only to those who are initially being saved. Once they're initially saved, then all their future sins are forgiven. But such a reading would undermine a Protestant's use of Hebrews 10:14 to prove that the future sins of a *Christian* are forgiven, and thus there would be no need to offer a rebuttal. A Catholic not only wouldn't contend with the idea that Christ's merits are continuously applied to those who are initially saved, but affirm it.

72 See Jacque Lafleur, *The Science of Salvation: Forty-Nine Instant Sermons Especially for Lay Pastors* (Fort Oglethorpe, GA: TEACH Services, Inc., 2009), 213; First Baptist Independence, "Baptism," www.fbionline.org; Word of Life Baptist Church, "Our Beliefs," www.wolbc.org.

73 Bernard Drachman and Kaufmann Kohler, "Ablution," *Jewish Encyclopedia*, www.jewishencyclopedia.com.

74 Kaufmann Kohler and Samuel Kraus, "Baptism," *Jewish Encyclopedia*, www.jewishencyclopedia.com.

75 Quote taken from Jimmy Akin, *The Fathers Know Best: Your Essential Guide to the Teachings of the Early Church* (El Cajon, CA: Catholic Answers Press, 2010).

76 See Geisler and MacKenzie, *Roman Catholics and Evangelicals*, 481.

77 Thomas Aquinas, *Summa Theologiae* III:68:9

78 *The Greek New Testament: SBL Edition*, ed. Michael W. Holmes; Electronic edition.

79   Martin Luther, *The Babylonian Captivity.*

80   2:22:4.

81   *Fragments from the Lost Writings of Irenaeus* 34

82   *Letters* 58:2.

83   See Geisler and MacKenzie, *Roman Catholics and Evangelicals*, 481, 483, 488.

84   See Craig Keener, "Holy Spirit," *The Lexham Bible Dictionary*, ed. John D. Barry et al. (Bellingham, WA: Lexham Press, 2016).

85   Ibid.

86   George R. Beasley-Murray, John, vol. 36, *Word Biblical Commentary* (Dallas: Word, Incorporated, 2002), 49; emphasis added.

87   For a survey of alternative explanations for the term "water" and ways to critique them, see my article "Defending Re-birth by Water," May 28, 2018, www.catholic.com.

88   See Geisler and MacKenzie, *Roman Catholics and Evangelicals*, 481–482.

89   See Jimmy Akin, *The Drama of Salvation: How God Rescues Us from Our Sins and Brings Us to Eternal Life* (El Cajon, CA: Catholic Answers Press, 2015), 140.

90   See Loraine Boettner, *Roman Catholicism* (Phillipsburg, NJ: Presbyterian and Reformed Publishing Company, 1962), 178; Matt Slick, "Transubstantiation and the Real Presence," https://carm.org/transubstantiation.

91   Brant Pitre, *Jesus and the Jewish Roots of the Eucharist: Unlocking the Secrets of the Last Supper* (New York: Doubleday, 2011), chap. 4.

92   See Geisler and MacKenzie, *Roman Catholics and Evangelicals*, 267; Ron Rhodes, *Reasoning from the Scriptures with Catholics*, 184; James White, *The Roman Catholic Controversy*, 176; James McCarthy, *The Gospel According to Rome*, 155.

93   J.N.D. Kelly, *Early Christian Doctrines*, 196–197. Cited in Jimmy Akin, *The Father's Know Best*, 299.

94   Joachim Jeremias, *The Eucharistic Words of Jesus* (Philadelphia: Trinity Press International, 1966), 252; emphasis in the original.

95   Max Thurian, *The Eucharistic Memorial*, trans. J. G. Davies (Richmond, VA: John Knox Press, 1962), 1:19; Quoted in Christian E. Wood, "Anamnesis and Allegory in Ambrose's de Sacramentis and de Mysteriis," *Letter & Spirit: The Bible and the Church Fathers: The Liturgical Context of Patristic Exegesis*, vol. 7 (2011): 56–57.

96   J.N.D. Kelly, *Early Christian Doctrines*, 196–197.

97   See Loraine Boettner, *Roman Catholicism* (Phillipsburg, NJ: Presbyterian and Reformed Publishing Company, 1962), 181–182; Todd Baker, *Exodus from Rome: A Biblical and Historical Critique of Roman Catholicism*, vol. 1 (Bloomington: iUniverse, 2014), 128; D. Stephen Long, Hebrews, *Belief: A Theological Commentary on the Bible* (Louisville, KY: Westminister John Knox Press, 2011), 130.

98   See Jimmy Akin, "The Priesthood Debate," www.jimmyakin.com.

99   Justin Martyr, *Dialogue with Trypho* 41; c. A.D. 155.

100 Ireaneus of Lyons, *Against Heresies* 4:17:5; c. A.D. 189.

101 See Loraine Boettner, *Roman Catholicism* (Phillipsburg, NJ: Presbyterian and Reformed Publishing Company, 1962), 176; Matt Slick, "Transubstantiation and the Real Presence," https://carm.org/transubstantiation.

102 Eusebius, *Church History* 3:39:14–15; emphasis added.

103 Thomas Aquinas, *Catena Aurea: Commentary on the Four Gospels, Collected out of the Works of the Fathers: St. Matthew*, Vol. 1, ed. J. H. Newman, Ed. (Oxford: John Henry Parker, 1841), 897.

104   See Loraine Boettner, *Roman Catholicism*, 202; Todd Baker, *Exodus from Rome*, 273.

105   See Loraine Boettner, *Roman Catholicism*, 205–206; Norman L. Geisler and Ralph
      E. MacKenzie, *Roman Catholics and Evangelicals*, 293; John MacArthur, *The Freedom
      and Power of Forgiveness* (Wheaton, IL: Crossway Books, 1998), 72; Steve Urick, *The
      Truth About Roman Catholicism: What Every Catholic Needs to Know* (Bloomington, IN:
      AuthorHouse , 2014); Joseph Nadeau, *Lies from the Pit* (Bloomington, IN: Westbow
      Press, 2016).

106   William Arndt et al., *A Greek-English Lexicon of the New Testament and Other Early
      Christian Literature*, 708.

107   Ibid., 351.

108   Brooke Westcott, *The Epistle of St. John* (New York: MacMillan and Co., 1902), 23.

109   4:14, 14:1.

110   See Colins and Walls, *Roman But Not Catholic*, 161; Geisler and MacKenzie, *Roman
      Catholics and Evangelicals*, 291.

111   Luther writes, "Because we are all priests of equal standing, no one must push
      himself forward and take it upon himself, without our consent and election, to do
      that for which we all have equal authority. For no one dare take upon himself what is
      common to all without the authority and consent of the community." Martin Luther,
      "To the Christian Nobility of the German Nation" in *Three Treatises*, 2nd ed., trans.
      Charles M. Jacobs (Minneapolis: Fortress Press, 1990), 14.

112   I am grateful to Jimmy Akin for this line of argument. See Jimmy Akin, "The
      Priesthood Debate," www.jimmyakin.com.

113   It's worth noting here is that in Catholic theology the Old Testament high priesthood
      correlates with the bishop, as well, because he participates in Jesus' priestly ministry
      in the fullest degree (CCC 1586).

114   *Apostolic Tradition* 9.

115   See William A. Heth, "Remarriage for Adultery or Desertion," in *Remarriage
      after Divorce in Today's Church*, ed. Mark L. Strauss and Paul E. Engle, *Zondervan
      Counterpoints Collection* (Grand Rapids, MI: Zondervan, 2006), 72; Jay Adams,
      Marriage, Divorce, and Remarriage in the Bible: A Fresh Look at What Scripture Teaches
      (Grand Rapids, MI: Zondervan, 1980), 54.

116   See Louw and Nida, *Greek-English Lexicon of the New Testament*, 770; William Arndt et
      al., *A Greek-English Lexicon of the New Testament and Other Early Christian Literature*, 854.

117   John P. Meier, *The Vision of Matthew: Christ, Church, and Morality in the First Gospel*
      (Eugene, OR: Wipf and Stock Publishers, 1991), 252.

118   Ibid., 249–250.

119   Ibid.

120   Ibid., 254.

121   See Jimmy Akin, *A Daily Defense*, 123.

122   See Ron Rhodes, *Reasoning from the Scriptures with Catholics*, 269–271.

123   I am grateful to Jimmy Akin for this line of argument.

124   See James McCarthy, *The Gospel According to Rome*, 197.

125   Pius IX, *Ineffabilis Deus*, 8 December 1854, www.ewtn.com.

126   See Geisler and MacKenzie, *Roman Catholics and Evangelicals*, 302; Ron Rhodes,
      Reasoning from the Scriptures with Catholics, 274–275; Waiss and McCarthy, *Letters
      Between a Catholic and an Evangelical*, 280.

127   There are two objections that some may pose to our interpretation of this passage.
      First, some may argue that because the term "son" is not used in Matthew 10:2–3, it

doesn't necessarily follow that Alphaeus is James' biological father. Alphaeus could simply be a brother of James or some other sort of relative. Although this is true, I think the context suggests filial relationship. Consider, for example, that the term "brother" (Greek—*adelophos*) is used to describe the relationship between Simon and Andrew, along with the relationship that "James of Zebedee" has with John. Given that Matthew is speaking of familial relations, it's reasonable to infer that Zebedee is the biological father of James. And if it's reasonable to infer that Zebedee is the biological father of James, then it's reasonable to make the same inference concerning Alphaeus and his relation to James. A second argument is that because the term "apostle" can be used in a looser sense, the "James" that Paul speaks of in Galatians 1:18–19 is not one of the twelve. Although it's true the term "apostle" can be used for individuals outside the twelve (e.g., Barnabas in Acts 14:14), the context suggests that Paul uses "apostle" in the proper sense. Consider that Paul goes up to Jerusalem to visit with *Cephas* after three years of preaching, and then immediately speaks of "the other apostles." To speak of "the other apostles" without qualification within the same breadth of speaking of "Cephas" lends itself to the interpretation that Paul is talking about the twelve. Moreover, just a few verses later, in Galatians 2:1–2, Paul informs us that after fourteen years of preaching among the Gentiles he went back to Jerusalem and laid before "those who were of repute," who Paul identifies as James, Cephas, and John in Gal. 2:9, the content of his preaching "lest somehow [he] should be running or had run in vain." If Paul visited the apostles proper in Jerusalem to check his preaching after fourteen years of preaching, then it's reasonable to conclude his initial visit to Jerusalem after the first three years of his preaching (Gal. 1:18–19) was of the same nature—a presentation of his preaching to "those who were of repute" lest he should preach in vain.

128 Athanasius, *De virginitate.*
129 Hilary of Poitiers, *Commentary on Matthew* I, 4.
130 See Jacob Milgrom, *Harper Collins Study Bible* n. Lev 16:29; citing Targum Pseudo-Jonthan; cf. Brant Pitre, "A Biblical Basis for Mary's Perpetual Virginity," March 13, 2008, www.thesacredpage.com.
131 See Geisler and MacKenzie, *Roman Catholics and Evangelicals*, 303; Ron Rhodes, *Reasoning from the Scriptures with Catholics*, 274–275; Waiss and McCarthy, *Letters Between a Catholic and an Evangelical*, 280; Colins and Walls, *Roman But Not Catholic*, 296.
132 See Eric Svendson, *Evangelical Answers*, 143–144.
133 Thanks to Tim Staples for this argument.
134 See Geisler and MacKenzie, *Roman Catholics and Evangelicals*, 322.
135 See Geisler and MacKenzie, *Roman Catholics and Evangelicals*, 319, 352; Waiss and McCarthy, *Letters Between a Catholic and an Evangelical*, 278; Colins and Walls, *Roman But Not Catholic*, 311.
136 See also: Acts 8:24; 2 Cor. 13:7; Gal. 5:13, 6:2; Eph. 4:32; Phil. 1:9; 1 Thess. 3:10–12, 4:9–18, 5:14–15, 25; 2 Thess. 1:3, 3:1; 1 Tim 2:1–4; 2 Tim 1:3–4; Heb. 13:18; James 5:16; 1 Pet. 1:22, 3:8; 1 John 4:7–21; 2 John 5.
137 See Lynda Howard-Munro, *A Rebuttal to Catholic Apologetics* (Mustang, OK: Tate Publishing, 2013), 163.
138 See "Necromancy," www.merriam-webster.com.
139 See Jimmy Akin, *A Daily Defense*, 150.
140 The major proponents of this challenge come from outside mainstream Protestantism, such as Seventh Day Adventists. See Philip Rodonioff, "Waking Up To Eternity," www.adentist.org. However, the challenge is found among non-Seventh Day Adventists.

See Peter Marshall, *Beliefs and the Dead in Reformation England* (Oxford:Oxford University Press, 2002), 211, footnote 138; Dave Armstrong, "Dialogue: Are Dead Saints Playing Harps or Interceding?" June 2, 2016, www.patheos.com; Eric Stoutz, "What Does Ecclesiastes Mean?" May 22, 2007, www.catholicexchange.com; Fr. John Echert, "Ecclesiastes 9:5," EWTN Catholic Q&A, http://www.ewtn.com/v/experts/showmessage.asp?number=327547&Pg=&Pgnu=&recnu=.

141   See Huldrych Zwingli, *Huldrych Zwingli Writings, Vol. One: The Defense of the Reformed Faith*, Pittsburgh Theological Monographs (Eugene, OR: Pickwick Publications, 1984), 173; Svendson, *Evangelical Answers*, 158–160.

142   Thomas Aquinas, *Summa Theologiae Suppl.* 72:1, ad 5.

143   Thomas Aquinas, *Summa Theologiae* I:12:7.

144   See W. Robert Godfrey, "What Do We Mean By Sola Scriptura," 13.

145   Research for these bible passages is taken from Jimmy Akin, *A Daily Defense*, 130.

146   Quoted in Jimmy Akin, *A Daily Defense*, 130.

147   See Geisler and MacKenzie, *Roman Catholics and Evangelicals*, 57–58, 141.

148   Louw and Nida, *Greek-English Lexicon of the New Testament*, 4.

149   Joseph Ratzinger, *Eschatology: Death and Eternal Life* (Washington, D.C: The Catholic University of America Press, 1988), 230.

150   This line of argumentation is taken from Jimmy Akin, *A Daily Defense*, 205.

151   See Ron Rhodes, *Reasoning from the Scriptures with Catholics*, 237–241; Colins and Walls, *Roman But Not Catholic*, 308.

152   *The Soul* 58.

153   See Hal Lindsey, *There's a New World Coming: An In-depth Analysis of the Book of Revelation* (Eugene, OR: Harvest House Publishers, 1984), 77–78.

154   *Decree of the Holy Office*, July 21, 1944. Quoted in *The Sources of Catholic Dogma*, eds. H. Denzinger, and K. Rahner, trans. R.J. Deferrari (St. Louis, MO: Herder Books Company, 1954), 625.

155   See John F. Walvoord, *Every Prophecy of the Bible: Clear Explanations for Uncertain Times* (Colorado Springs: David C. Cook, 1990), 606.

156   See Augustine, *City of God*, 20.7; quoted in *Revelation*, Ancient Christian Commentary on Scripture, ed., C. Weinrich William (Downers Grove, IL: InterVarsity Press, 2005), 322.

157   1) The Possessed Boy (Mark 9:14–29), 2) A passing reference to the exorcism of Mary Magdalene (Luke 8:2), 3) The Gerasene Demoniac (Mark 5:1–20), 4) The Demoniac in the Capernaum Synagogue (Mark 1:23–28), 5) The Mute and Blind demoniac in the Q tradition (Q – Matt 12:24/Luke 11:14–15), 6) The Mute Demoniac (Matt 9:32–33), and 7) The Syrophoenician Woman (Mark 7:24–30/Matt 15:21–28).

158   See Augustine, *City of God*, 20.7; quoted in Revelation, 322.

159   Thomas Aquinas, *Summa Contra Gentiles* 3.83.

160   See Loraine Boettner, *Roman Catholicism*, 276, 307; Andrew Wommack, *Who Told You That You Were Naked?: A Study of the Conscience* (Tulsa, OK: Harrison House Publishers, 2018); Adam Clarke, "Commentary on 1 Timothy 4:3," The Adam Clarke Commentary, 1832, www.studylight.org; Albert Barnes, "Commentary on 1 Timothy 4:3," Barnes' Notes on the New Testament, 1870, www.studylight.org.

161   Exceptions to the general rule of celibacy for ordained clergy are sometimes made in the Latin rite—for example, for married Protestant clergy who convert to Catholicism and wish to be ordained. For Eastern rites, which have a long tradition of married clergy, a married man may be ordained as a priest but unmarried priests must remain celibate.

162 For Protestants who use this verse against Catholics, see Ron Rhodes, *Reasoning from the Scriptures with Catholics*, 112; Waiss and McCarthy, *Letters Between a Catholic and an Evangelical*, 80; Colins and Walls, *Roman But Not Catholic*, 188.

163 See Jimmy Akin, *A Daily Defense*, 32.

164 Ibid.

165 See Geisler and MacKenzie, *Roman Catholics and Evangelicals*, 343, 354; Ron Rhodes, *Reasoning from the Scriptures with Catholics*, 238.

166 Martin Luther wrote, "For Christian faith and life can well exist without the intolerable laws of the pope. In fact, faith cannot properly exist unless there are fewer of these Romanist laws or unless they are even abolished altogether. In baptism we have become free and have been made subject only to God's word. Why should we become bound by the word of any man? As St. Paul says, 'You have become free; do not become a bondservant of men,' that is, of those men who rule by man-made laws" (*Luther's Works, Vol. 44: The Christian in Society I*, ed. Jaroslav Jan Pelikan, Hilton C. Oswald, and Helmut T. Lehmann, vol. 44 (Philadelphia: Fortress Press, 1999), 198).

167 I am thankful to Jimmy Akin for his research on this response. See Jimmy Akin, *A Daily Defense*, 87.

168 See Loraine Boettner, *Roman Catholicism*, 285; Luis Munoz, Birth, *Criminal History and Judgment of the Roman C. Church* (Bloomington, IN: Balboa Press, 2012), 107.

169 See William Arndt et al., *A Greek-English Lexicon of the New Testament and Other Early Christian Literature*, 172.

170 J.P. Louw, and E.A. Nida, *Greek-English lexicon of the New Testament: Based on Semantic Domains*, 398.

171 See Geisler and Thomas Howe, *When Critics Ask: A Popular Handbook on Bible Difficulties*, available online at http://crusadefortruth.com/links/PDFS/When_Critics_Ask.pdf.

172 See J. Swanson, *Dictionary of Biblical Languages with Semantic Domains: Hebrew (Old Testament)*, electronic ed. (Oak Harbor: Logos Research Systems, Inc., 1997); F. Brown, S.R. Driver, and C.A. Briggs, *Enhanced Brown-Driver-Briggs Hebrew and English Lexicon* (Oxford: Clarendon Press, 1977), 1016.

173 See Geisler and Thomas Howe, *When Critics Ask*, http://crusadefortruth.com/links/PDFS/When_Critics_Ask.pdf.

174 See Trent Horn, "The Bible Doesn't Forbid Alcohol," July 31, 2014, www.catholic.com.

175 M. Leahy, "Amos," in *A Catholic Commentary on Holy Scripture*, eds. B. Orchard & E.F. Sutcliffe (New York: Thomas Nelson and Sons, 1953), 663.

176 See Geisler and MacKenzie, *Roman Catholics and Evangelicals*, 321–322, 325–326; Waiss and McCarthy, *Letters Between a Catholic and an Evangelical*, 278.

177 See Jimmy Akin, *A Daily Defense*, 43.

What Is Catholic Answers?

Catholic Answers is a media ministry that serves Christ by explaining and defending the Catholic faith:

- We help Catholics grow in their faith
- We bring former Catholics home
- We lead non-Catholics into the fullness of the truth

There are many ways we help people:

 Catholic Answers Live is America's most popular Catholic radio program

 Catholic Answers Press publishes faith-building books, booklets, magazines, and audio resources

 Catholic Answers Studios creates television programs, DVDs, and online videos

 Our website, Catholic.com hosts hundreds of thousands of online resources, free to use

 Catholic Answers Events conducts seminars, conferences, and pilgrimages

Catholic Answers is an independent, nonprofit organization supported by your donations.

Visit us online and learn how we can help you.

Your journey starts at:
catholic.com